TAILS DON'T LIE

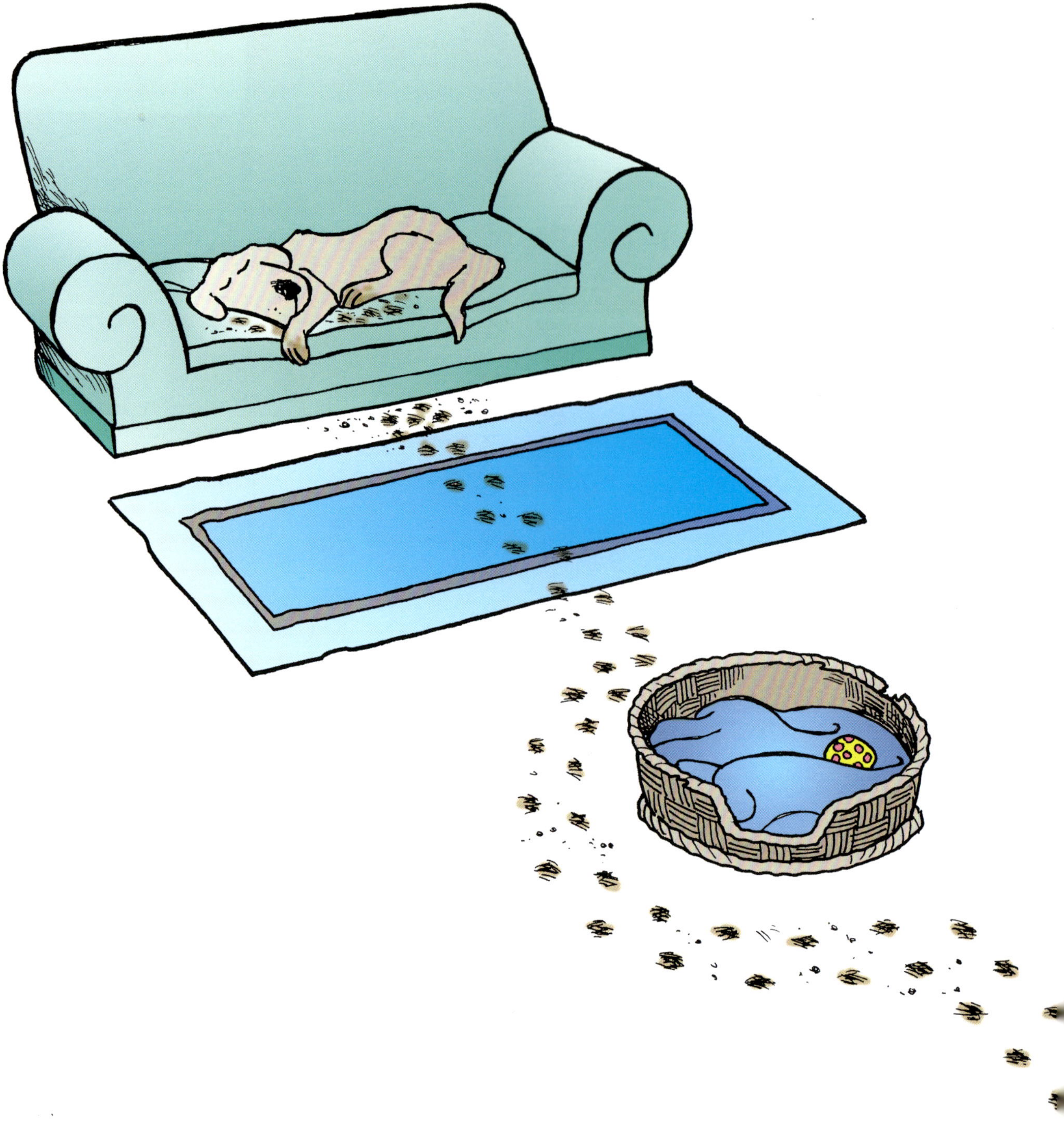

TAILS DON'T LIE 2

A Pack of Dog Cartoons

ONLINE DATING
NAME: SPOT
AGE: 5 YEARS
BREED: MUTT
LIKES: WADING IN MUDDY DITCHES

ADRIAN RAESIDE

HARBOUR PUBLISHING

This book is dedicated to anyone who has rescued an animal.

Koko, a rescue dog, and his best buddy, Sakura, brought endless joy and inspiration. They have both since passed over to the Rainbow Bridge but they live on in our hearts and in The Other Coast.

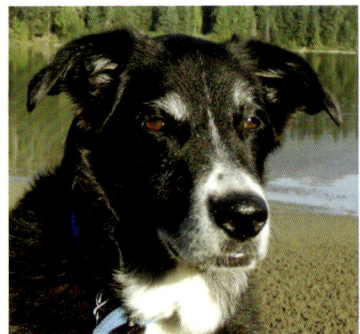

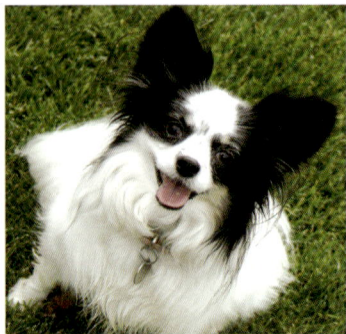

1 2 3 4 5 — 21 20 19 18 17

HARBOUR PUBLISHING CO. LTD.
P.O. Box 219, Madeira Park, BC,
V0N 2H0, Canada
www.harbourpublishing.com

Book cover and page layout
by Teresa Karbashewski.

This book was printed with soy-based inks on chlorine-free paper made from 10% post-consumer waste.

Printed and bound in Canada.

Library and Archives Canada Cataloguing in Publication

Raeside, Adrian, 1957-
[Cartoons. Selections]
Tails don't lie 2 : a pack of dog cartoons / Adrian Raeside.
Issued in print and electronic formats.

ISBN 978-1-55017-793-0 (softcover).–ISBN 978-1-55017-794-7 (HTML)

1. Dogs–Caricatures and cartoons. 2. Canadian wit and humor, Pictorial. I. Title. II. Title: Tails do not lie two.

NC1449.R34A4 2017 741.5'6971 C2016-907502-8
C2016-907503-6

Harbour Publishing acknowledges the support of the Canada Council for the Arts, which last year invested $153 million to bring the arts to Canadians throughout the country. We also gratefully acknowledge financial support from the Government of Canada through the Canada Book Fund and from the Province of British Columbia through the BC Arts Council and the Book Publishing Tax Credit.

Canada Council for the Arts Conseil des Arts du Canada

Canada

BRITISH COLUMBIA ARTS COUNCIL
An agency of the Province of British Columbia

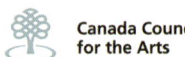

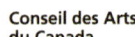

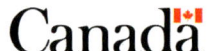

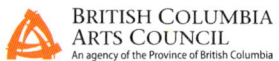

Introduction

I've always thought dogs' tails are fascinating. They're so incredibly versatile. They use them to communicate everything from the furious, full-body-wiggling "I'm so happy to see you I could burst!" wag, the side-to-side "I'm not sure who you are but I'm pretty sure I smell a treat in your pocket" wag, and the "N-O-O-O! Is that the vet's office we're pulling up to?" under-the-bum tuck. They also keep noses warm on cold nights (unless they have been docked) and they are excellent at conveniently sweeping food off low tables.

Tails Don't Lie 2 features the philosophical, ditch-wading, farting, shedding, bed-hogging, hairy scroungers who inhabit my *Other Coast* comic strip. They reveal why dogs covet the driver's seat, what would happen if dogs went on space missions (do aliens have dogs?), the humiliation of tail-docking, if purebreds are really canine snobs, the immense importance of trees to a dog, and ask the eternal question: Why isn't squirrel-chasing included in dog agility courses?

If you have a dog, I hope you will spot yours in *Tails Don't Lie 2*. If you don't have a dog, visit your local animal shelter. There's a dog there waiting for you. And, as anyone who has rescued a dog will tell you, rescue dogs give the best face-licks!

—ADRIAN RAESIDE

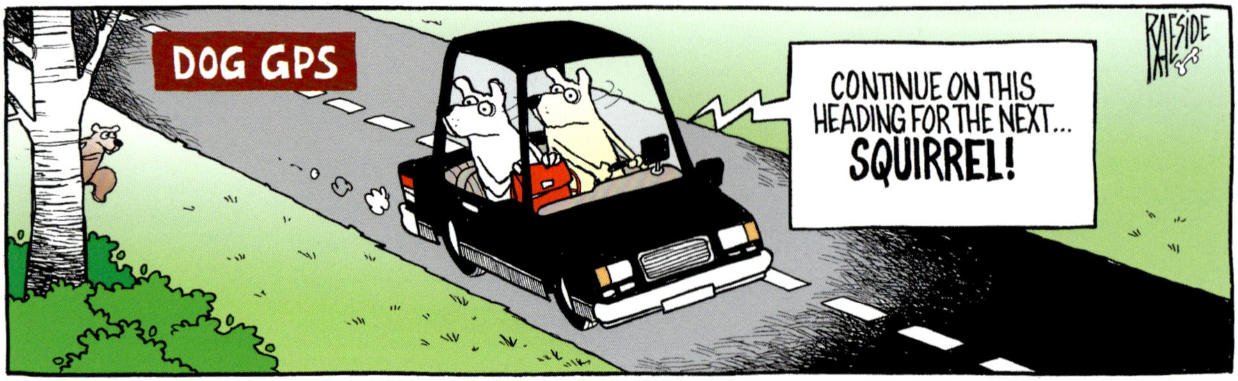
DOG GPS
CONTINUE ON THIS HEADING FOR THE NEXT... SQUIRREL!
RAESIDE

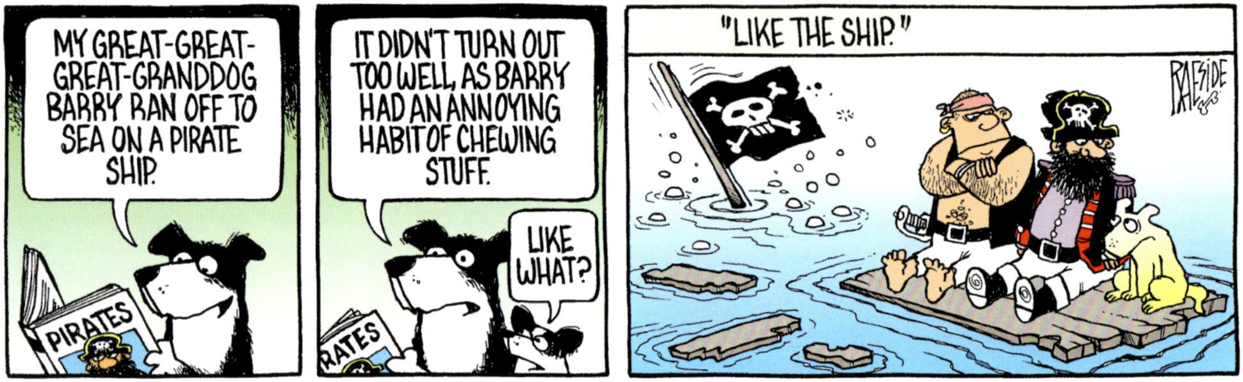
MY GREAT-GREAT-GREAT-GRANDDOG BARRY RAN OFF TO SEA ON A PIRATE SHIP.
PIRATES
IT DIDN'T TURN OUT TOO WELL, AS BARRY HAD AN ANNOYING HABIT OF CHEWING STUFF.
LIKE WHAT?
RATES
"LIKE THE SHIP."
RAESIDE

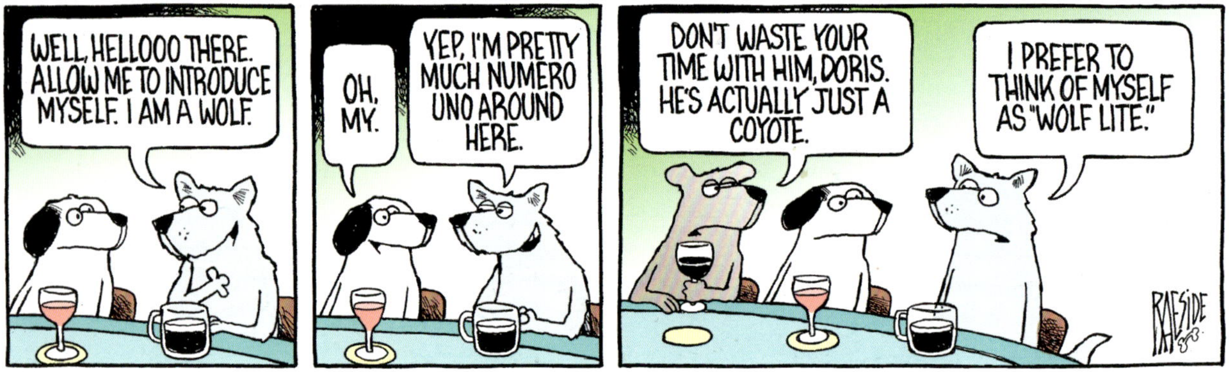
WELL, HELLOOO THERE. ALLOW ME TO INTRODUCE MYSELF. I AM A WOLF.
OH, MY.
YEP, I'M PRETTY MUCH NUMERO UNO AROUND HERE.
DON'T WASTE YOUR TIME WITH HIM, DORIS. HE'S ACTUALLY JUST A COYOTE.
I PREFER TO THINK OF MYSELF AS "WOLF LITE."
RAESIDE

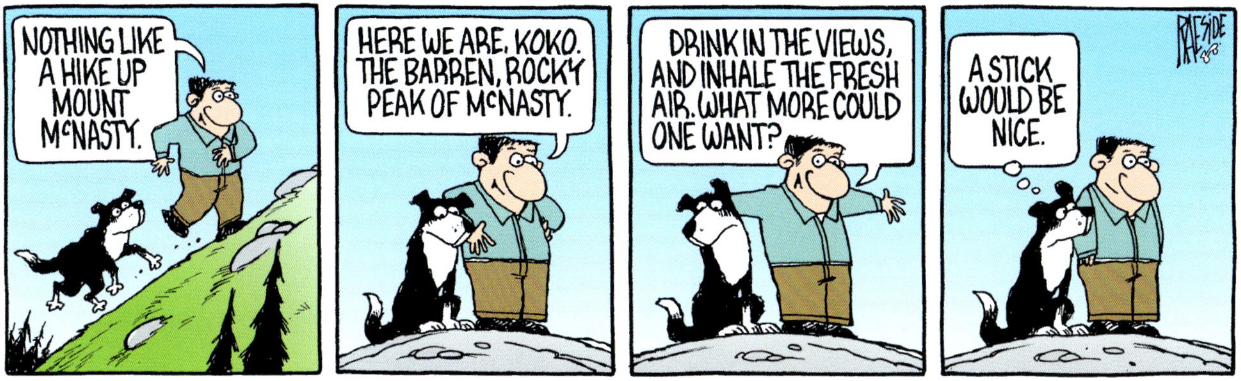
NOTHING LIKE A HIKE UP MOUNT McNASTY.
HERE WE ARE, KOKO. THE BARREN, ROCKY PEAK OF McNASTY.
DRINK IN THE VIEWS, AND INHALE THE FRESH AIR. WHAT MORE COULD ONE WANT?
A STICK WOULD BE NICE.

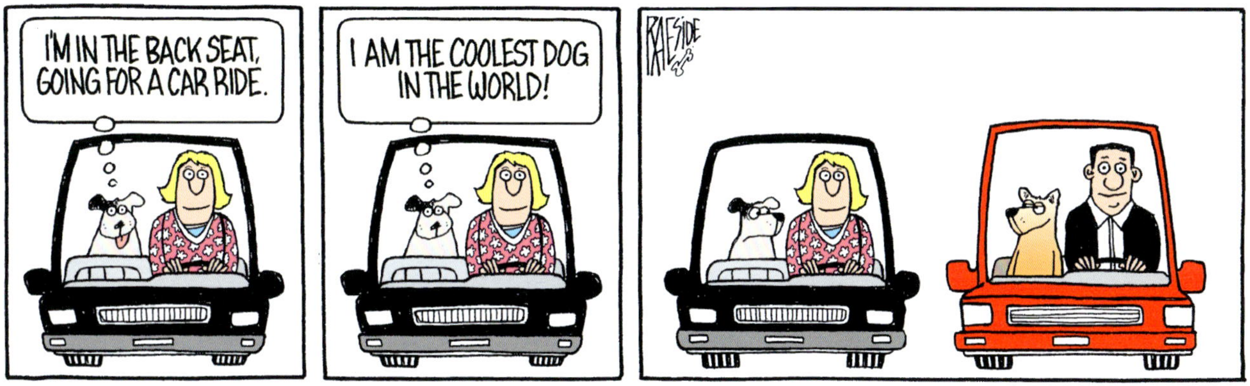
I'M IN THE BACK SEAT, GOING FOR A CAR RIDE.
I AM THE COOLEST DOG IN THE WORLD!

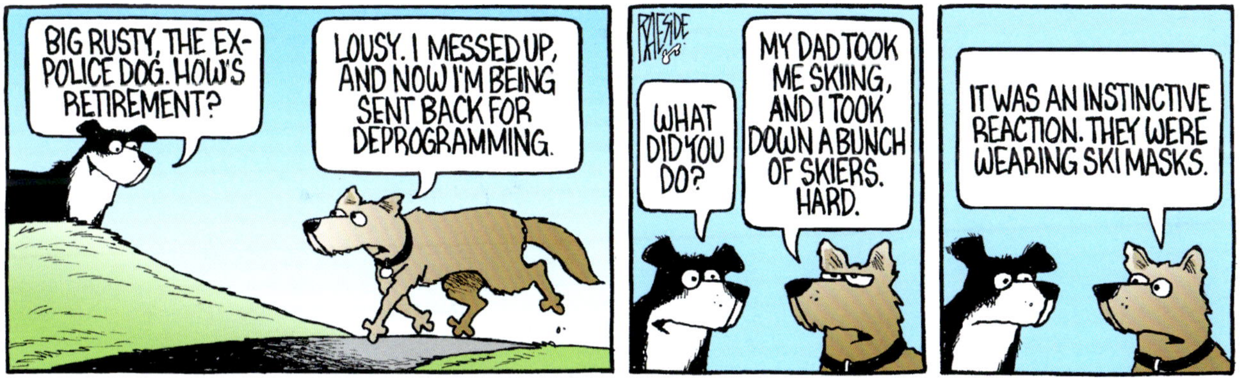
BIG RUSTY, THE EX-POLICE DOG. HOW'S RETIREMENT?
LOUSY. I MESSED UP, AND NOW I'M BEING SENT BACK FOR DEPROGRAMMING.
WHAT DID YOU DO?
MY DAD TOOK ME SKIING, AND I TOOK DOWN A BUNCH OF SKIERS. HARD.
IT WAS AN INSTINCTIVE REACTION. THEY WERE WEARING SKI MASKS.

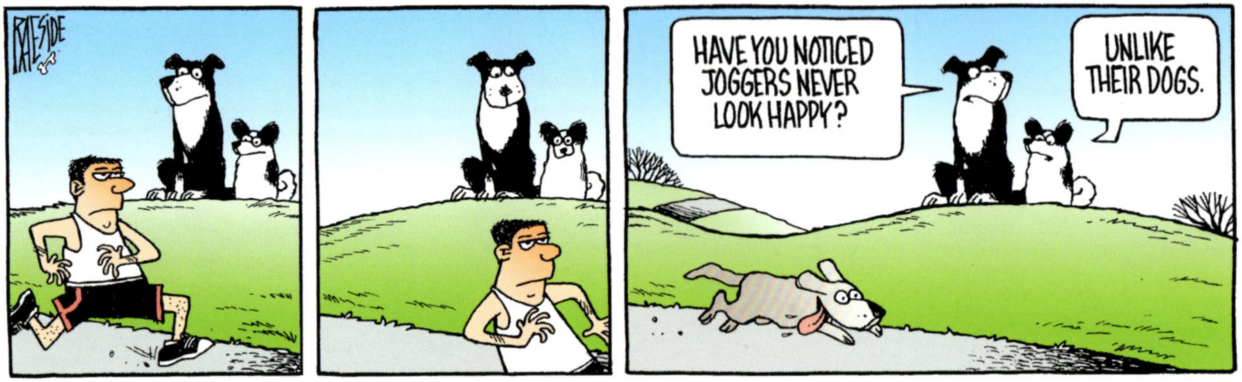
RAESIDE
HAVE YOU NOTICED JOGGERS NEVER LOOK HAPPY?
UNLIKE THEIR DOGS.

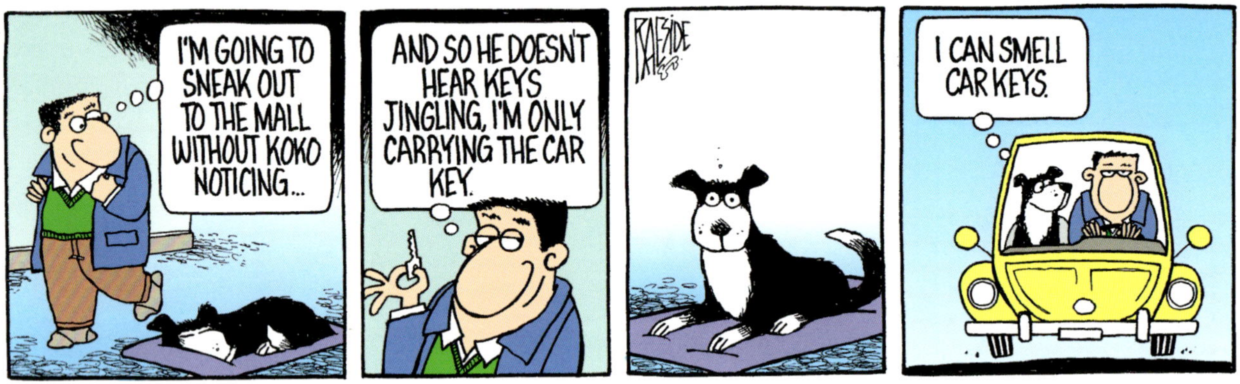
I'M GOING TO SNEAK OUT TO THE MALL WITHOUT KOKO NOTICING...
AND SO HE DOESN'T HEAR KEYS JINGLING, I'M ONLY CARRYING THE CAR KEY.
RAESIDE
I CAN SMELL CAR KEYS.

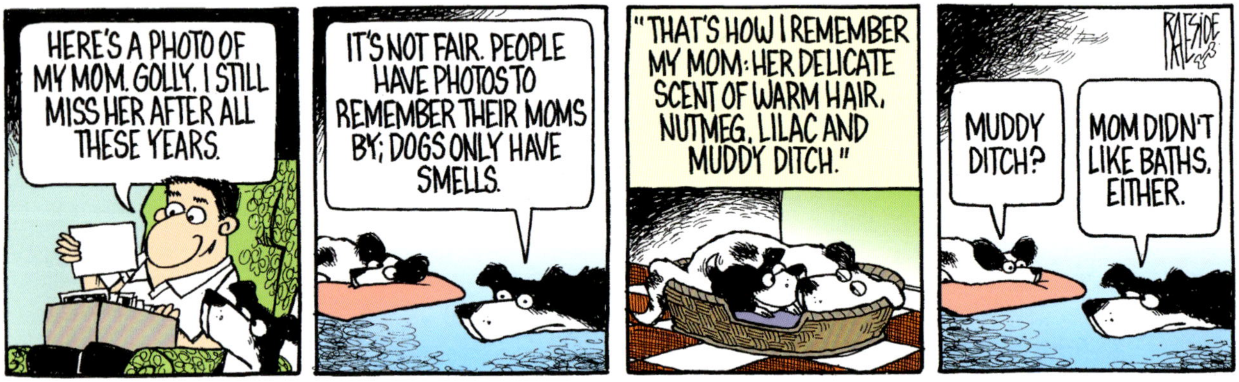
HERE'S A PHOTO OF MY MOM. GOLLY, I STILL MISS HER AFTER ALL THESE YEARS.
IT'S NOT FAIR. PEOPLE HAVE PHOTOS TO REMEMBER THEIR MOMS BY; DOGS ONLY HAVE SMELLS.
"THAT'S HOW I REMEMBER MY MOM: HER DELICATE SCENT OF WARM HAIR, NUTMEG, LILAC AND MUDDY DITCH."
RAESIDE
MUDDY DITCH?
MOM DIDN'T LIKE BATHS, EITHER.

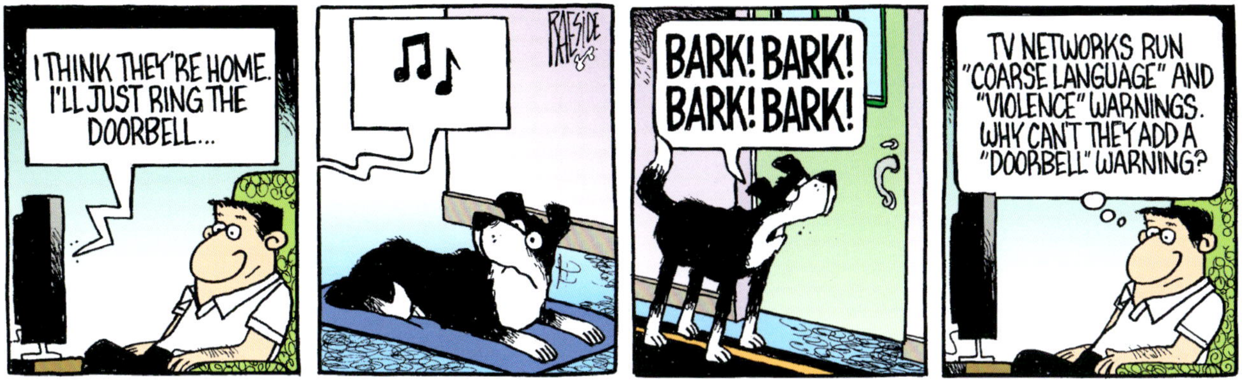
I THINK THEY'RE HOME. I'LL JUST RING THE DOORBELL...
RAESIDE
BARK! BARK! BARK! BARK!
TV NETWORKS RUN "COARSE LANGUAGE" AND "VIOLENCE" WARNINGS. WHY CAN'T THEY ADD A "DOORBELL" WARNING?

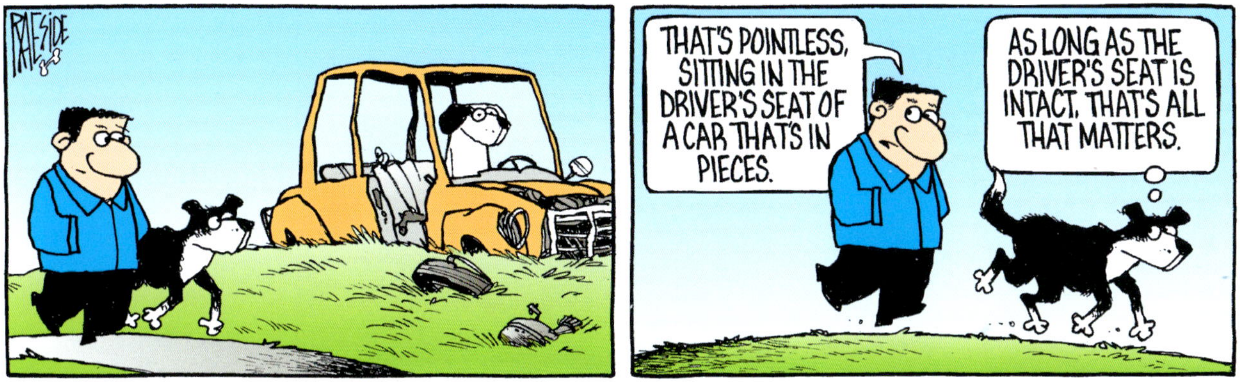
RAESIDE
THAT'S POINTLESS, SITTING IN THE DRIVER'S SEAT OF A CAR THAT'S IN PIECES.
AS LONG AS THE DRIVER'S SEAT IS INTACT, THAT'S ALL THAT MATTERS.

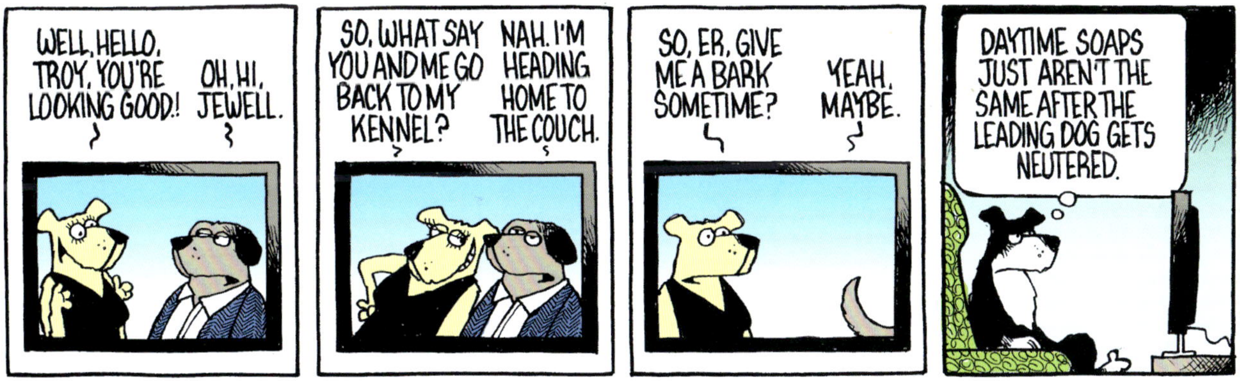
WELL, HELLO, TROY. YOU'RE LOOKING GOOD!
OH, HI, JEWELL.
SO, WHAT SAY YOU AND ME GO BACK TO MY KENNEL?
NAH. I'M HEADING HOME TO THE COUCH.
SO, ER, GIVE ME A BARK SOMETIME?
YEAH, MAYBE.
DAYTIME SOAPS JUST AREN'T THE SAME AFTER THE LEADING DOG GETS NEUTERED.

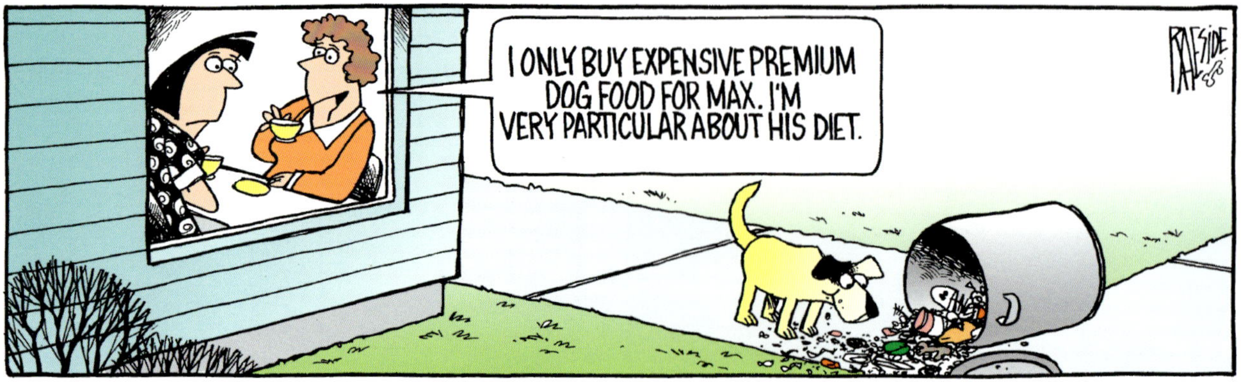
I ONLY BUY EXPENSIVE PREMIUM DOG FOOD FOR MAX. I'M VERY PARTICULAR ABOUT HIS DIET.

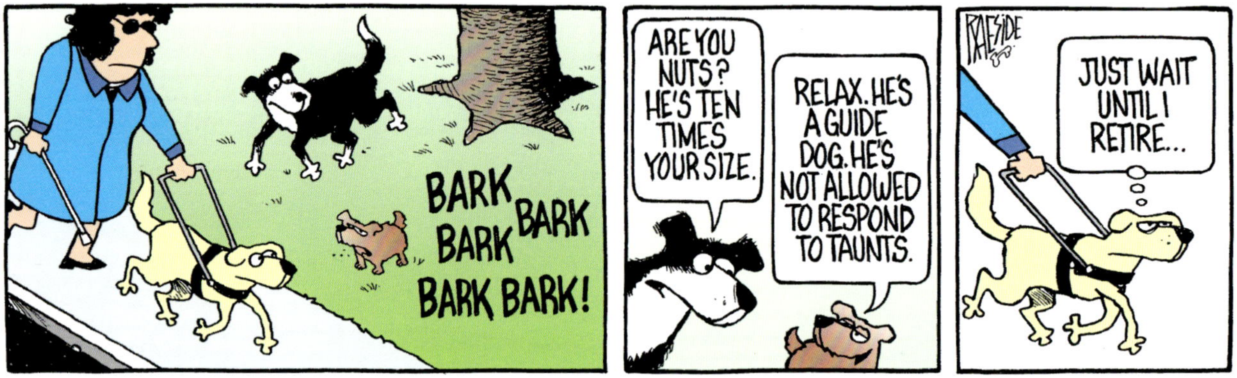
BARK BARK BARK BARK BARK!
ARE YOU NUTS? HE'S TEN TIMES YOUR SIZE.
RELAX. HE'S A GUIDE DOG. HE'S NOT ALLOWED TO RESPOND TO TAUNTS.
JUST WAIT UNTIL I RETIRE...

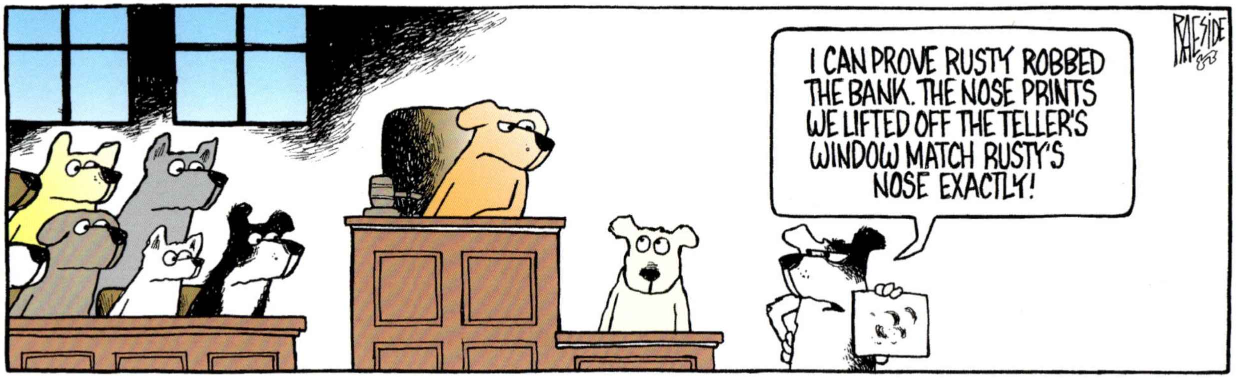
I CAN PROVE RUSTY ROBBED THE BANK. THE NOSE PRINTS WE LIFTED OFF THE TELLER'S WINDOW MATCH RUSTY'S NOSE EXACTLY!

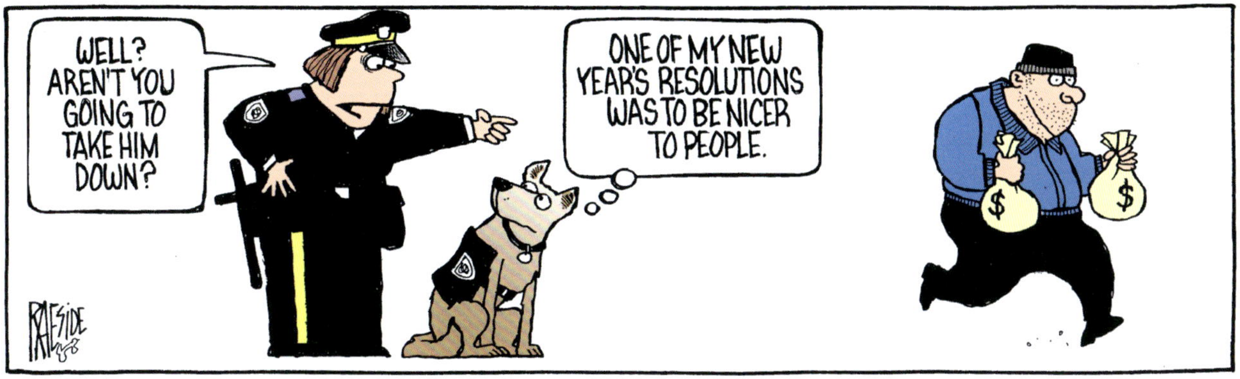
WELL? AREN'T YOU GOING TO TAKE HIM DOWN?
ONE OF MY NEW YEAR'S RESOLUTIONS WAS TO BE NICER TO PEOPLE.

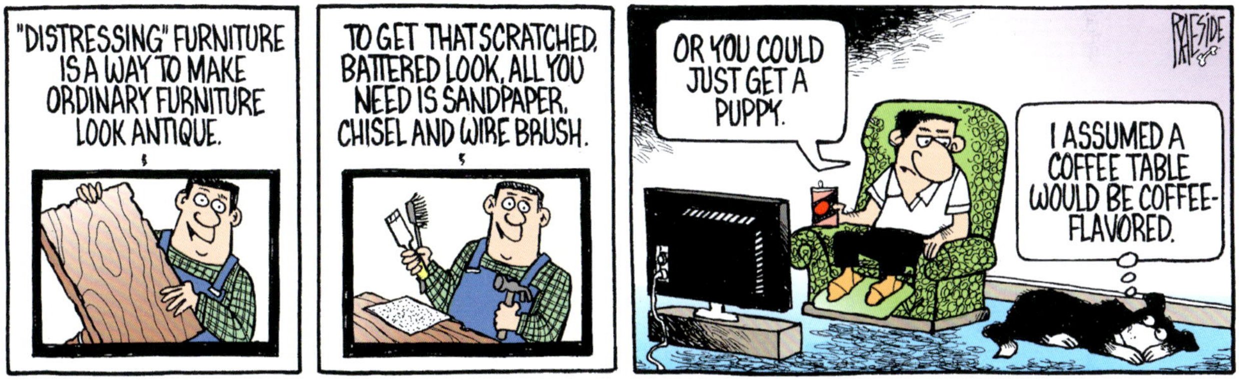
"DISTRESSING" FURNITURE IS A WAY TO MAKE ORDINARY FURNITURE LOOK ANTIQUE.
TO GET THAT SCRATCHED, BATTERED LOOK, ALL YOU NEED IS SANDPAPER, CHISEL AND WIRE BRUSH.
OR YOU COULD JUST GET A PUPPY.
I ASSUMED A COFFEE TABLE WOULD BE COFFEE-FLAVORED.

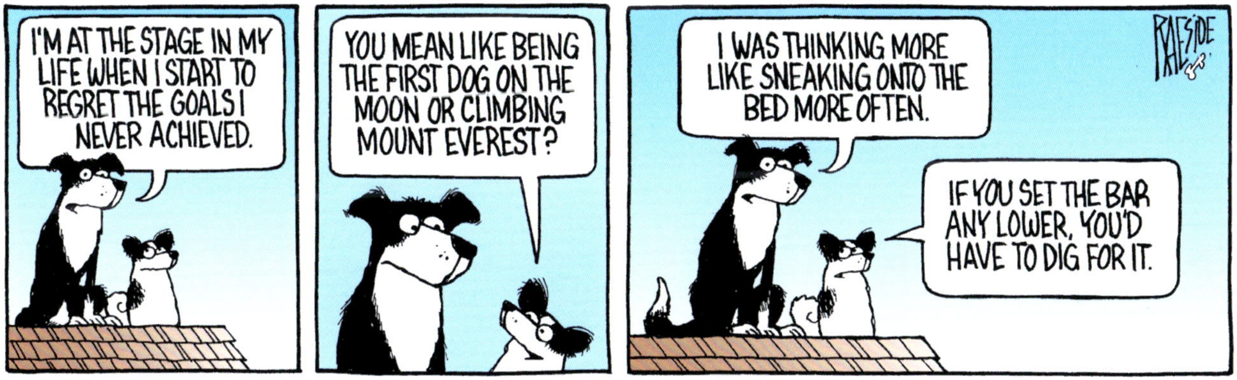
I'M AT THE STAGE IN MY LIFE WHEN I START TO REGRET THE GOALS I NEVER ACHIEVED.
YOU MEAN LIKE BEING THE FIRST DOG ON THE MOON OR CLIMBING MOUNT EVEREST?
I WAS THINKING MORE LIKE SNEAKING ONTO THE BED MORE OFTEN.
IF YOU SET THE BAR ANY LOWER, YOU'D HAVE TO DIG FOR IT.

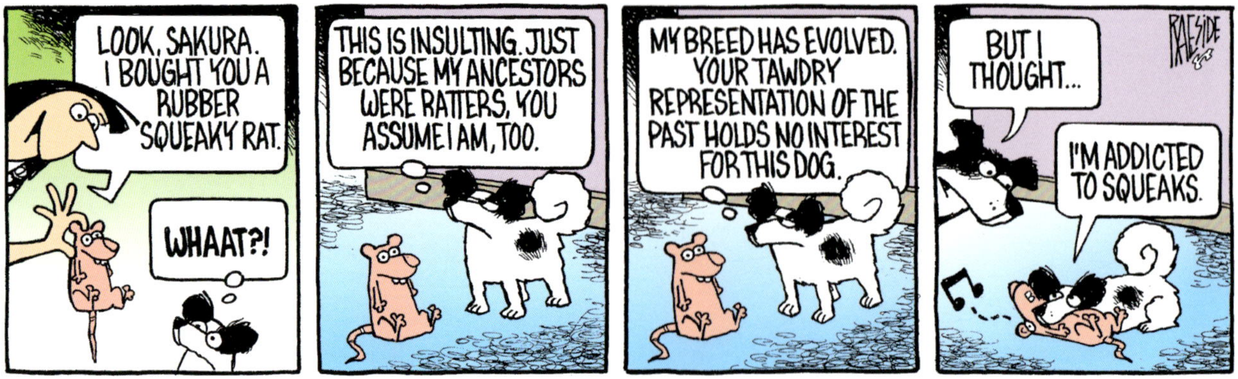
LOOK, SAKURA. I BOUGHT YOU A RUBBER SQUEAKY RAT.
WHAAT?!
THIS IS INSULTING. JUST BECAUSE MY ANCESTORS WERE RATTERS, YOU ASSUME I AM, TOO.
MY BREED HAS EVOLVED. YOUR TAWDRY REPRESENTATION OF THE PAST HOLDS NO INTEREST FOR THIS DOG.
BUT I THOUGHT...
I'M ADDICTED TO SQUEAKS.

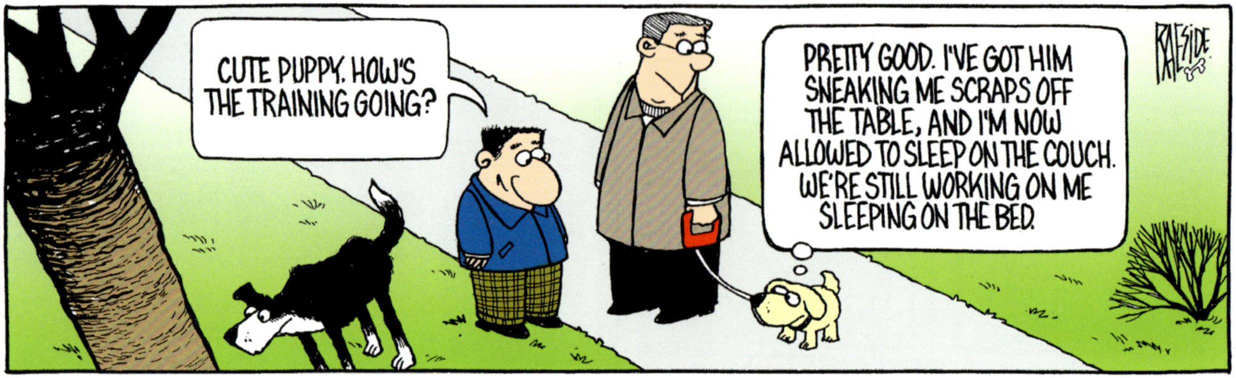
CUTE PUPPY. HOW'S THE TRAINING GOING?
PRETTY GOOD. I'VE GOT HIM SNEAKING ME SCRAPS OFF THE TABLE, AND I'M NOW ALLOWED TO SLEEP ON THE COUCH. WE'RE STILL WORKING ON ME SLEEPING ON THE BED.

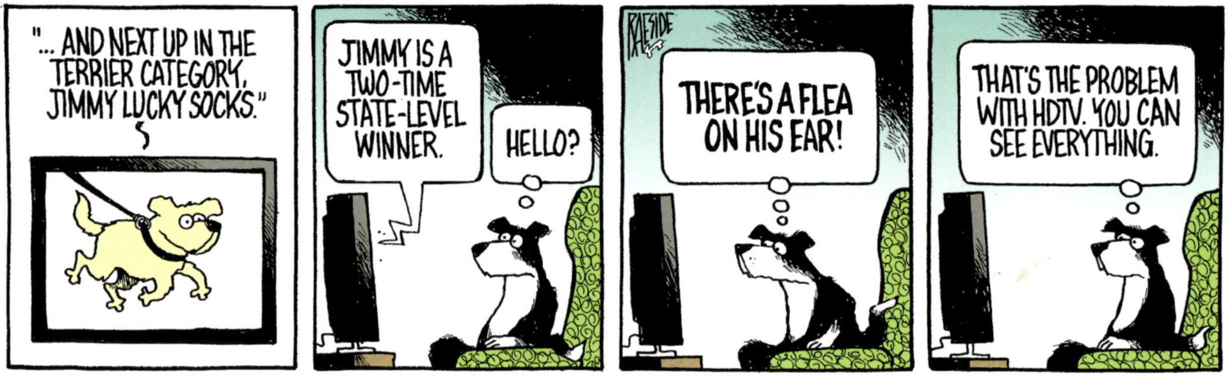
"... AND NEXT UP IN THE TERRIER CATEGORY, JIMMY LUCKY SOCKS."
JIMMY IS A TWO-TIME STATE-LEVEL WINNER.
HELLO?
THERE'S A FLEA ON HIS EAR!
THAT'S THE PROBLEM WITH HDTV. YOU CAN SEE EVERYTHING.

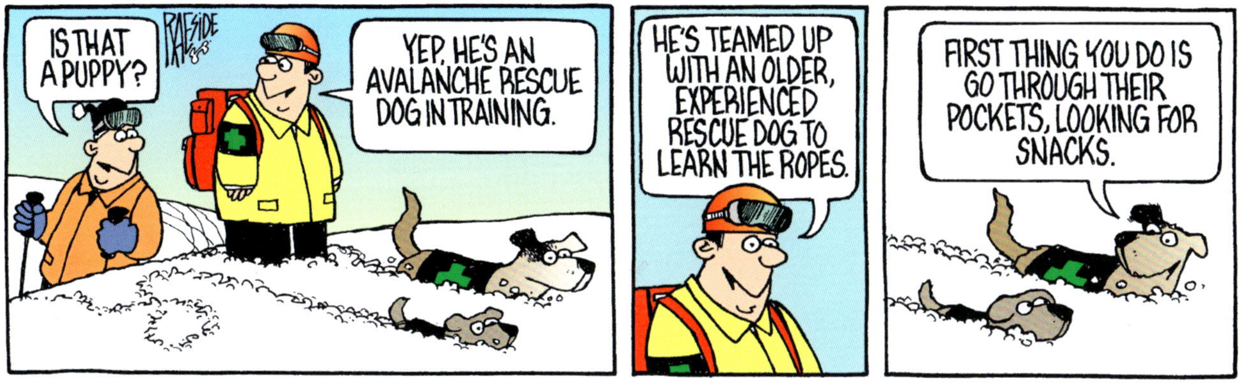
IS THAT A PUPPY?
YEP, HE'S AN AVALANCHE RESCUE DOG IN TRAINING.
HE'S TEAMED UP WITH AN OLDER, EXPERIENCED RESCUE DOG TO LEARN THE ROPES.
FIRST THING YOU DO IS GO THROUGH THEIR POCKETS, LOOKING FOR SNACKS.

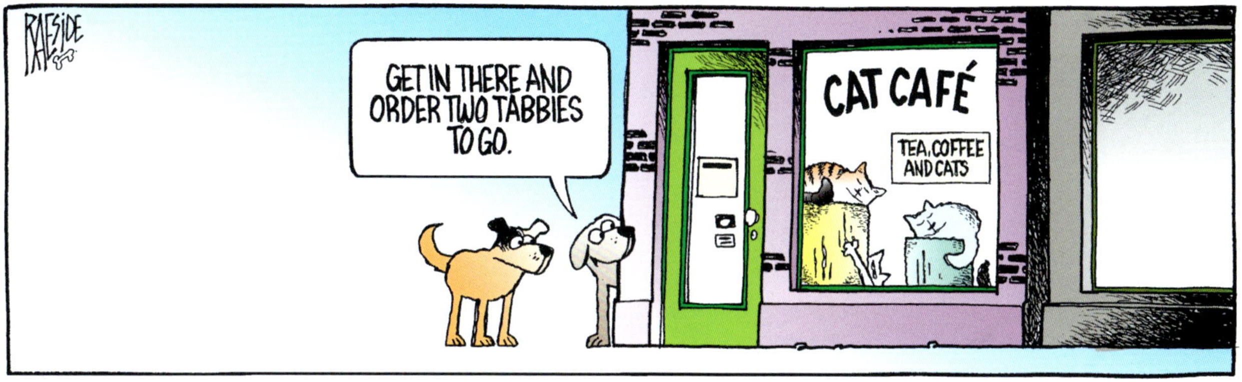
GET IN THERE AND ORDER TWO TABBIES TO GO.
CAT CAFÉ
TEA, COFFEE AND CATS

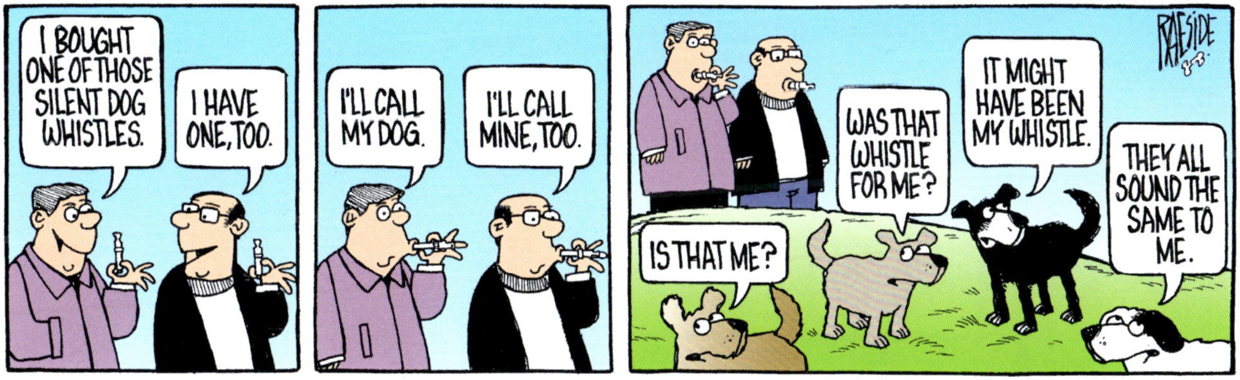
I BOUGHT ONE OF THOSE SILENT DOG WHISTLES.
I HAVE ONE, TOO.
I'LL CALL MY DOG.
I'LL CALL MINE, TOO.
IS THAT ME?
WAS THAT WHISTLE FOR ME?
IT MIGHT HAVE BEEN MY WHISTLE.
THEY ALL SOUND THE SAME TO ME.

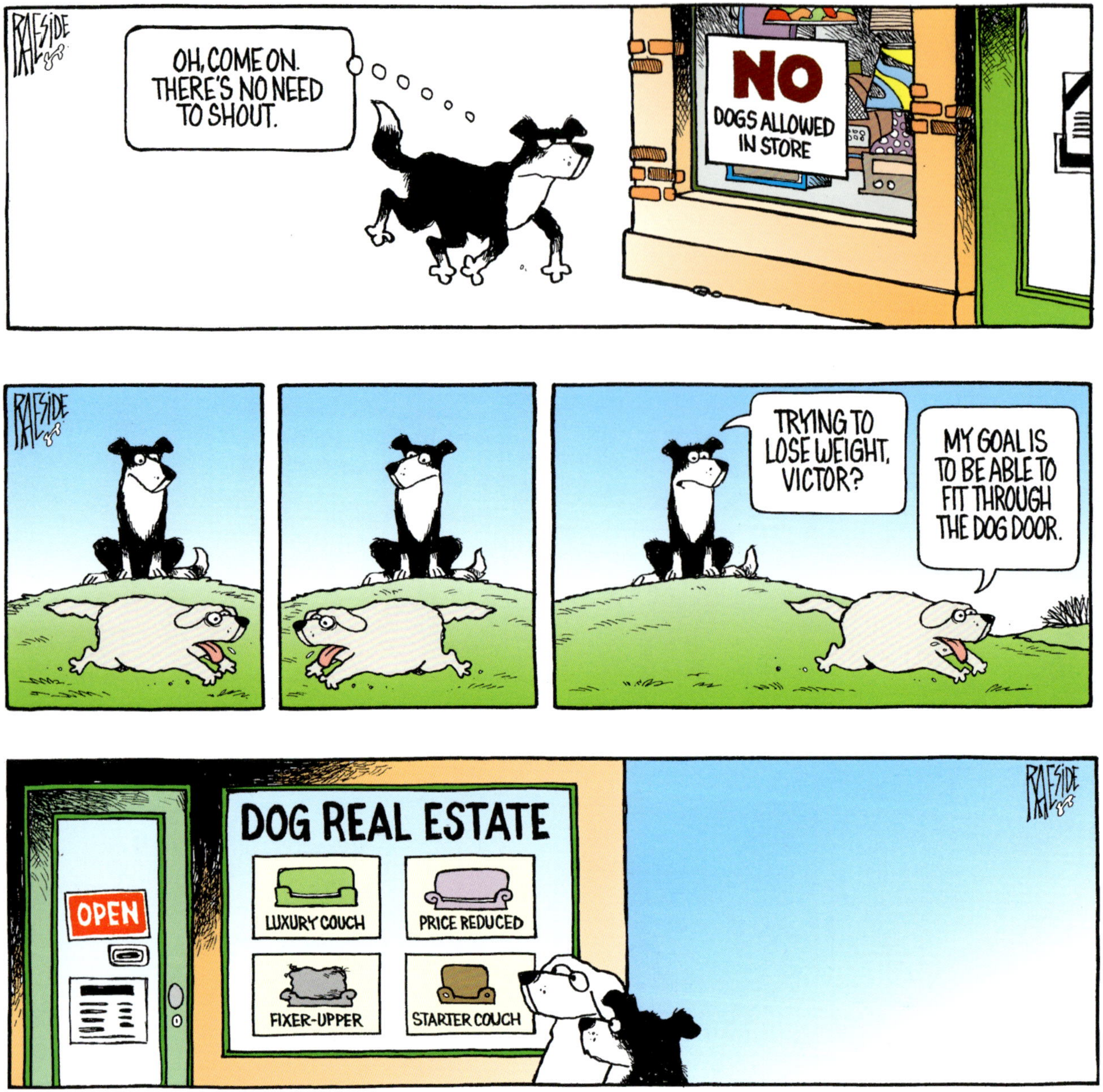
OH, COME ON. THERE'S NO NEED TO SHOUT.
NO
DOGS ALLOWED IN STORE
TRYING TO LOSE WEIGHT, VICTOR?
MY GOAL IS TO BE ABLE TO FIT THROUGH THE DOG DOOR.
OPEN
DOG REAL ESTATE
LUXURY COUCH
PRICE REDUCED
FIXER-UPPER
STARTER COUCH

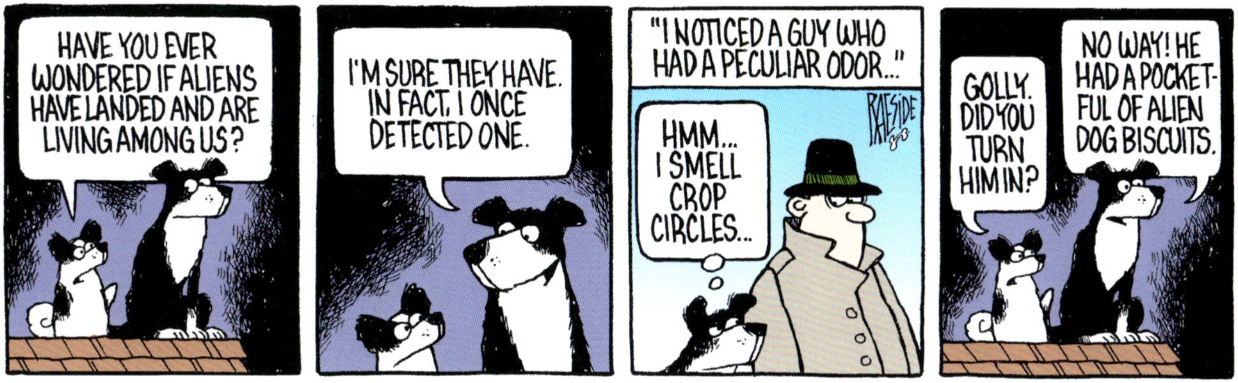
HAVE YOU EVER WONDERED IF ALIENS HAVE LANDED AND ARE LIVING AMONG US?
I'M SURE THEY HAVE. IN FACT, I ONCE DETECTED ONE.
"I NOTICED A GUY WHO HAD A PECULIAR ODOR..."
HMM... I SMELL CROP CIRCLES...
GOLLY. DID YOU TURN HIM IN?
NO WAY! HE HAD A POCKET-FUL OF ALIEN DOG BISCUITS.

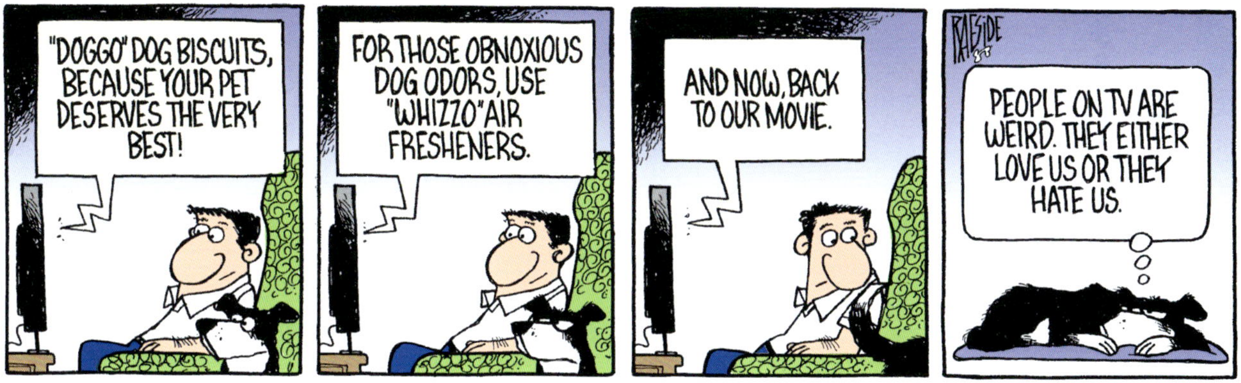
"DOGGO" DOG BISCUITS, BECAUSE YOUR PET DESERVES THE VERY BEST!
FOR THOSE OBNOXIOUS DOG ODORS, USE "WHIZZO" AIR FRESHENERS.
AND NOW, BACK TO OUR MOVIE.
PEOPLE ON TV ARE WEIRD. THEY EITHER LOVE US OR THEY HATE US.

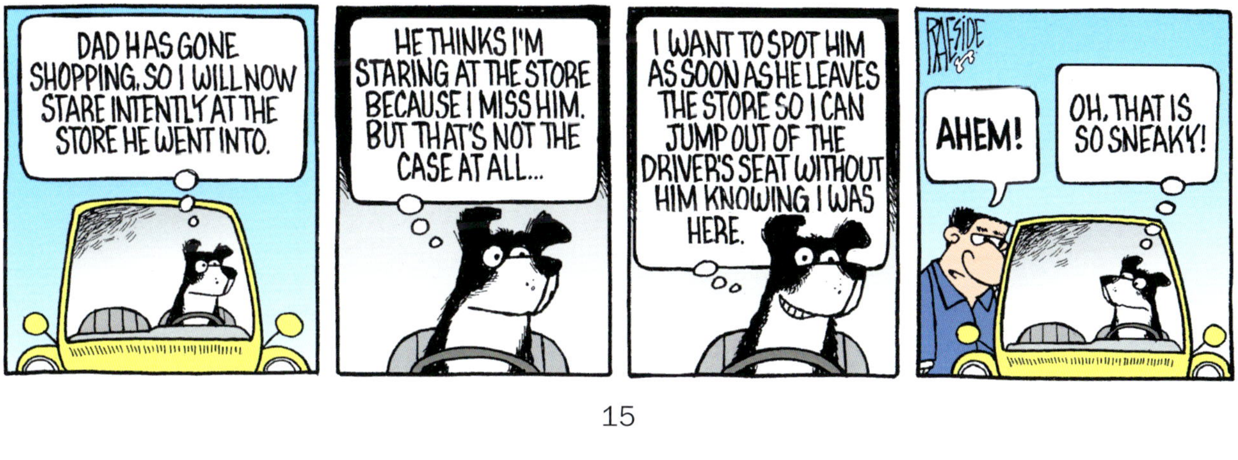
DAD HAS GONE SHOPPING, SO I WILL NOW STARE INTENTLY AT THE STORE HE WENT INTO.
HE THINKS I'M STARING AT THE STORE BECAUSE I MISS HIM. BUT THAT'S NOT THE CASE AT ALL...
I WANT TO SPOT HIM AS SOON AS HE LEAVES THE STORE SO I CAN JUMP OUT OF THE DRIVER'S SEAT WITHOUT HIM KNOWING I WAS HERE.
AHEM!
OH, THAT IS SO SNEAKY!

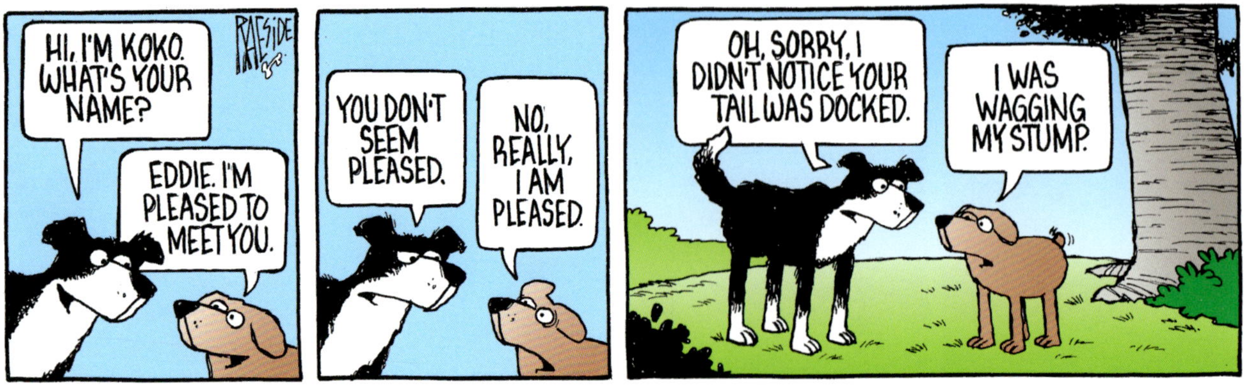
HI, I'M KOKO. WHAT'S YOUR NAME?
EDDIE. I'M PLEASED TO MEET YOU.
YOU DON'T SEEM PLEASED.
NO, REALLY, I AM PLEASED.
OH, SORRY, I DIDN'T NOTICE YOUR TAIL WAS DOCKED.
I WAS WAGGING MY STUMP.

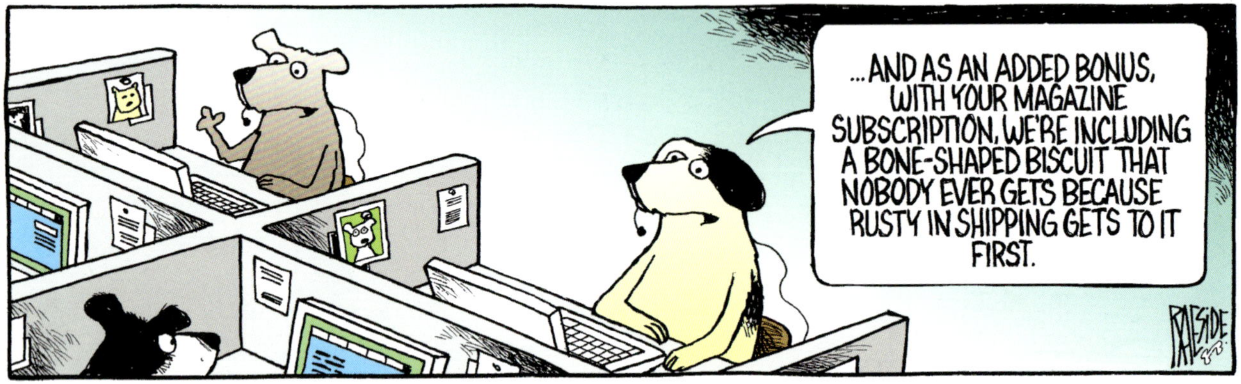
...AND AS AN ADDED BONUS, WITH YOUR MAGAZINE SUBSCRIPTION, WE'RE INCLUDING A BONE-SHAPED BISCUIT THAT NOBODY EVER GETS BECAUSE RUSTY IN SHIPPING GETS TO IT FIRST.

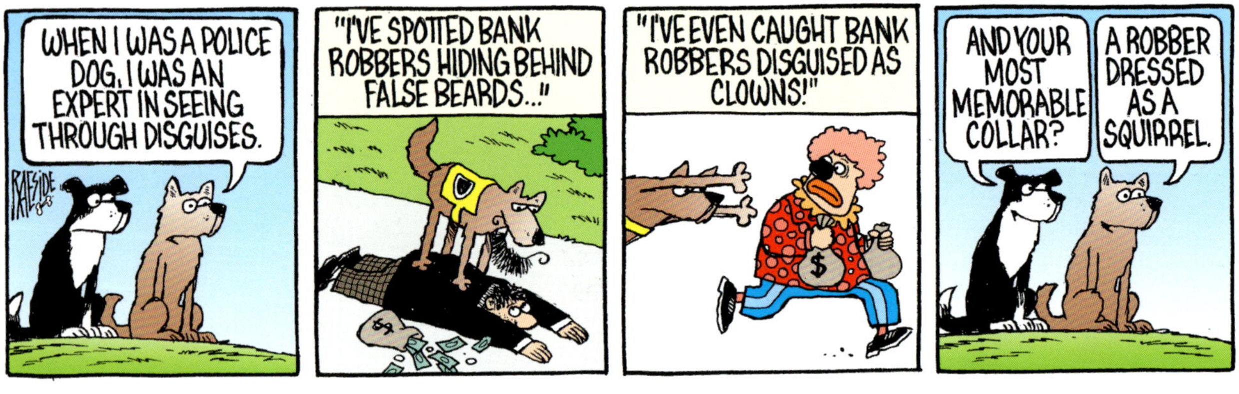
WHEN I WAS A POLICE DOG, I WAS AN EXPERT IN SEEING THROUGH DISGUISES.
"I'VE SPOTTED BANK ROBBERS HIDING BEHIND FALSE BEARDS..."
"I'VE EVEN CAUGHT BANK ROBBERS DISGUISED AS CLOWNS!"
AND YOUR MOST MEMORABLE COLLAR?
A ROBBER DRESSED AS A SQUIRREL.

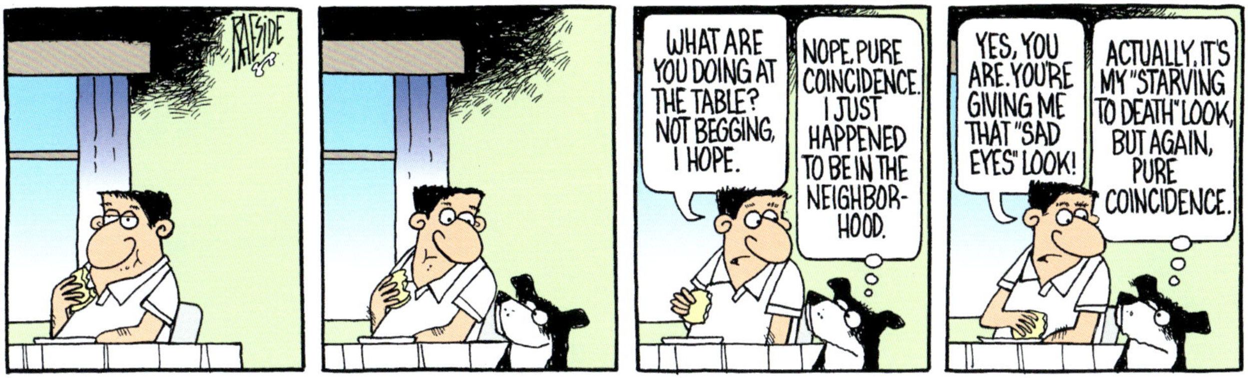
WHAT ARE YOU DOING AT THE TABLE? NOT BEGGING, I HOPE.
NOPE, PURE COINCIDENCE. I JUST HAPPENED TO BE IN THE NEIGHBORHOOD.
YES, YOU ARE. YOU'RE GIVING ME THAT "SAD EYES" LOOK!
ACTUALLY, IT'S MY "STARVING TO DEATH" LOOK, BUT AGAIN, PURE COINCIDENCE.

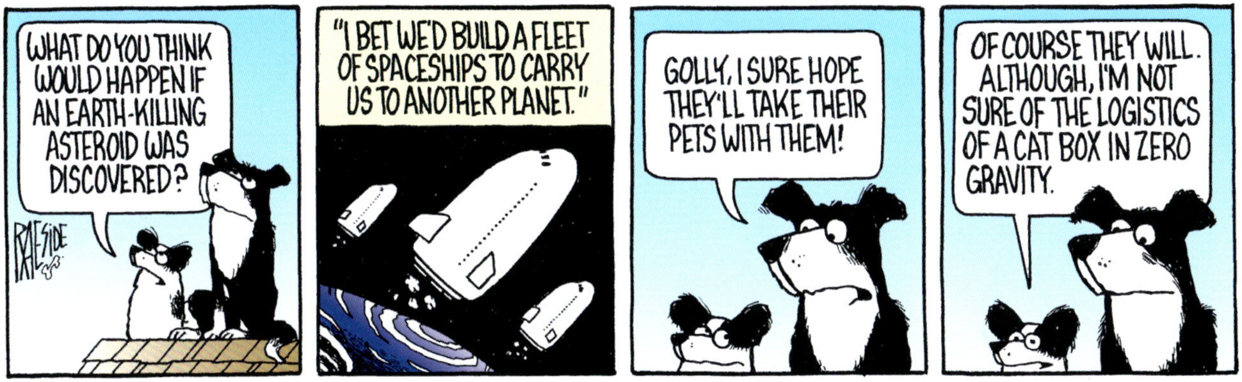
WHAT DO YOU THINK WOULD HAPPEN IF AN EARTH-KILLING ASTEROID WAS DISCOVERED?
"I BET WE'D BUILD A FLEET OF SPACESHIPS TO CARRY US TO ANOTHER PLANET."
GOLLY, I SURE HOPE THEY'LL TAKE THEIR PETS WITH THEM!
OF COURSE THEY WILL. ALTHOUGH, I'M NOT SURE OF THE LOGISTICS OF A CAT BOX IN ZERO GRAVITY.

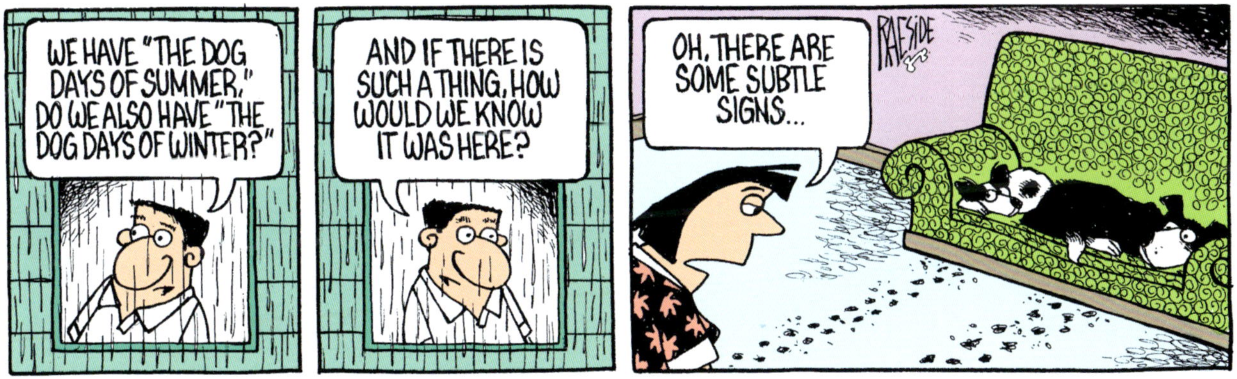
WE HAVE "THE DOG DAYS OF SUMMER," DO WE ALSO HAVE "THE DOG DAYS OF WINTER?"
AND IF THERE IS SUCH A THING, HOW WOULD WE KNOW IT WAS HERE?
OH, THERE ARE SOME SUBTLE SIGNS...

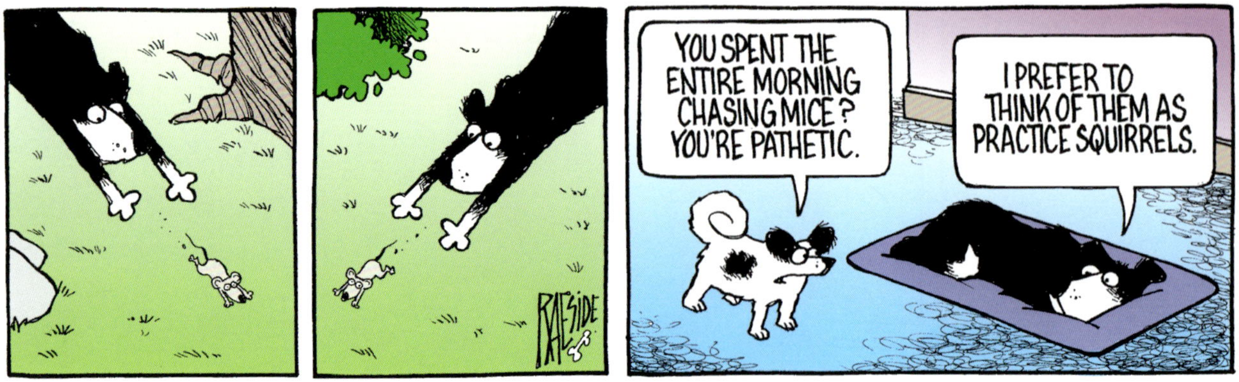
YOU SPENT THE ENTIRE MORNING CHASING MICE? YOU'RE PATHETIC.
I PREFER TO THINK OF THEM AS PRACTICE SQUIRRELS.

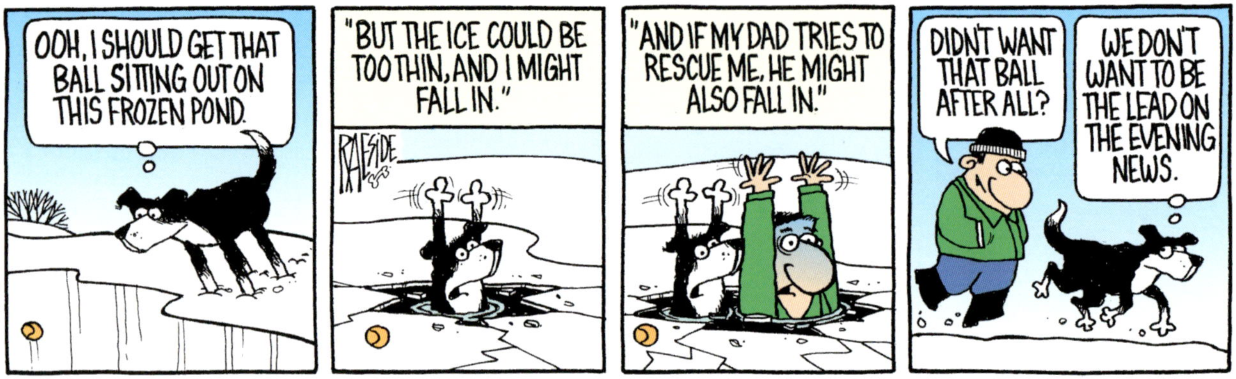
OOH, I SHOULD GET THAT BALL SITTING OUT ON THIS FROZEN POND.
"BUT THE ICE COULD BE TOO THIN, AND I MIGHT FALL IN."
"AND IF MY DAD TRIES TO RESCUE ME, HE MIGHT ALSO FALL IN."
DIDN'T WANT THAT BALL AFTER ALL?
WE DON'T WANT TO BE THE LEAD ON THE EVENING NEWS.

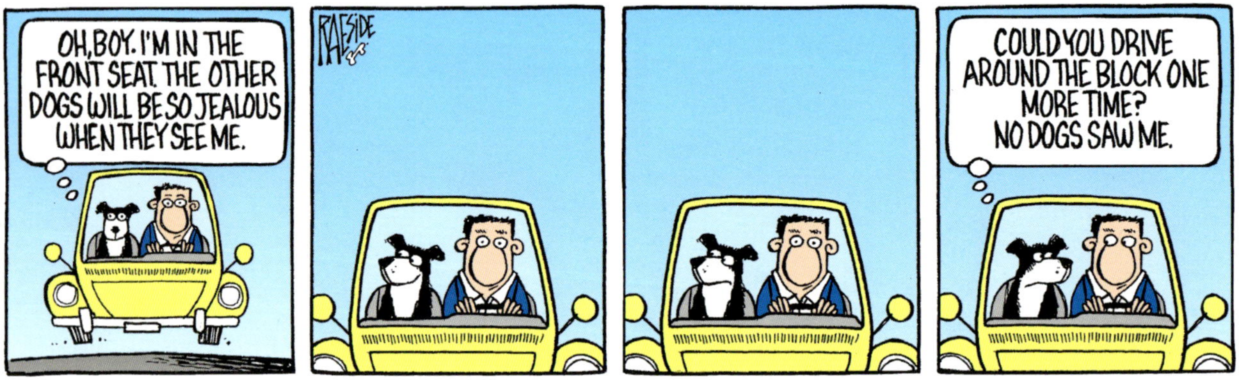
OH, BOY. I'M IN THE FRONT SEAT. THE OTHER DOGS WILL BE SO JEALOUS WHEN THEY SEE ME.
COULD YOU DRIVE AROUND THE BLOCK ONE MORE TIME? NO DOGS SAW ME.

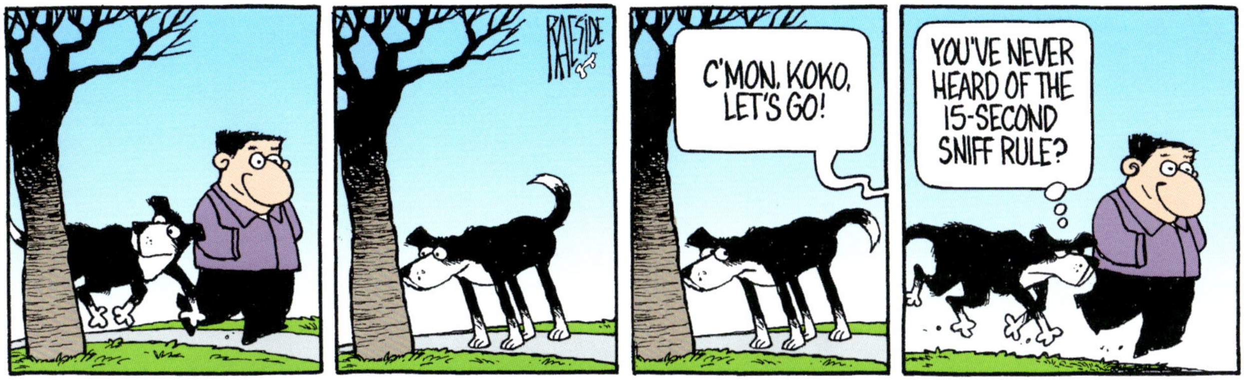
C'MON, KOKO, LET'S GO!
YOU'VE NEVER HEARD OF THE 15-SECOND SNIFF RULE?

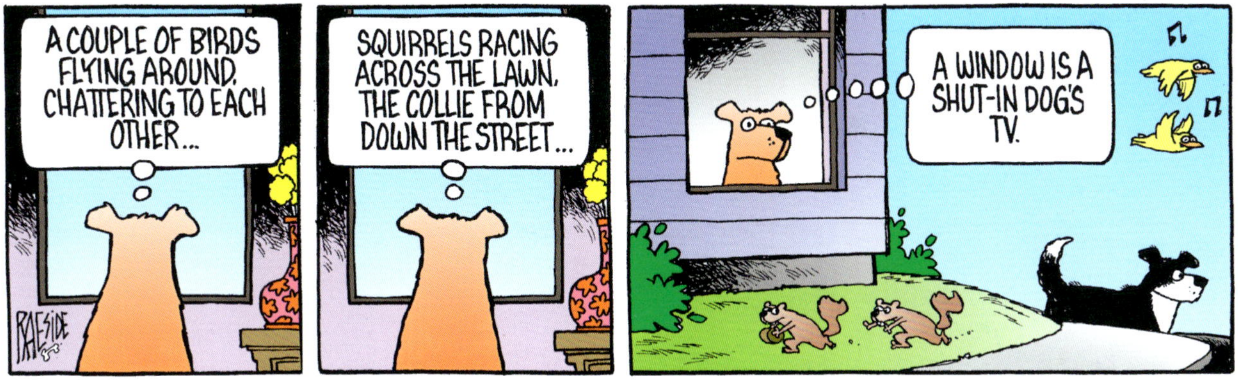
A COUPLE OF BIRDS FLYING AROUND, CHATTERING TO EACH OTHER...
SQUIRRELS RACING ACROSS THE LAWN, THE COLLIE FROM DOWN THE STREET...
A WINDOW IS A SHUT-IN DOG'S TV.

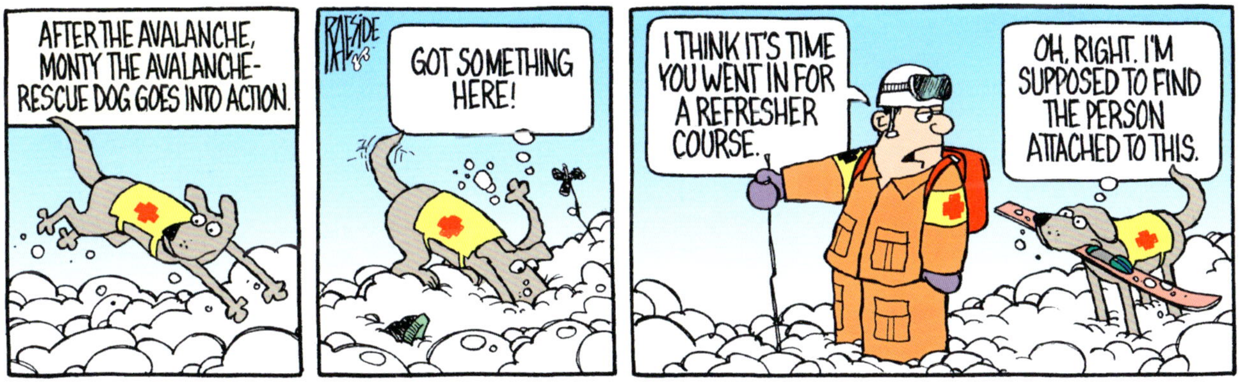
AFTER THE AVALANCHE, MONTY THE AVALANCHE-RESCUE DOG GOES INTO ACTION.
GOT SOMETHING HERE!
I THINK IT'S TIME YOU WENT IN FOR A REFRESHER COURSE.
OH, RIGHT. I'M SUPPOSED TO FIND THE PERSON ATTACHED TO THIS.

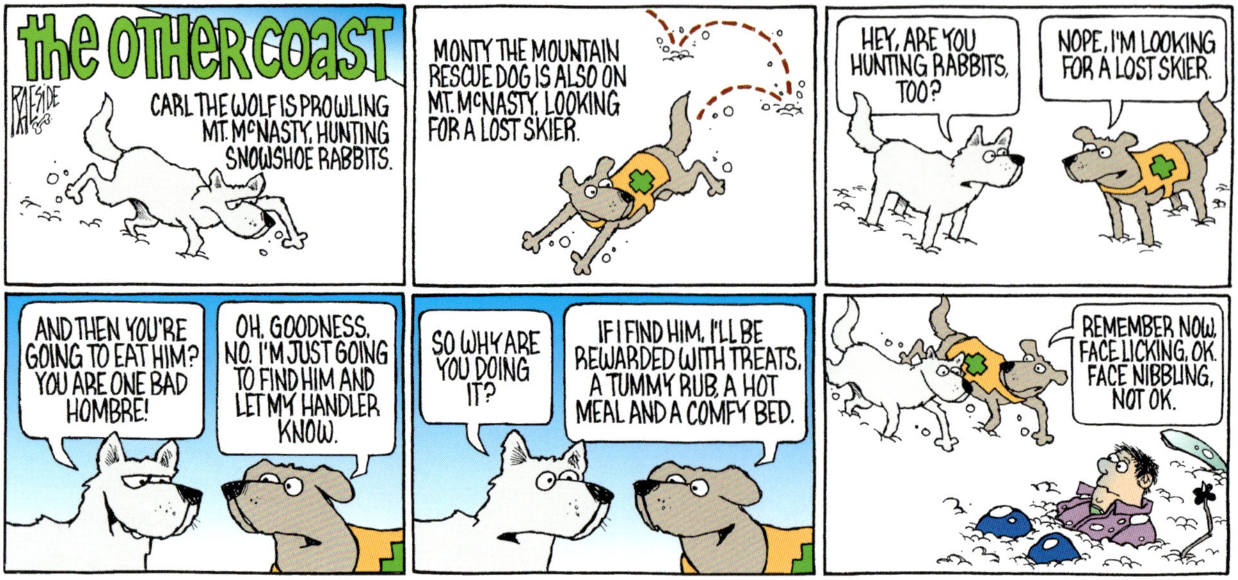
the OTHER COAST
RAESIDE
CARL THE WOLF IS PROWLING MT. McNASTY, HUNTING SNOWSHOE RABBITS.
MONTY THE MOUNTAIN RESCUE DOG IS ALSO ON MT. McNASTY, LOOKING FOR A LOST SKIER.
HEY, ARE YOU HUNTING RABBITS, TOO?
NOPE, I'M LOOKING FOR A LOST SKIER.
AND THEN YOU'RE GOING TO EAT HIM? YOU ARE ONE BAD HOMBRE!
OH, GOODNESS, NO. I'M JUST GOING TO FIND HIM AND LET MY HANDLER KNOW.
SO WHY ARE YOU DOING IT?
IF I FIND HIM, I'LL BE REWARDED WITH TREATS, A TUMMY RUB, A HOT MEAL AND A COMFY BED.
REMEMBER NOW, FACE LICKING, OK. FACE NIBBLING, NOT OK.

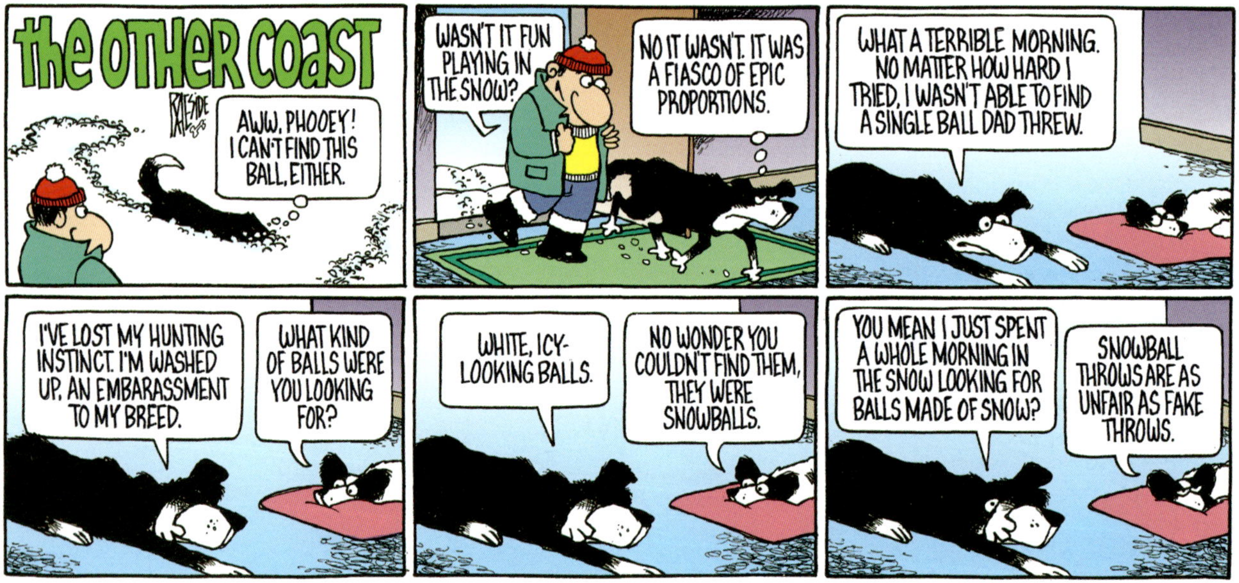
the OTHER COAST
RAESIDE
AWW, PHOOEY! I CAN'T FIND THIS BALL, EITHER.
WASN'T IT FUN PLAYING IN THE SNOW?
NO IT WASN'T. IT WAS A FIASCO OF EPIC PROPORTIONS.
WHAT A TERRIBLE MORNING. NO MATTER HOW HARD I TRIED, I WASN'T ABLE TO FIND A SINGLE BALL DAD THREW.
I'VE LOST MY HUNTING INSTINCT. I'M WASHED UP, AN EMBARASSMENT TO MY BREED.
WHAT KIND OF BALLS WERE YOU LOOKING FOR?
WHITE, ICY-LOOKING BALLS.
NO WONDER YOU COULDN'T FIND THEM, THEY WERE SNOWBALLS.
YOU MEAN I JUST SPENT A WHOLE MORNING IN THE SNOW LOOKING FOR BALLS MADE OF SNOW?
SNOWBALL THROWS ARE AS UNFAIR AS FAKE THROWS.

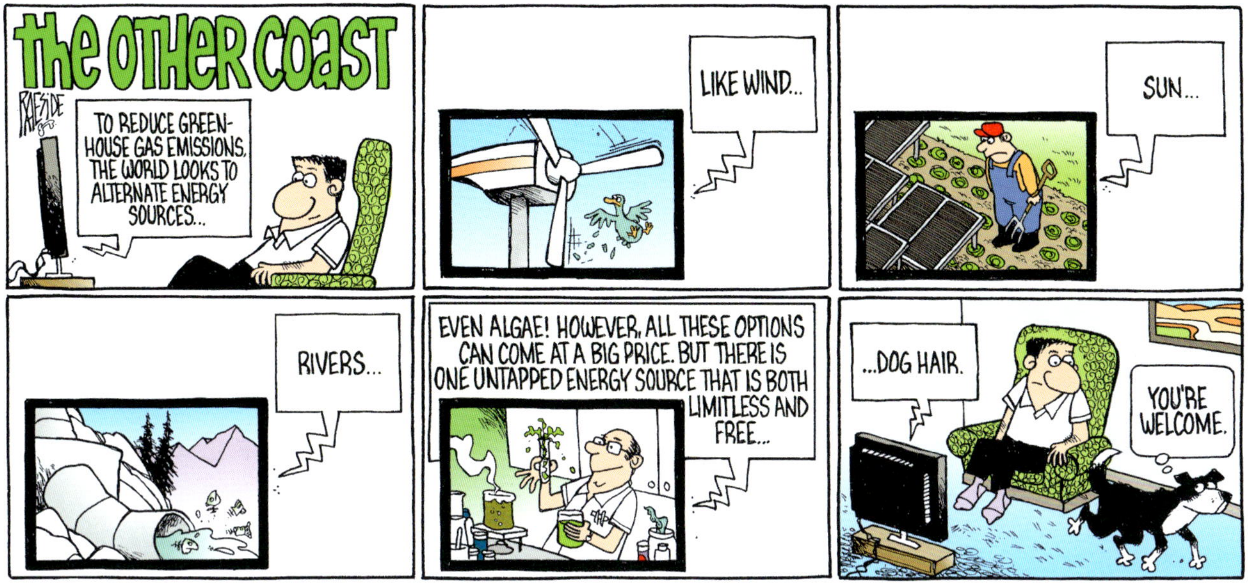
the OTHER COAST
RAESIDE
TO REDUCE GREENHOUSE GAS EMISSIONS, THE WORLD LOOKS TO ALTERNATE ENERGY SOURCES...
LIKE WIND...
SUN...
RIVERS...
EVEN ALGAE! HOWEVER, ALL THESE OPTIONS CAN COME AT A BIG PRICE. BUT THERE IS ONE UNTAPPED ENERGY SOURCE THAT IS BOTH LIMITLESS AND FREE...
...DOG HAIR.
YOU'RE WELCOME.

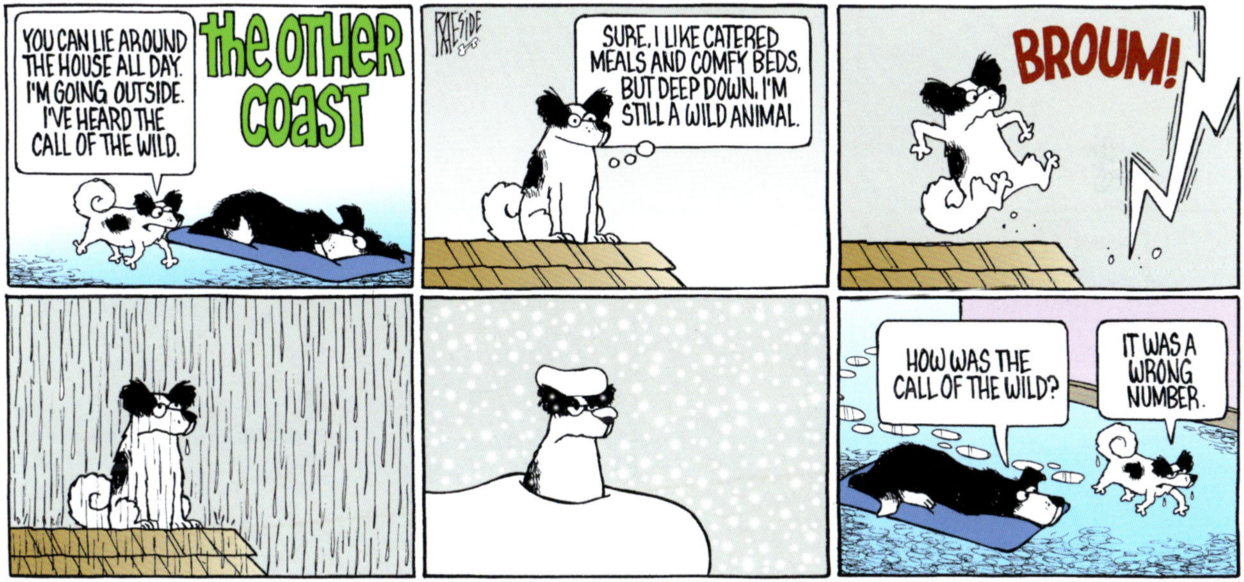
YOU CAN LIE AROUND THE HOUSE ALL DAY. I'M GOING OUTSIDE. I'VE HEARD THE CALL OF THE WILD.
the OTHER COAST
RAESIDE
SURE, I LIKE CATERED MEALS AND COMFY BEDS, BUT DEEP DOWN, I'M STILL A WILD ANIMAL.
BROUM!
HOW WAS THE CALL OF THE WILD?
IT WAS A WRONG NUMBER.

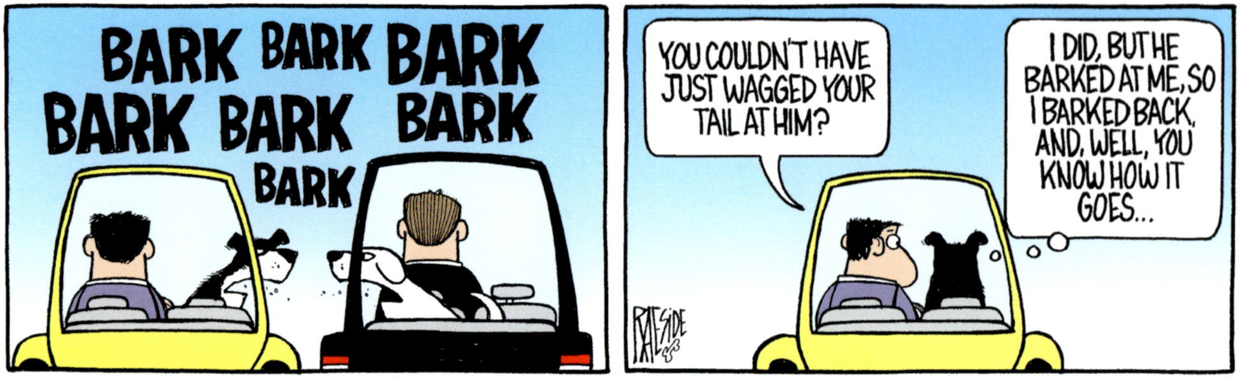
BARK BARK BARK
BARK BARK BARK
BARK
YOU COULDN'T HAVE JUST WAGGED YOUR TAIL AT HIM?
I DID, BUT HE BARKED AT ME, SO I BARKED BACK, AND, WELL, YOU KNOW HOW IT GOES...

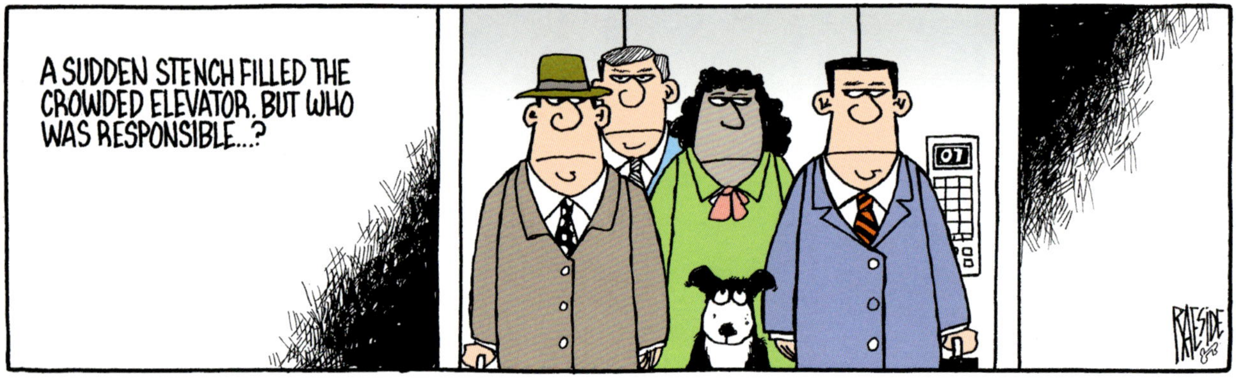
A SUDDEN STENCH FILLED THE CROWDED ELEVATOR. BUT WHO WAS RESPONSIBLE...?
01

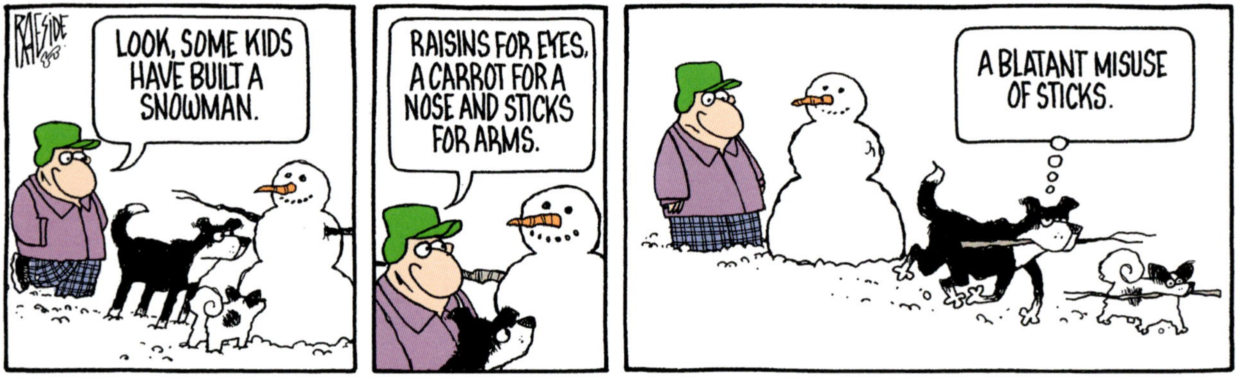
LOOK, SOME KIDS HAVE BUILT A SNOWMAN.
RAISINS FOR EYES, A CARROT FOR A NOSE AND STICKS FOR ARMS.
A BLATANT MISUSE OF STICKS.

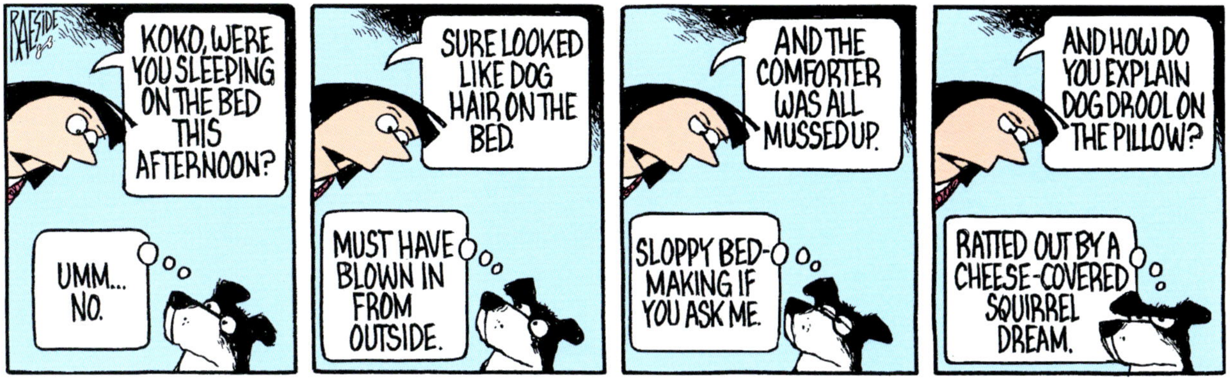
KOKO, WERE YOU SLEEPING ON THE BED THIS AFTERNOON?
UMM... NO.
SURE LOOKED LIKE DOG HAIR ON THE BED.
MUST HAVE BLOWN IN FROM OUTSIDE.
AND THE COMFORTER WAS ALL MUSSED UP.
SLOPPY BED-MAKING IF YOU ASK ME.
AND HOW DO YOU EXPLAIN DOG DROOL ON THE PILLOW?
RATTED OUT BY A CHEESE-COVERED SQUIRREL DREAM.

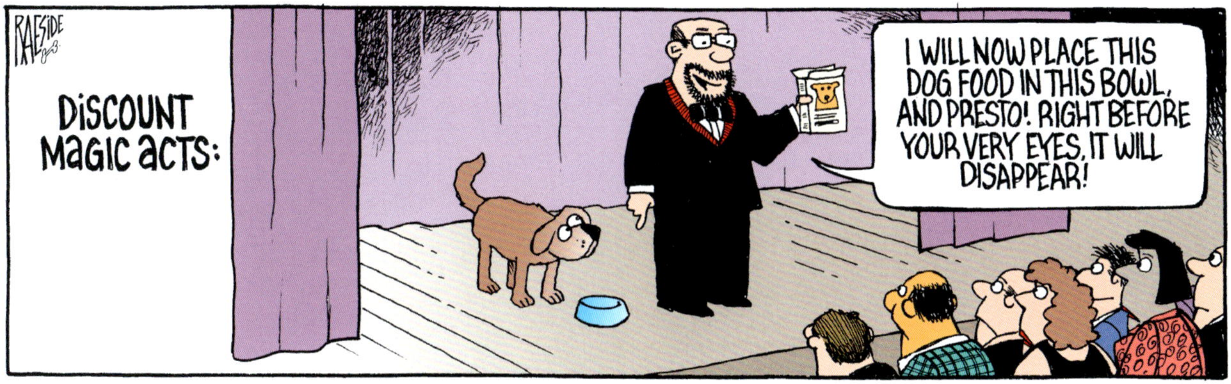
DISCOUNT MAGIC ACTS:
I WILL NOW PLACE THIS DOG FOOD IN THIS BOWL, AND PRESTO!. RIGHT BEFORE YOUR VERY EYES, IT WILL DISAPPEAR!

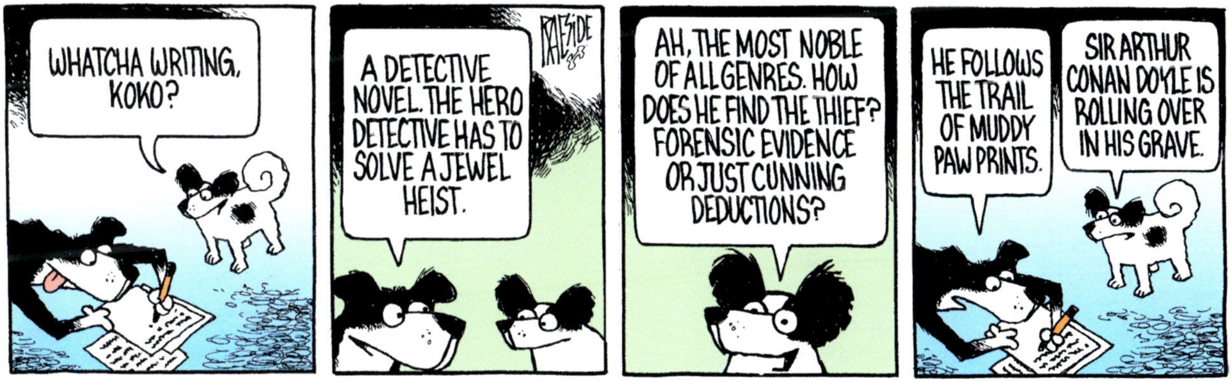
WHATCHA WRITING, KOKO?
A DETECTIVE NOVEL. THE HERO DETECTIVE HAS TO SOLVE A JEWEL HEIST.
AH, THE MOST NOBLE OF ALL GENRES. HOW DOES HE FIND THE THIEF? FORENSIC EVIDENCE OR JUST CUNNING DEDUCTIONS?
HE FOLLOWS THE TRAIL OF MUDDY PAW PRINTS.
SIR ARTHUR CONAN DOYLE IS ROLLING OVER IN HIS GRAVE.

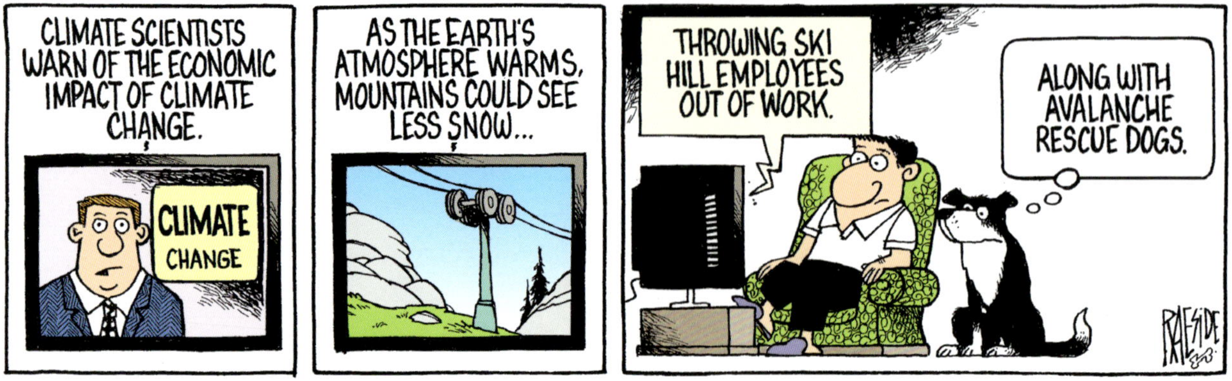
CLIMATE SCIENTISTS WARN OF THE ECONOMIC IMPACT OF CLIMATE CHANGE.
CLIMATE CHANGE
AS THE EARTH'S ATMOSPHERE WARMS, MOUNTAINS COULD SEE LESS SNOW...
THROWING SKI HILL EMPLOYEES OUT OF WORK.
ALONG WITH AVALANCHE RESCUE DOGS.

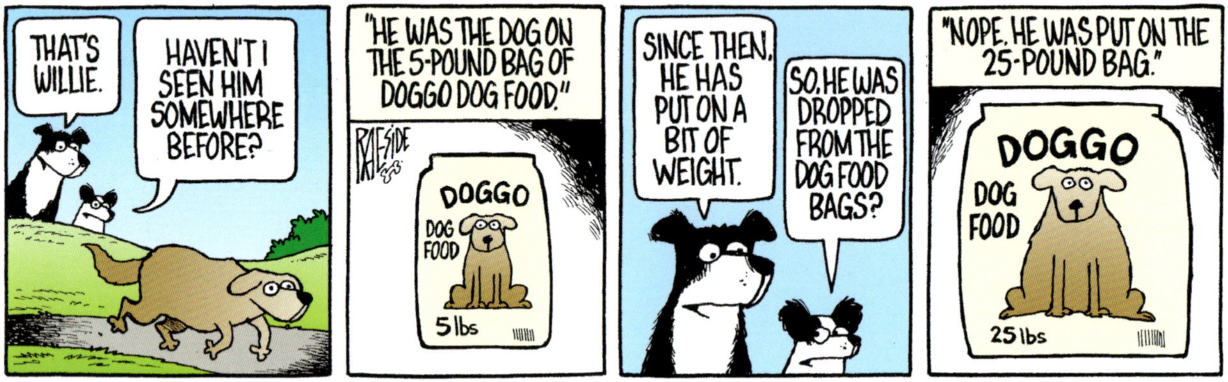
THAT'S WILLIE.
HAVEN'T I SEEN HIM SOMEWHERE BEFORE?
"HE WAS THE DOG ON THE 5-POUND BAG OF DOGGO DOG FOOD."
DOGGO
DOG FOOD
5 lbs
SINCE THEN, HE HAS PUT ON A BIT OF WEIGHT.
SO, HE WAS DROPPED FROM THE DOG FOOD BAGS?
"NOPE. HE WAS PUT ON THE 25-POUND BAG."
DOGGO
DOG FOOD
25 lbs

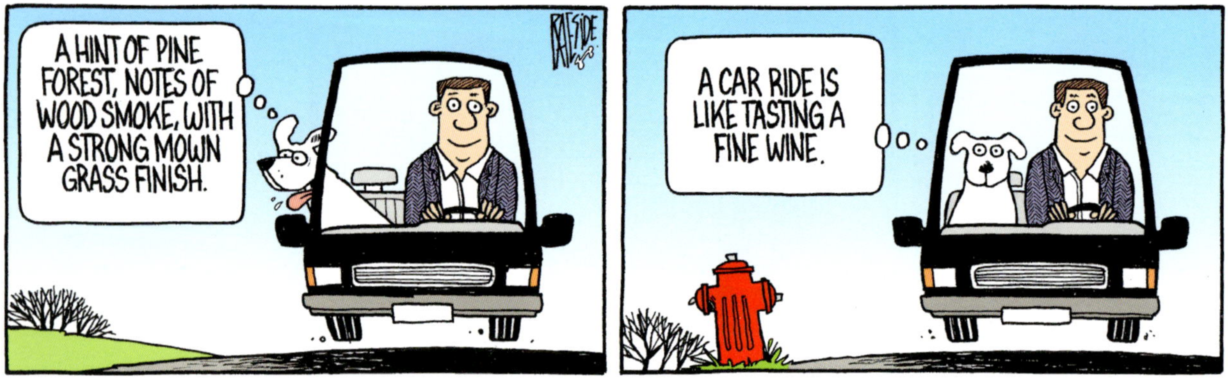
A HINT OF PINE FOREST, NOTES OF WOOD SMOKE, WITH A STRONG MOWN GRASS FINISH.
A CAR RIDE IS LIKE TASTING A FINE WINE.

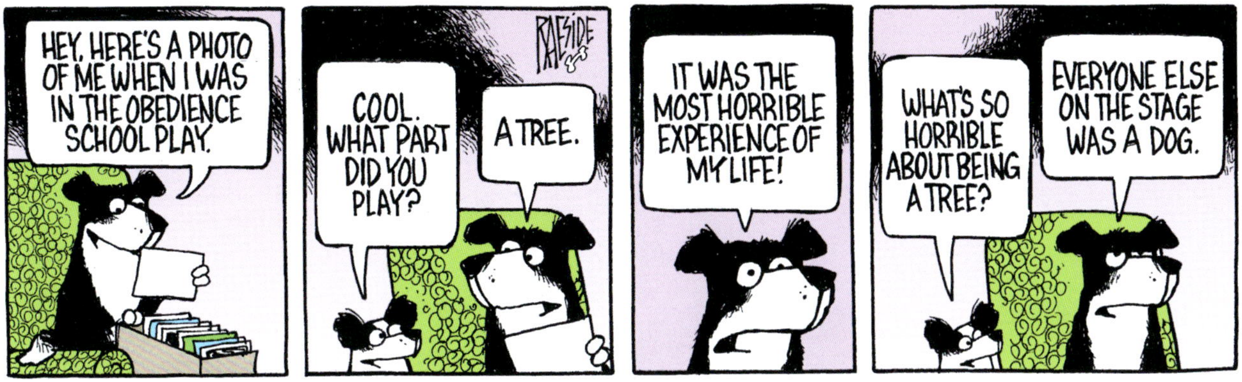
HEY, HERE'S A PHOTO OF ME WHEN I WAS IN THE OBEDIENCE SCHOOL PLAY.
COOL. WHAT PART DID YOU PLAY?
A TREE.
IT WAS THE MOST HORRIBLE EXPERIENCE OF MY LIFE!
WHAT'S SO HORRIBLE ABOUT BEING A TREE?
EVERYONE ELSE ON THE STAGE WAS A DOG.

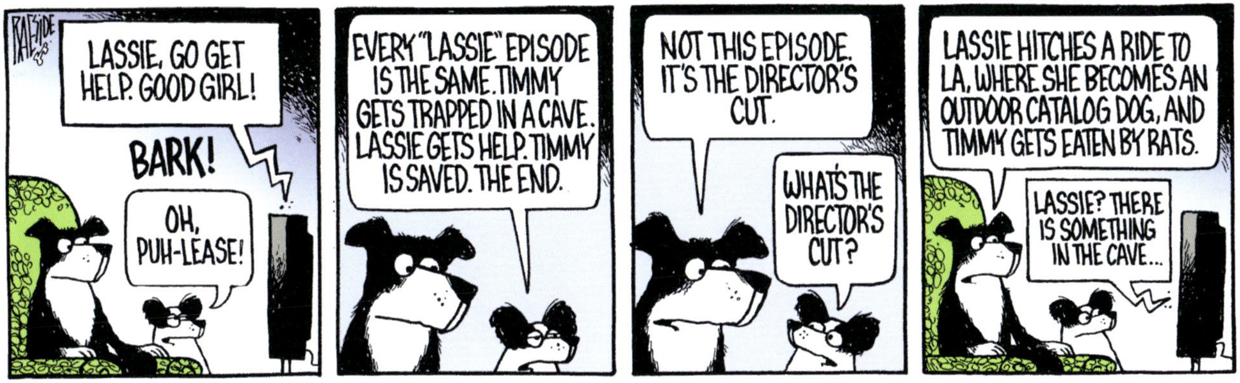
LASSIE, GO GET HELP. GOOD GIRL!
BARK!
OH, PUH-LEASE!
EVERY "LASSIE" EPISODE IS THE SAME. TIMMY GETS TRAPPED IN A CAVE. LASSIE GETS HELP. TIMMY IS SAVED. THE END.
NOT THIS EPISODE. IT'S THE DIRECTOR'S CUT.
WHAT'S THE DIRECTOR'S CUT?
LASSIE HITCHES A RIDE TO LA, WHERE SHE BECOMES AN OUTDOOR CATALOG DOG, AND TIMMY GETS EATEN BY RATS.
LASSIE? THERE IS SOMETHING IN THE CAVE...

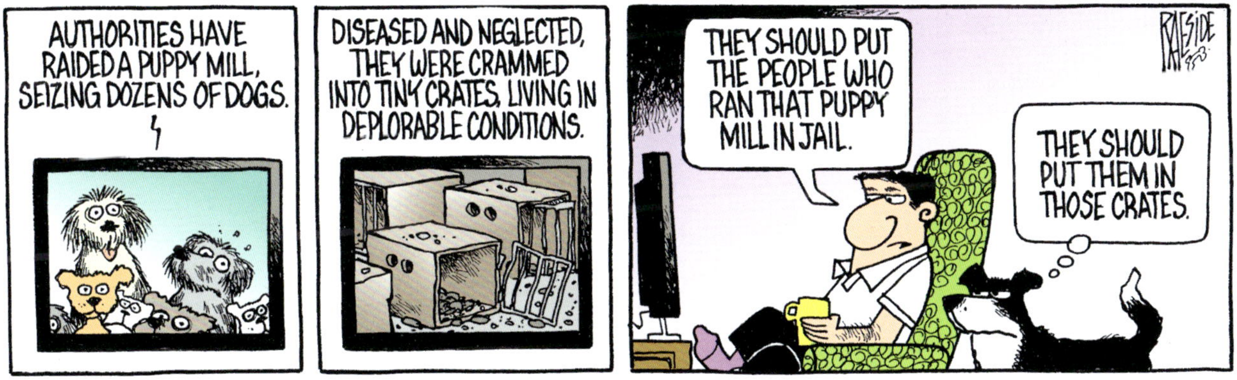
AUTHORITIES HAVE RAIDED A PUPPY MILL, SEIZING DOZENS OF DOGS.
DISEASED AND NEGLECTED, THEY WERE CRAMMED INTO TINY CRATES, LIVING IN DEPLORABLE CONDITIONS.
THEY SHOULD PUT THE PEOPLE WHO RAN THAT PUPPY MILL IN JAIL.
THEY SHOULD PUT THEM IN THOSE CRATES.

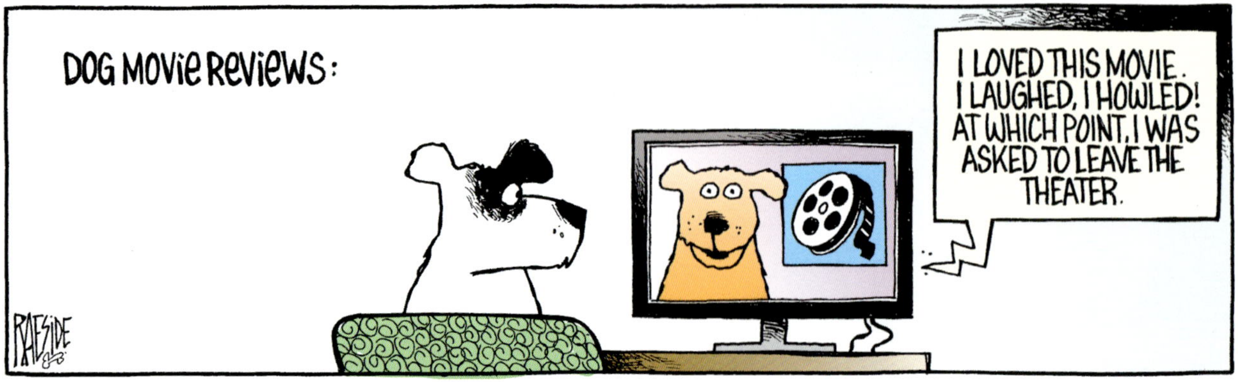
DOG MOVIE REVIEWS:
I LOVED THIS MOVIE. I LAUGHED, I HOWLED! AT WHICH POINT, I WAS ASKED TO LEAVE THE THEATER.
RAESIDE

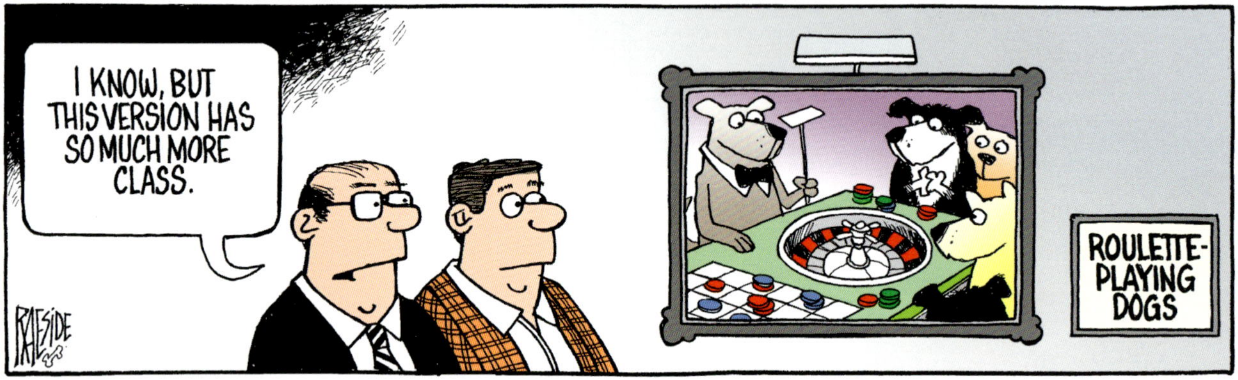
I KNOW, BUT THIS VERSION HAS SO MUCH MORE CLASS.
ROULETTE-PLAYING DOGS
RAESIDE

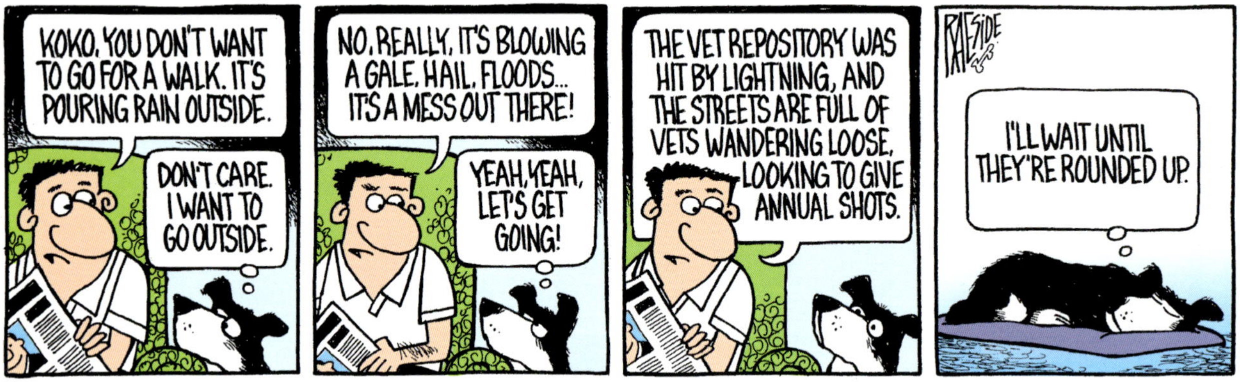
KOKO, YOU DON'T WANT TO GO FOR A WALK. IT'S POURING RAIN OUTSIDE.
DON'T CARE. I WANT TO GO OUTSIDE.
NO, REALLY, IT'S BLOWING A GALE, HAIL, FLOODS... IT'S A MESS OUT THERE!
YEAH, YEAH, LET'S GET GOING!
THE VET REPOSITORY WAS HIT BY LIGHTNING, AND THE STREETS ARE FULL OF VETS WANDERING LOOSE, LOOKING TO GIVE ANNUAL SHOTS.
RAESIDE
I'LL WAIT UNTIL THEY'RE ROUNDED UP.

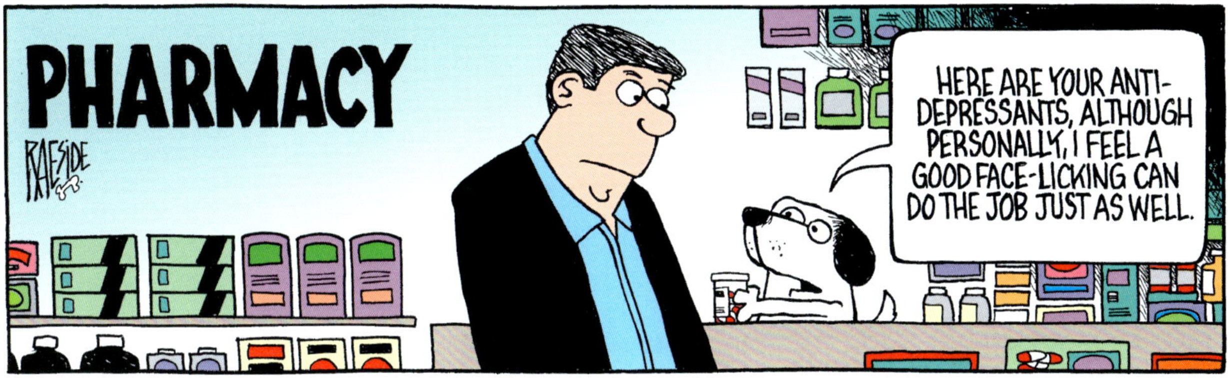
PHARMACY
RAESIDE
HERE ARE YOUR ANTI-DEPRESSANTS, ALTHOUGH PERSONALLY, I FEEL A GOOD FACE-LICKING CAN DO THE JOB JUST AS WELL.

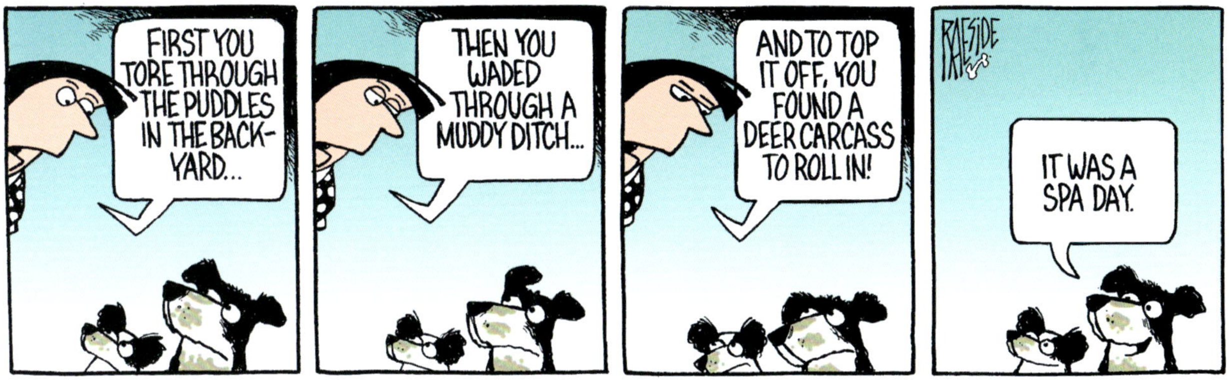
FIRST YOU TORE THROUGH THE PUDDLES IN THE BACK-YARD...
THEN YOU WADED THROUGH A MUDDY DITCH...
AND TO TOP IT OFF, YOU FOUND A DEER CARCASS TO ROLL IN!
RAESIDE
IT WAS A SPA DAY.

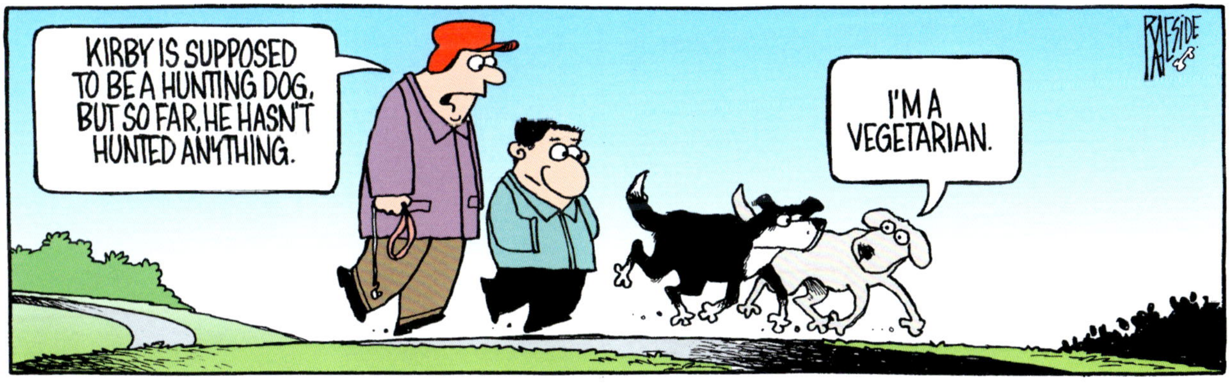
KIRBY IS SUPPOSED TO BE A HUNTING DOG, BUT SO FAR, HE HASN'T HUNTED ANYTHING.
I'M A VEGETARIAN.
RAESIDE

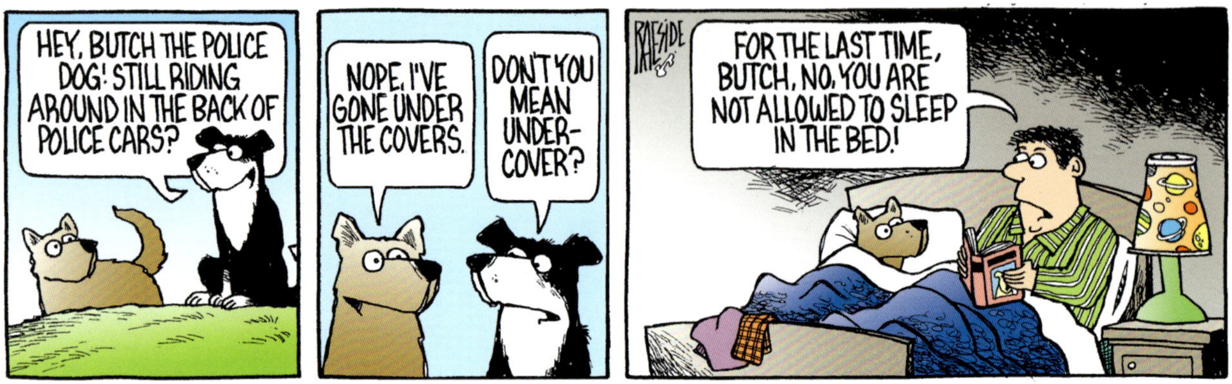
HEY, BUTCH THE POLICE DOG! STILL RIDING AROUND IN THE BACK OF POLICE CARS?
NOPE, I'VE GONE UNDER THE COVERS.
DON'T YOU MEAN UNDER-COVER?
RAESIDE
FOR THE LAST TIME, BUTCH, NO, YOU ARE NOT ALLOWED TO SLEEP IN THE BED!

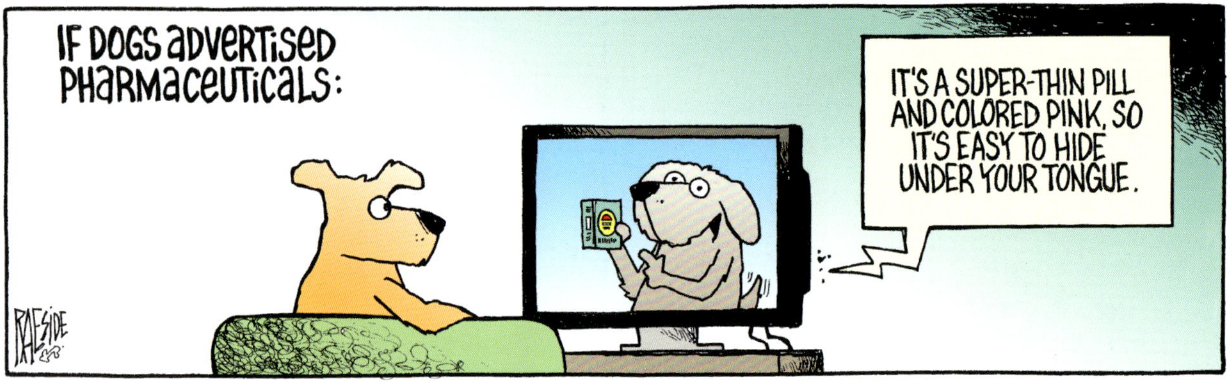
IF DOGS ADVERTISED PHARMACEUTICALS:
IT'S A SUPER-THIN PILL AND COLORED PINK, SO IT'S EASY TO HIDE UNDER YOUR TONGUE.
RAESIDE

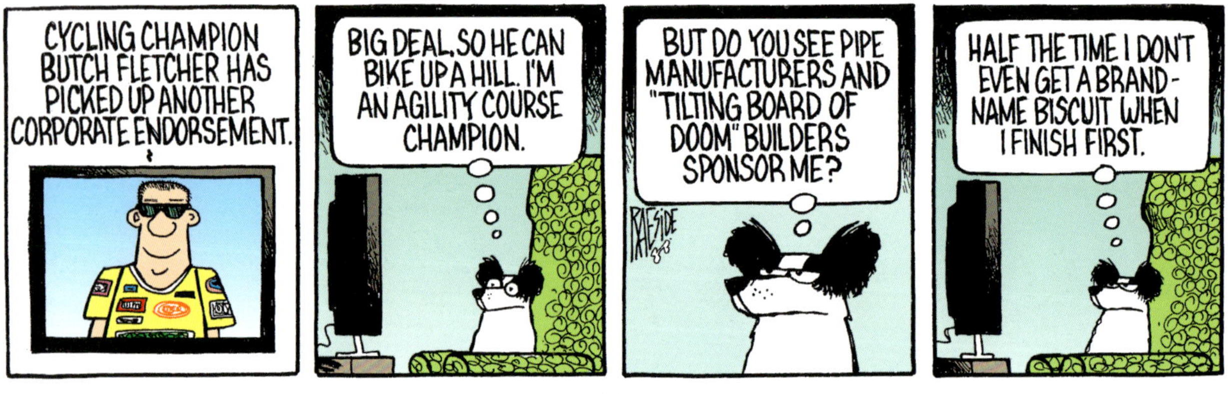
CYCLING CHAMPION BUTCH FLETCHER HAS PICKED UP ANOTHER CORPORATE ENDORSEMENT.
BIG DEAL, SO HE CAN BIKE UP A HILL. I'M AN AGILITY COURSE CHAMPION.
BUT DO YOU SEE PIPE MANUFACTURERS AND "TILTING BOARD OF DOOM" BUILDERS SPONSOR ME?
RAESIDE
HALF THE TIME I DON'T EVEN GET A BRAND-NAME BISCUIT WHEN I FINISH FIRST.

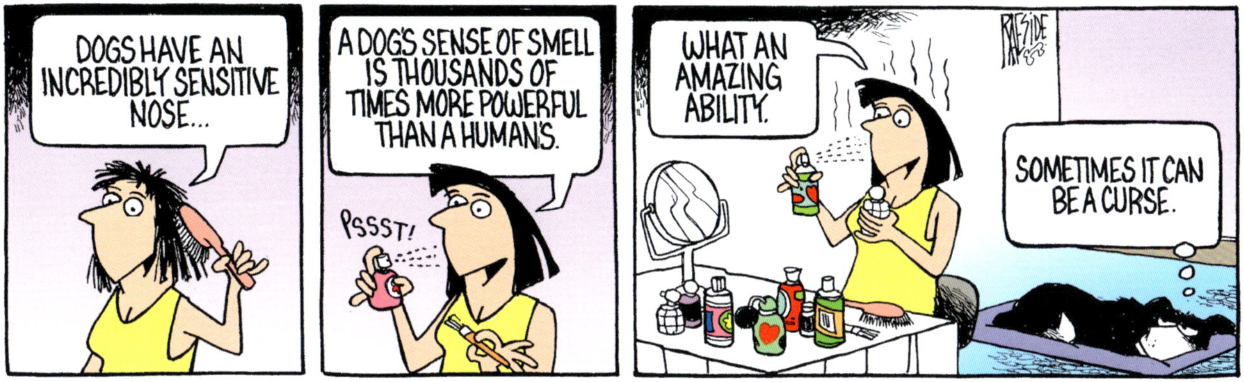
DOGS HAVE AN INCREDIBLY SENSITIVE NOSE...
A DOG'S SENSE OF SMELL IS THOUSANDS OF TIMES MORE POWERFUL THAN A HUMAN'S.
PSSST!
WHAT AN AMAZING ABILITY.
SOMETIMES IT CAN BE A CURSE.

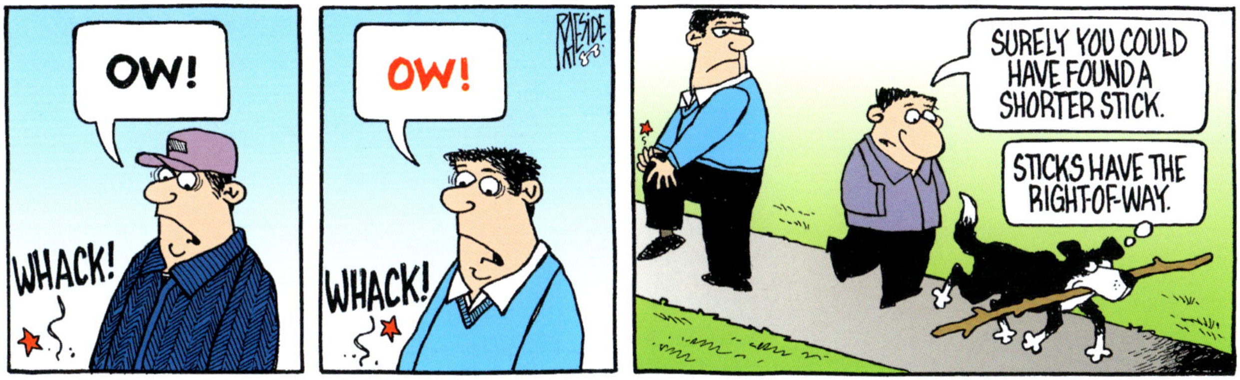
OW!
WHACK!
OW!
WHACK!
SURELY YOU COULD HAVE FOUND A SHORTER STICK.
STICKS HAVE THE RIGHT-OF-WAY.

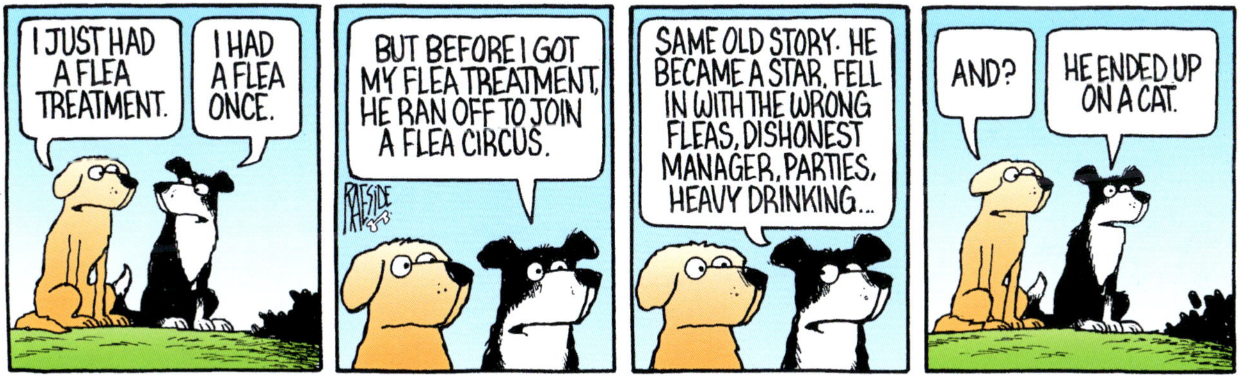
I JUST HAD A FLEA TREATMENT.
I HAD A FLEA ONCE.
BUT BEFORE I GOT MY FLEA TREATMENT, HE RAN OFF TO JOIN A FLEA CIRCUS.
SAME OLD STORY. HE BECAME A STAR, FELL IN WITH THE WRONG FLEAS, DISHONEST MANAGER, PARTIES, HEAVY DRINKING...
AND?
HE ENDED UP ON A CAT.

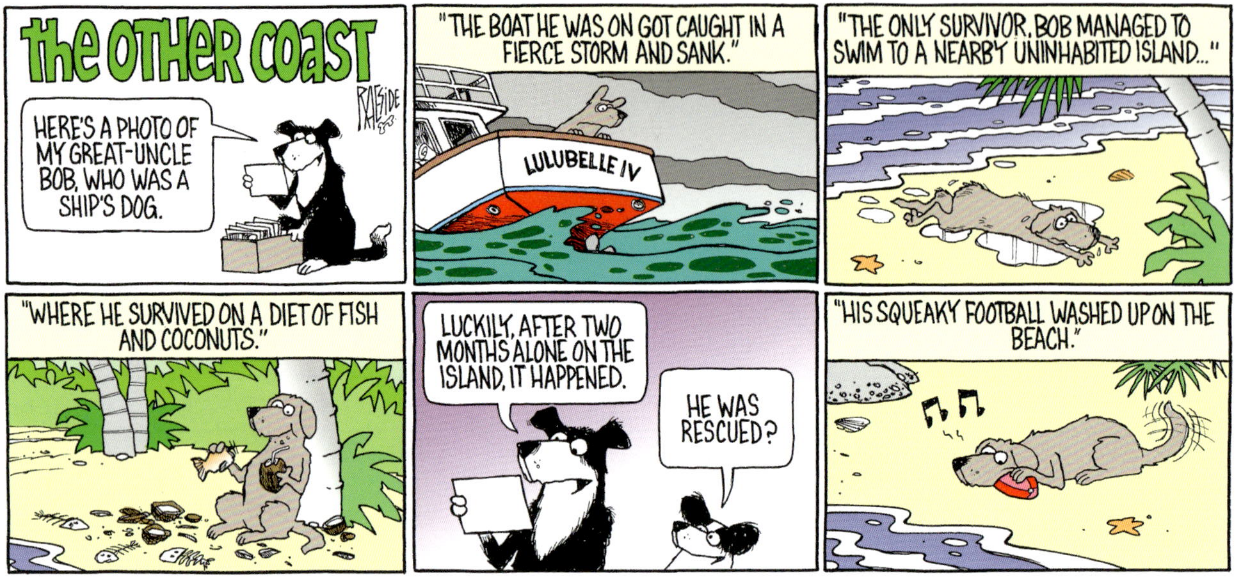
the OTHER COAST
RAESIDE
HERE'S A PHOTO OF MY GREAT-UNCLE BOB, WHO WAS A SHIP'S DOG.
"THE BOAT HE WAS ON GOT CAUGHT IN A FIERCE STORM AND SANK."
LULUBELLE IV
"THE ONLY SURVIVOR, BOB MANAGED TO SWIM TO A NEARBY UNINHABITED ISLAND..."
"WHERE HE SURVIVED ON A DIET OF FISH AND COCONUTS."
LUCKILY, AFTER TWO MONTHS ALONE ON THE ISLAND, IT HAPPENED.
HE WAS RESCUED?
"HIS SQUEAKY FOOTBALL WASHED UP ON THE BEACH."

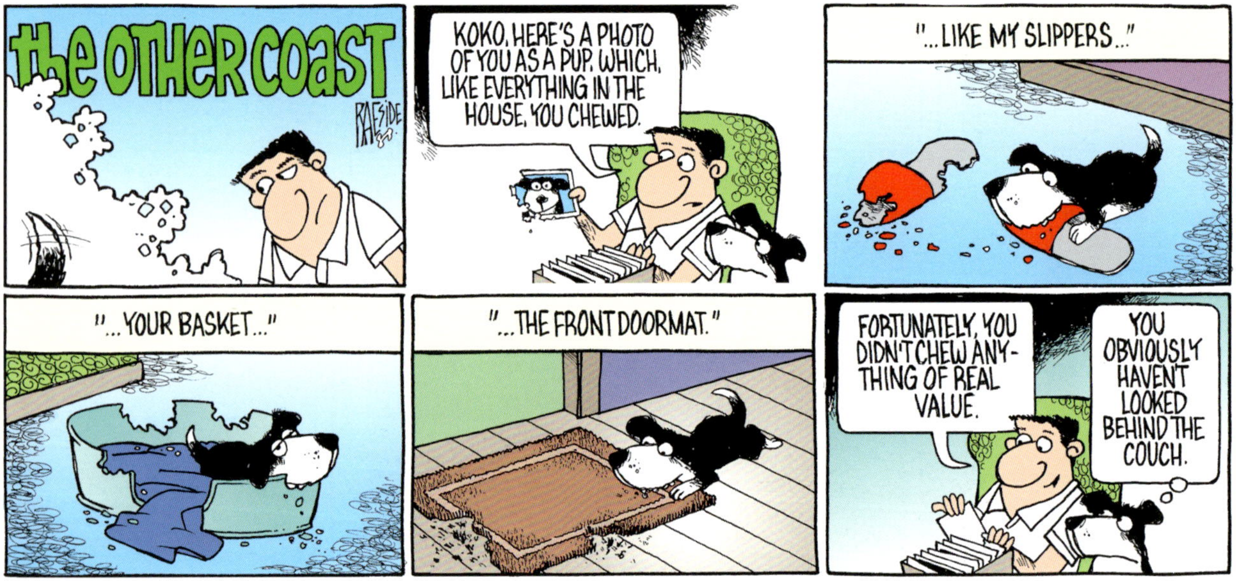
the OTHER COAST
RAESIDE
KOKO, HERE'S A PHOTO OF YOU AS A PUP, WHICH, LIKE EVERYTHING IN THE HOUSE, YOU CHEWED.
"...LIKE MY SLIPPERS..."
"...YOUR BASKET..."
"...THE FRONT DOORMAT."
FORTUNATELY, YOU DIDN'T CHEW ANYTHING OF REAL VALUE.
YOU OBVIOUSLY HAVEN'T LOOKED BEHIND THE COUCH.

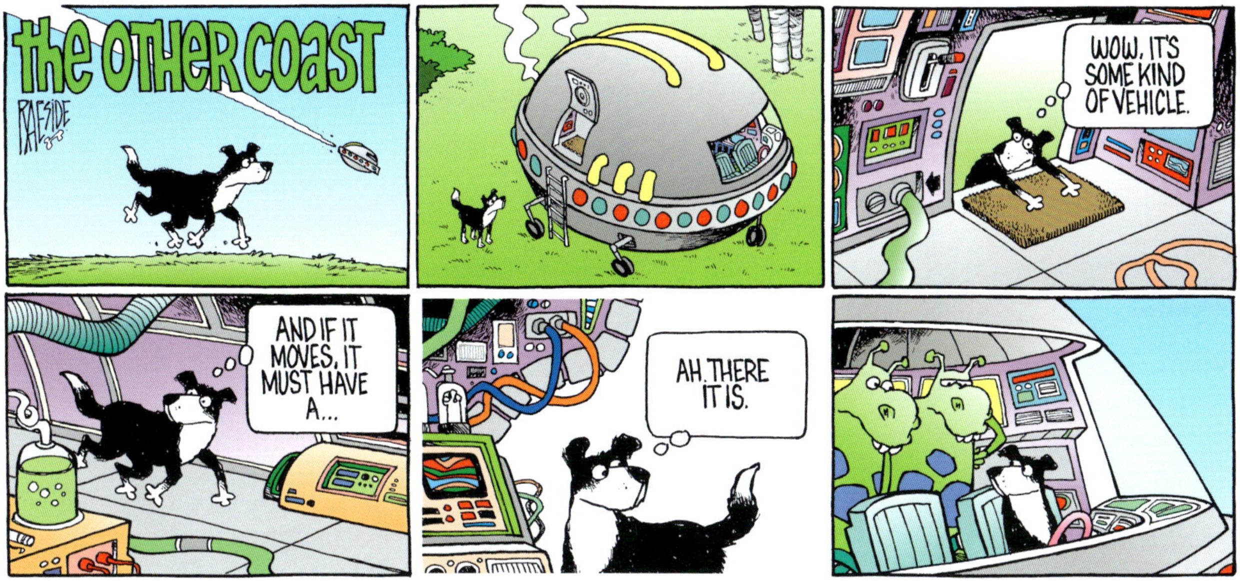
the OTHER COAST
RAESIDE
WOW, IT'S SOME KIND OF VEHICLE.
AND IF IT MOVES, IT MUST HAVE A...
AH. THERE IT IS.

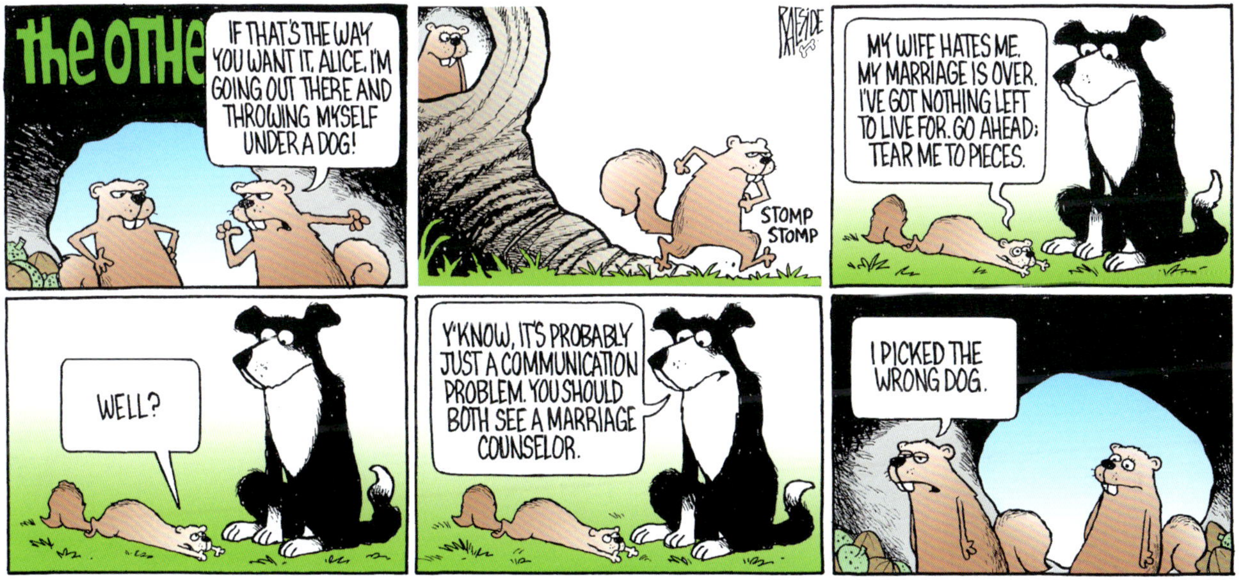
the OTHE
IF THAT'S THE WAY YOU WANT IT, ALICE, I'M GOING OUT THERE AND THROWING MYSELF UNDER A DOG!
RAESIDE
STOMP STOMP
MY WIFE HATES ME. MY MARRIAGE IS OVER. I'VE GOT NOTHING LEFT TO LIVE FOR. GO AHEAD; TEAR ME TO PIECES.
WELL?
Y'KNOW, IT'S PROBABLY JUST A COMMUNICATION PROBLEM. YOU SHOULD BOTH SEE A MARRIAGE COUNSELOR.
I PICKED THE WRONG DOG.

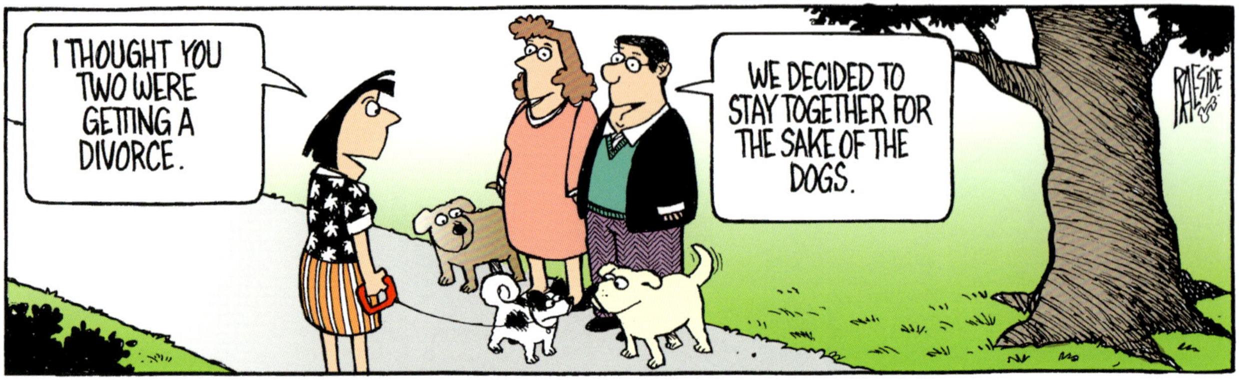
I THOUGHT YOU TWO WERE GETTING A DIVORCE.
WE DECIDED TO STAY TOGETHER FOR THE SAKE OF THE DOGS.
RAESIDE

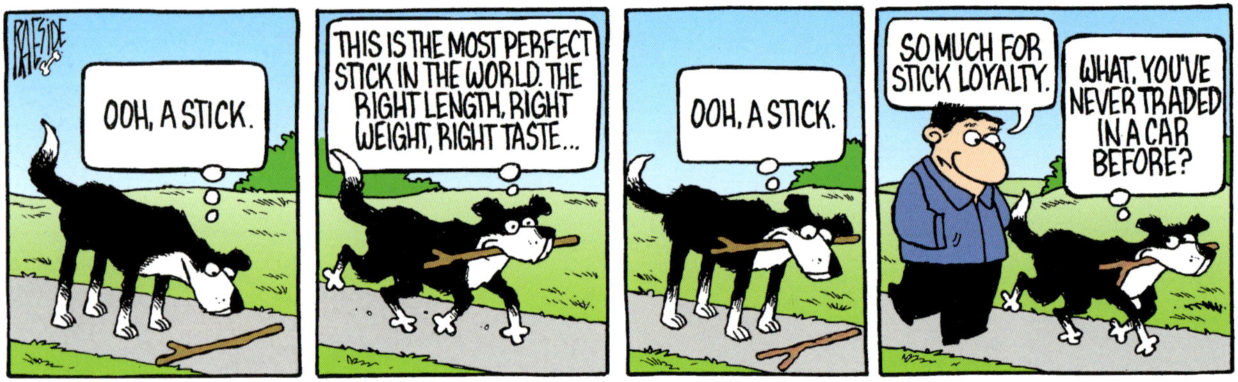
RAESIDE
OOH, A STICK.
THIS IS THE MOST PERFECT STICK IN THE WORLD. THE RIGHT LENGTH, RIGHT WEIGHT, RIGHT TASTE...
OOH, A STICK.
SO MUCH FOR STICK LOYALTY.
WHAT, YOU'VE NEVER TRADED IN A CAR BEFORE?

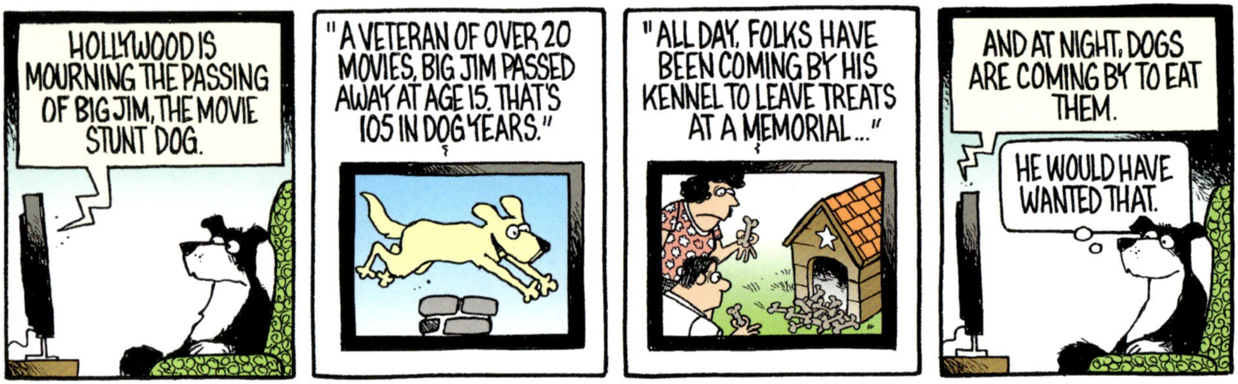
HOLLYWOOD IS MOURNING THE PASSING OF BIG JIM, THE MOVIE STUNT DOG.
"A VETERAN OF OVER 20 MOVIES, BIG JIM PASSED AWAY AT AGE 15. THAT'S 105 IN DOG YEARS."
"ALL DAY, FOLKS HAVE BEEN COMING BY HIS KENNEL TO LEAVE TREATS AT A MEMORIAL..."
AND AT NIGHT, DOGS ARE COMING BY TO EAT THEM.
HE WOULD HAVE WANTED THAT.

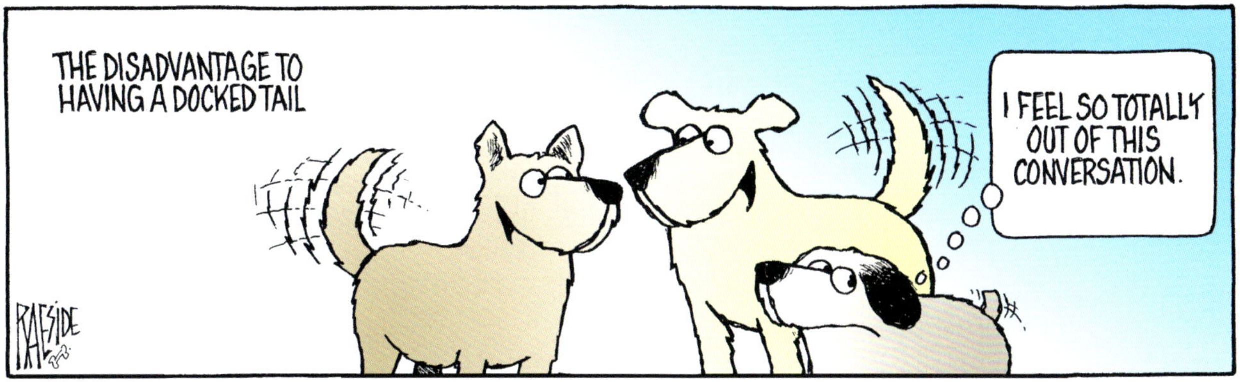
THE DISADVANTAGE TO HAVING A DOCKED TAIL
I FEEL SO TOTALLY OUT OF THIS CONVERSATION.

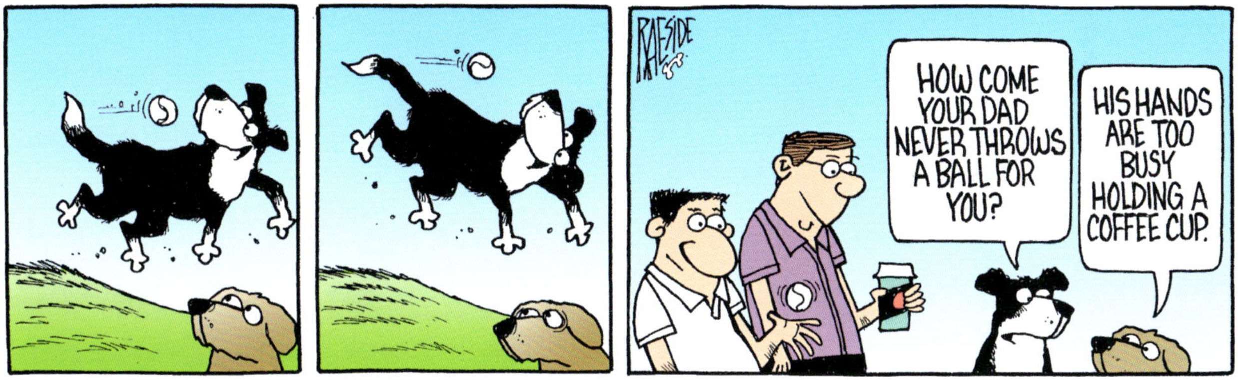
HOW COME YOUR DAD NEVER THROWS A BALL FOR YOU?
HIS HANDS ARE TOO BUSY HOLDING A COFFEE CUP.

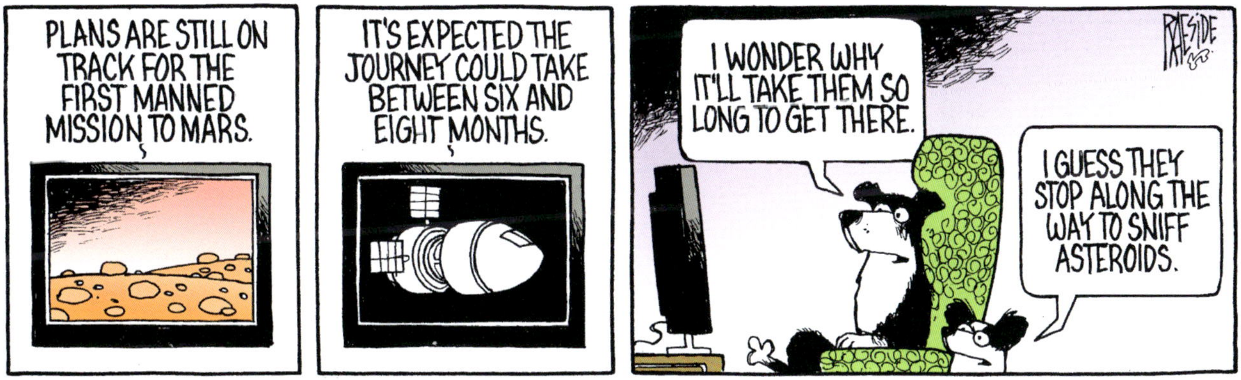
PLANS ARE STILL ON TRACK FOR THE FIRST MANNED MISSION TO MARS.
IT'S EXPECTED THE JOURNEY COULD TAKE BETWEEN SIX AND EIGHT MONTHS.
I WONDER WHY IT'LL TAKE THEM SO LONG TO GET THERE.
I GUESS THEY STOP ALONG THE WAY TO SNIFF ASTEROIDS.

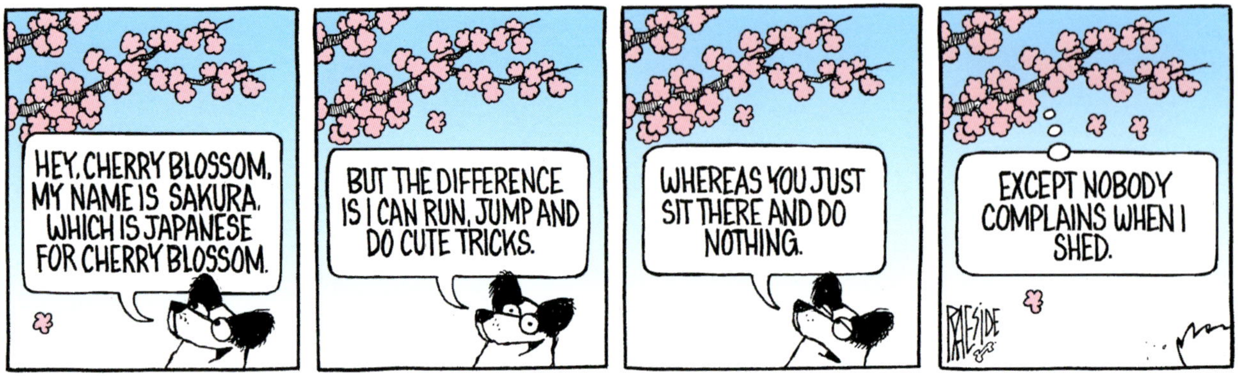
HEY, CHERRY BLOSSOM, MY NAME IS SAKURA, WHICH IS JAPANESE FOR CHERRY BLOSSOM.
BUT THE DIFFERENCE IS I CAN RUN, JUMP AND DO CUTE TRICKS.
WHEREAS YOU JUST SIT THERE AND DO NOTHING.
EXCEPT NOBODY COMPLAINS WHEN I SHED.

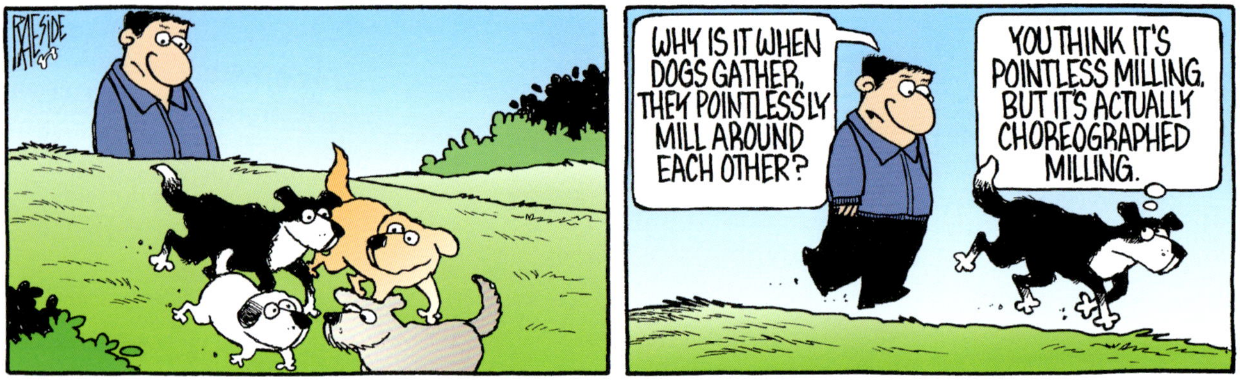
WHY IS IT WHEN DOGS GATHER, THEY POINTLESSLY MILL AROUND EACH OTHER?
YOU THINK IT'S POINTLESS MILLING. BUT IT'S ACTUALLY CHOREOGRAPHED MILLING.

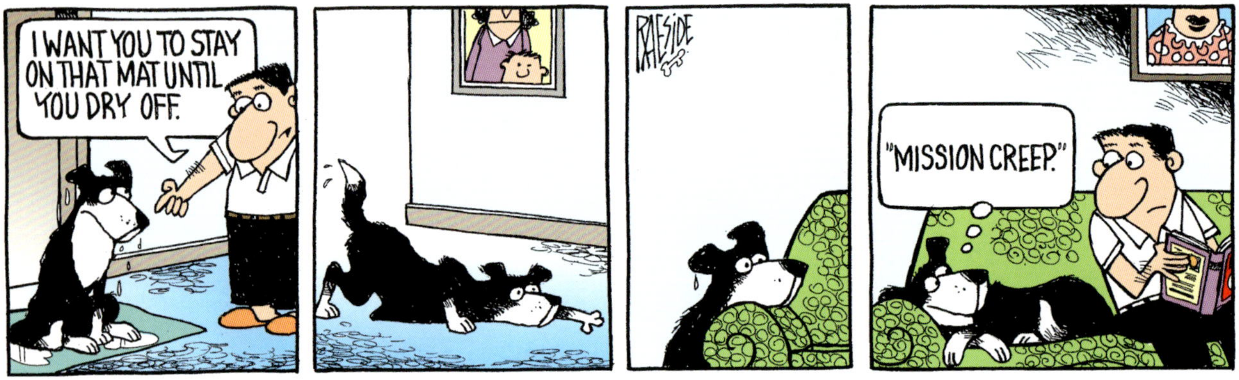
I WANT YOU TO STAY ON THAT MAT UNTIL YOU DRY OFF.
"MISSION CREEP."

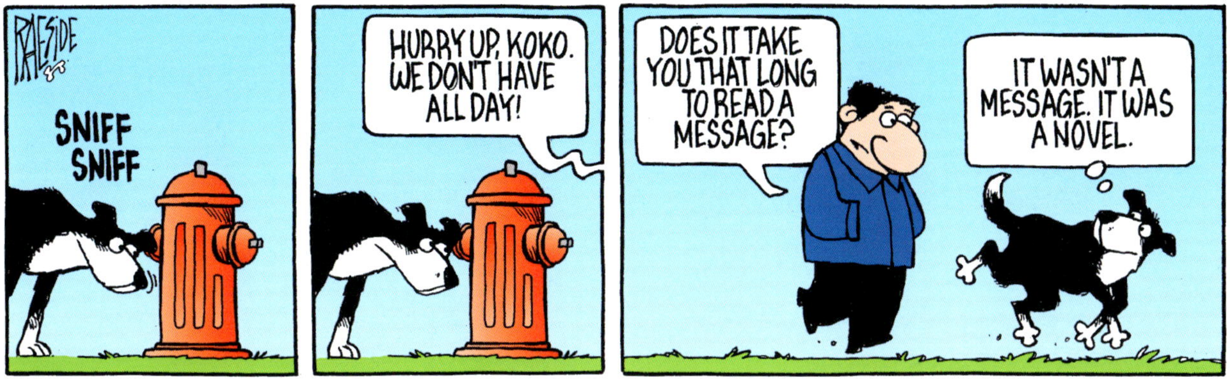
RAESIDE
SNIFF SNIFF
HURRY UP, KOKO. WE DON'T HAVE ALL DAY!
DOES IT TAKE YOU THAT LONG TO READ A MESSAGE?
IT WASN'T A MESSAGE. IT WAS A NOVEL.

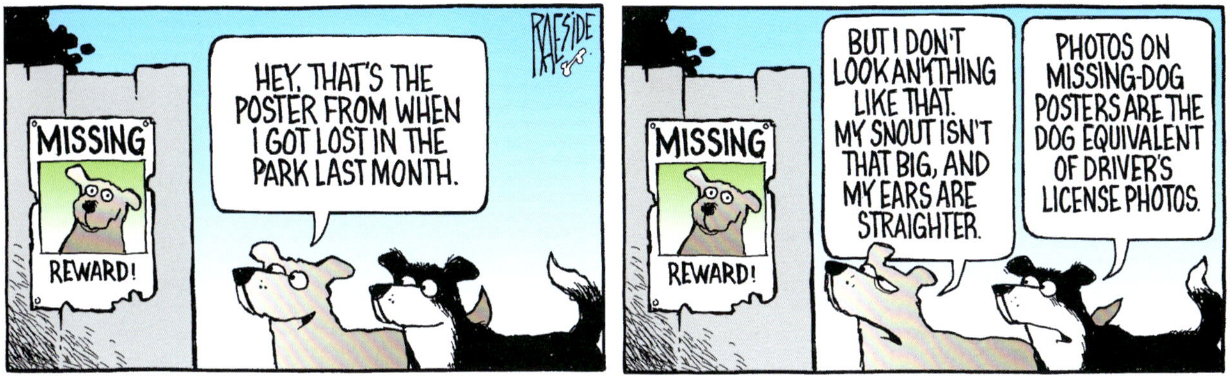
RAESIDE
MISSING
REWARD!
HEY, THAT'S THE POSTER FROM WHEN I GOT LOST IN THE PARK LAST MONTH.
MISSING
REWARD!
BUT I DON'T LOOK ANYTHING LIKE THAT. MY SNOUT ISN'T THAT BIG, AND MY EARS ARE STRAIGHTER.
PHOTOS ON MISSING-DOG POSTERS ARE THE DOG EQUIVALENT OF DRIVER'S LICENSE PHOTOS.

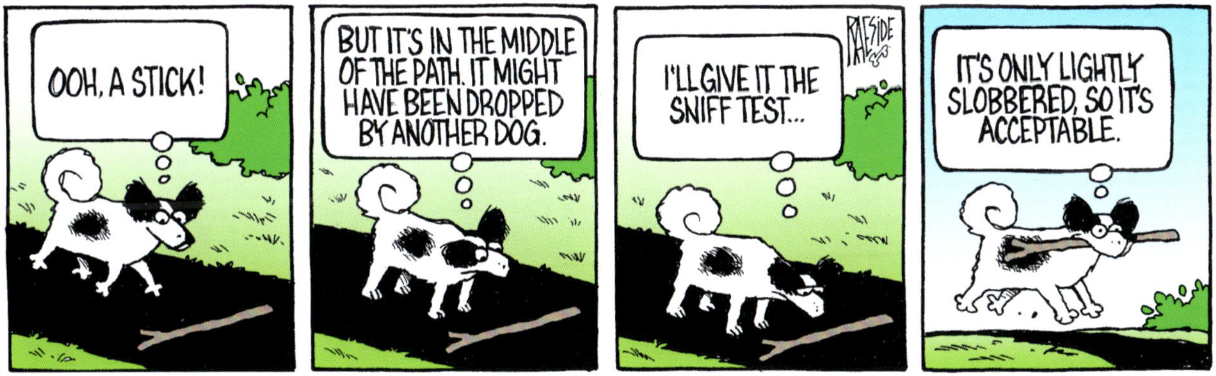
OOH, A STICK!
BUT IT'S IN THE MIDDLE OF THE PATH. IT MIGHT HAVE BEEN DROPPED BY ANOTHER DOG.
RAESIDE
I'LL GIVE IT THE SNIFF TEST...
IT'S ONLY LIGHTLY SLOBBERED, SO IT'S ACCEPTABLE.

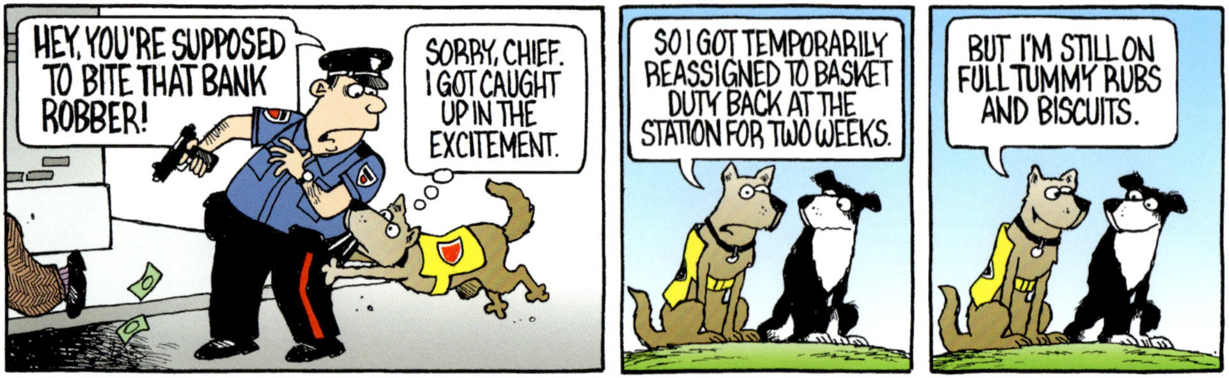
HEY, YOU'RE SUPPOSED TO BITE THAT BANK ROBBER!
SORRY, CHIEF. I GOT CAUGHT UP IN THE EXCITEMENT.
SO I GOT TEMPORARILY REASSIGNED TO BASKET DUTY BACK AT THE STATION FOR TWO WEEKS.
BUT I'M STILL ON FULL TUMMY RUBS AND BISCUITS.

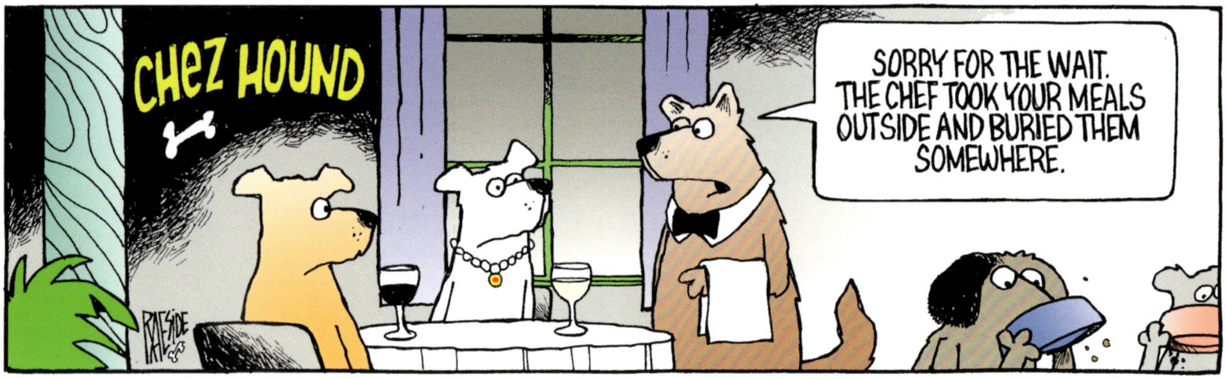
CHEZ HOUND
SORRY FOR THE WAIT. THE CHEF TOOK YOUR MEALS OUTSIDE AND BURIED THEM SOMEWHERE.

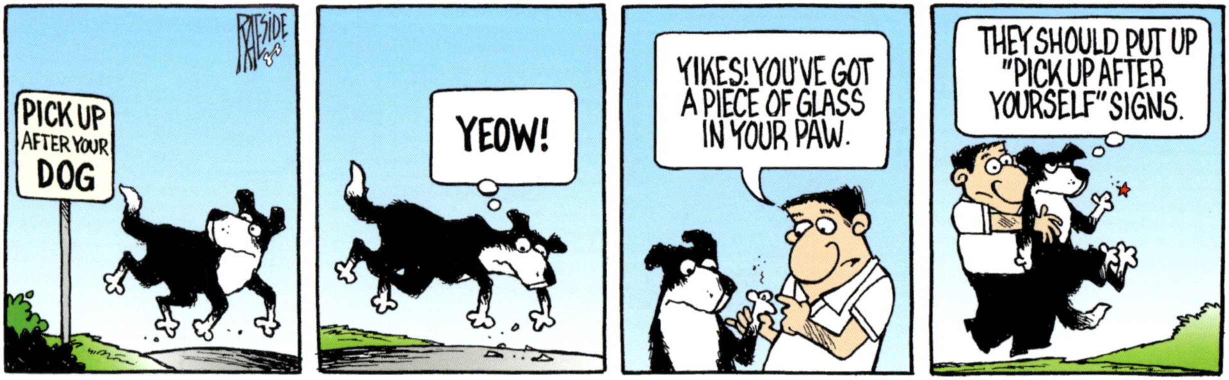
PICK UP AFTER YOUR DOG
YEOW!
YIKES! YOU'VE GOT A PIECE OF GLASS IN YOUR PAW.
THEY SHOULD PUT UP "PICK UP AFTER YOURSELF" SIGNS.

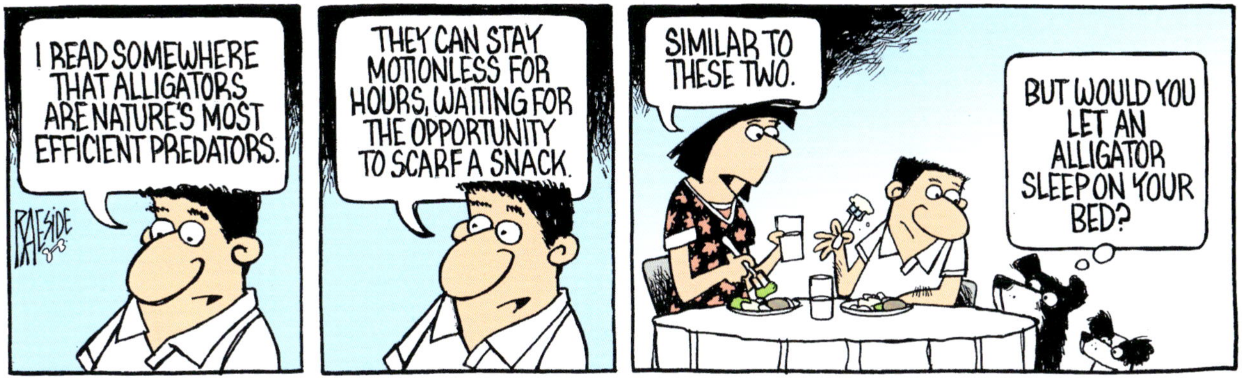
I READ SOMEWHERE THAT ALLIGATORS ARE NATURE'S MOST EFFICIENT PREDATORS.
RAESIDE
THEY CAN STAY MOTIONLESS FOR HOURS, WAITING FOR THE OPPORTUNITY TO SCARF A SNACK.
SIMILAR TO THESE TWO.
BUT WOULD YOU LET AN ALLIGATOR SLEEP ON YOUR BED?

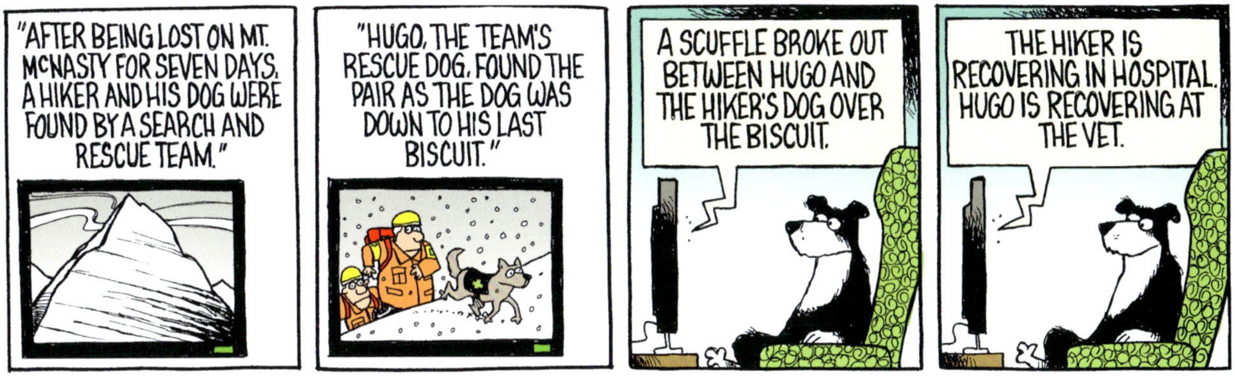
"AFTER BEING LOST ON MT. McNASTY FOR SEVEN DAYS, A HIKER AND HIS DOG WERE FOUND BY A SEARCH AND RESCUE TEAM."
"HUGO, THE TEAM'S RESCUE DOG, FOUND THE PAIR AS THE DOG WAS DOWN TO HIS LAST BISCUIT."
A SCUFFLE BROKE OUT BETWEEN HUGO AND THE HIKER'S DOG OVER THE BISCUIT.
THE HIKER IS RECOVERING IN HOSPITAL. HUGO IS RECOVERING AT THE VET.

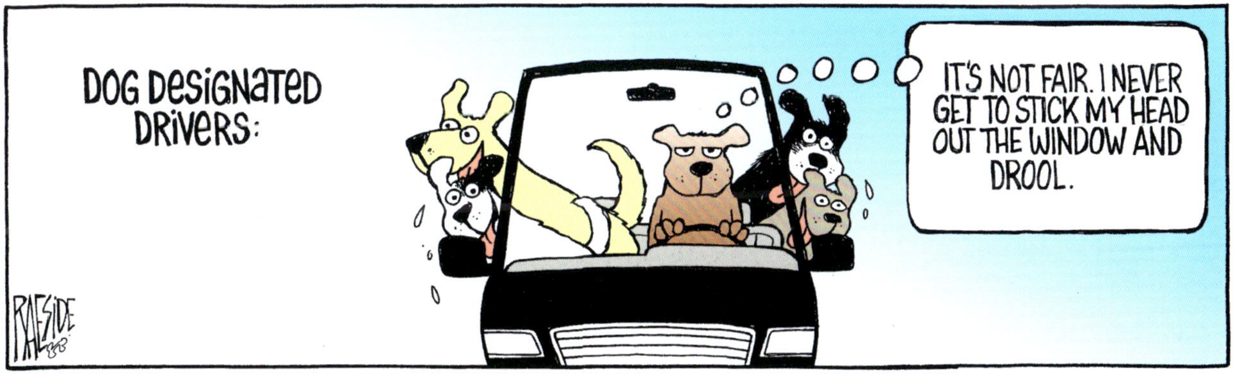
DOG DESIGNATED DRIVERS:
IT'S NOT FAIR. I NEVER GET TO STICK MY HEAD OUT THE WINDOW AND DROOL.
RAESIDE

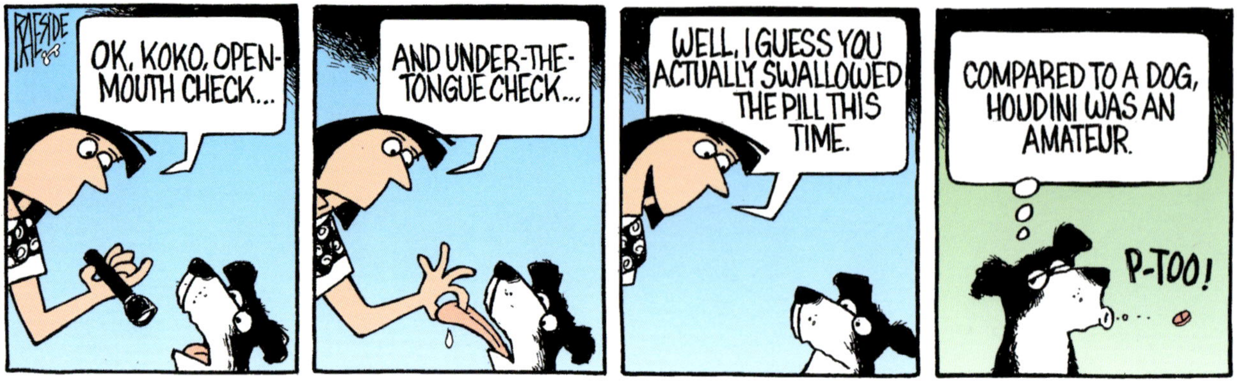
OK, KOKO, OPEN-MOUTH CHECK...
AND UNDER-THE-TONGUE CHECK...
WELL, I GUESS YOU ACTUALLY SWALLOWED THE PILL THIS TIME.
COMPARED TO A DOG, HOUDINI WAS AN AMATEUR.
P-TOO!

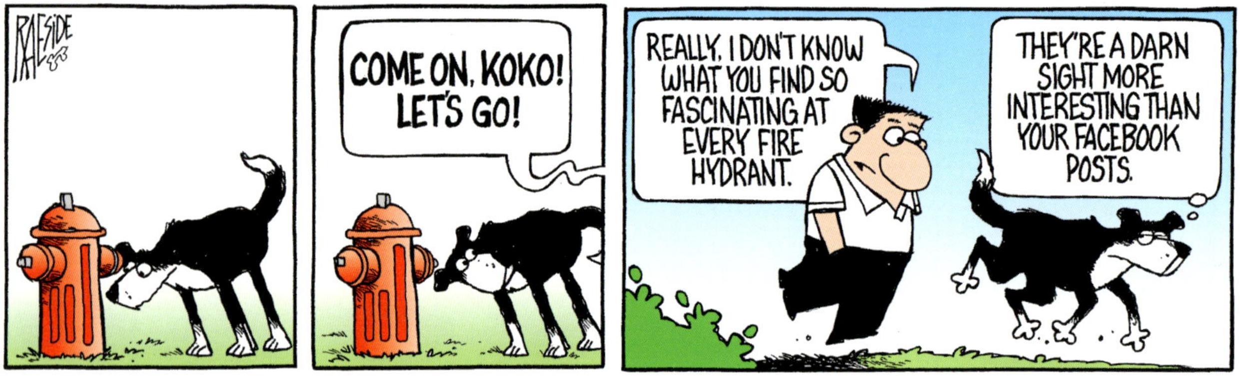
COME ON, KOKO! LET'S GO!
REALLY, I DON'T KNOW WHAT YOU FIND SO FASCINATING AT EVERY FIRE HYDRANT.
THEY'RE A DARN SIGHT MORE INTERESTING THAN YOUR FACEBOOK POSTS.

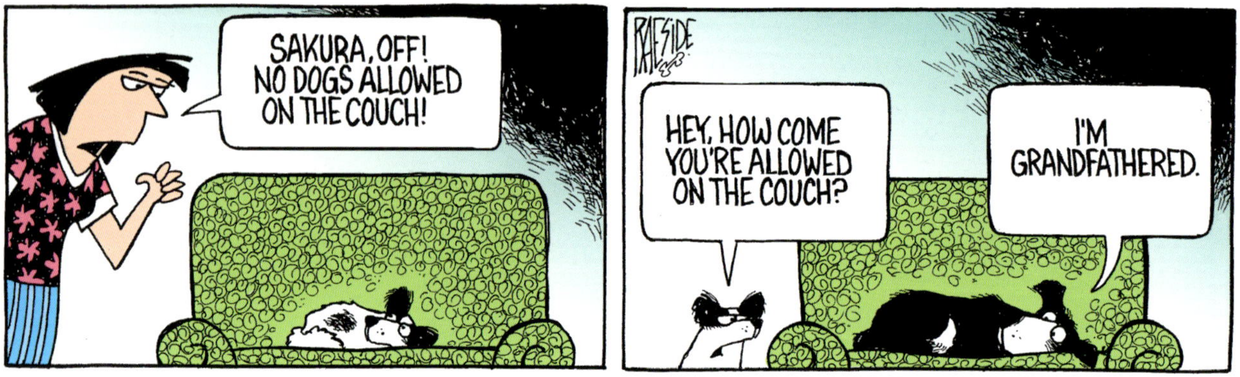
SAKURA, OFF! NO DOGS ALLOWED ON THE COUCH!
HEY, HOW COME YOU'RE ALLOWED ON THE COUCH?
I'M GRANDFATHERED.

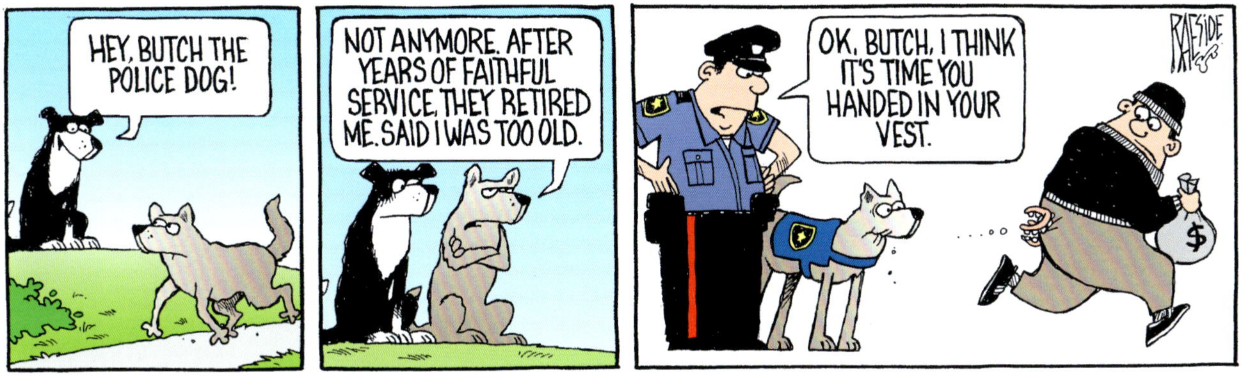
HEY, BUTCH THE POLICE DOG!
NOT ANYMORE. AFTER YEARS OF FAITHFUL SERVICE, THEY RETIRED ME. SAID I WAS TOO OLD.
OK, BUTCH, I THINK IT'S TIME YOU HANDED IN YOUR VEST.
$

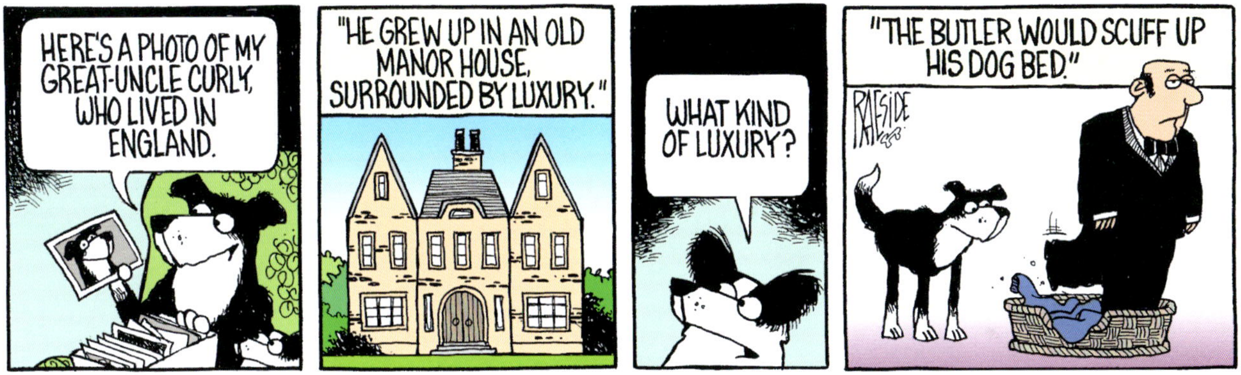
HERE'S A PHOTO OF MY GREAT-UNCLE CURLY, WHO LIVED IN ENGLAND.
"HE GREW UP IN AN OLD MANOR HOUSE, SURROUNDED BY LUXURY."
WHAT KIND OF LUXURY?
"THE BUTLER WOULD SCUFF UP HIS DOG BED."

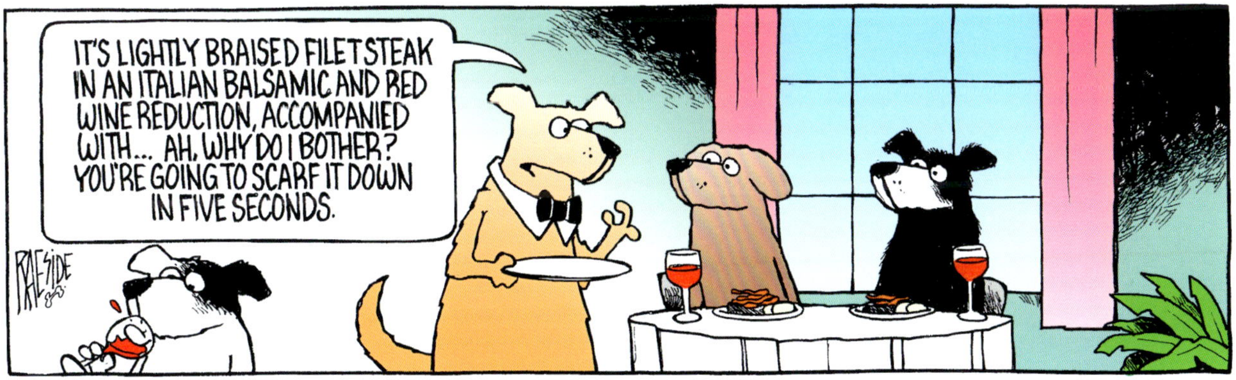
IT'S LIGHTLY BRAISED FILET STEAK IN AN ITALIAN BALSAMIC AND RED WINE REDUCTION, ACCOMPANIED WITH... AH, WHY DO I BOTHER? YOU'RE GOING TO SCARF IT DOWN IN FIVE SECONDS.

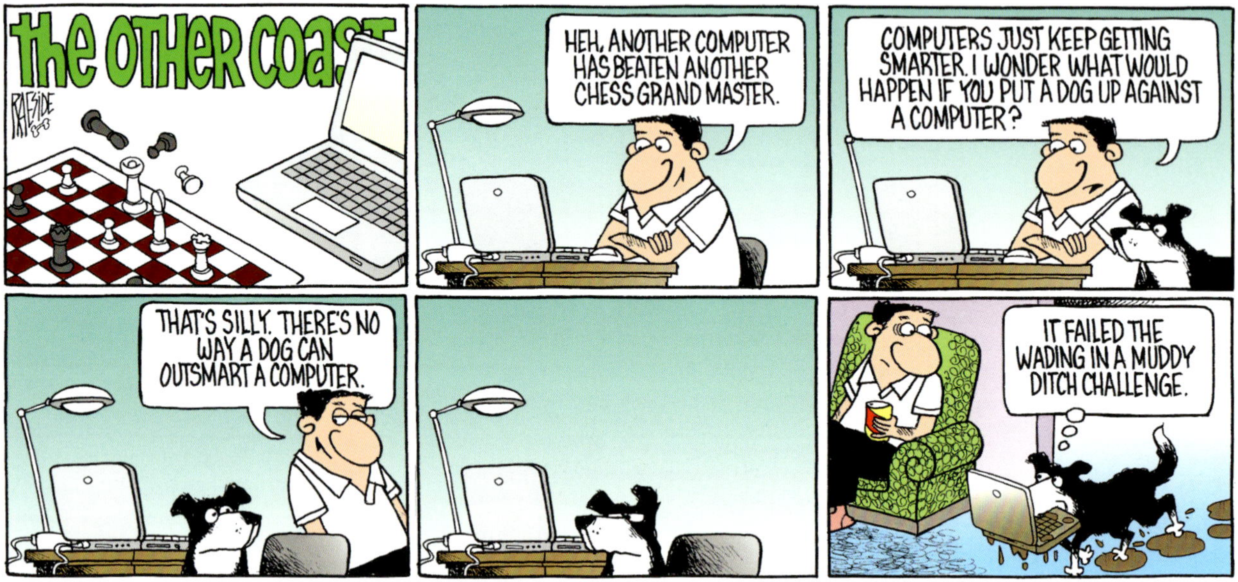
the OTHER COAST
RAESIDE
HEH, ANOTHER COMPUTER HAS BEATEN ANOTHER CHESS GRAND MASTER.
COMPUTERS JUST KEEP GETTING SMARTER. I WONDER WHAT WOULD HAPPEN IF YOU PUT A DOG UP AGAINST A COMPUTER?
THAT'S SILLY. THERE'S NO WAY A DOG CAN OUTSMART A COMPUTER.
IT FAILED THE WADING IN A MUDDY DITCH CHALLENGE.

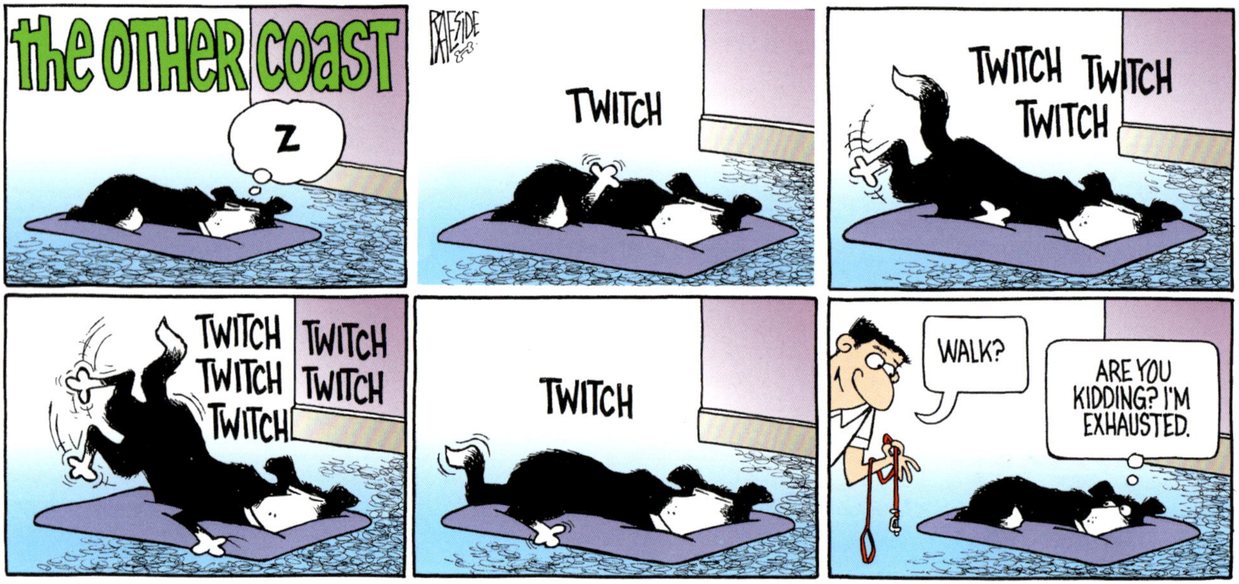
the OTHER COAST
Z
RAESIDE
TWITCH
TWITCH TWITCH
TWITCH
TWITCH
TWITCH
TWITCH
TWITCH
TWITCH
TWITCH
WALK?
ARE YOU KIDDING? I'M EXHAUSTED.

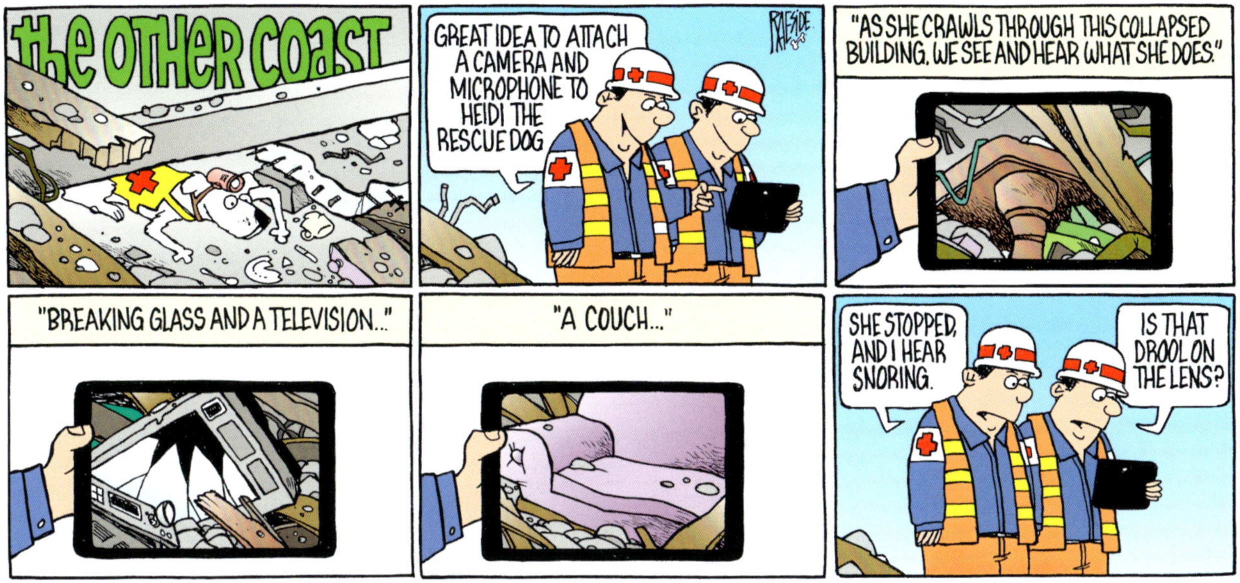
the OTHER COAST
GREAT IDEA TO ATTACH A CAMERA AND MICROPHONE TO HEIDI THE RESCUE DOG
"AS SHE CRAWLS THROUGH THIS COLLAPSED BUILDING, WE SEE AND HEAR WHAT SHE DOES."
"BREAKING GLASS AND A TELEVISION..."
"A COUCH..."
SHE STOPPED, AND I HEAR SNORING.
IS THAT DROOL ON THE LENS?

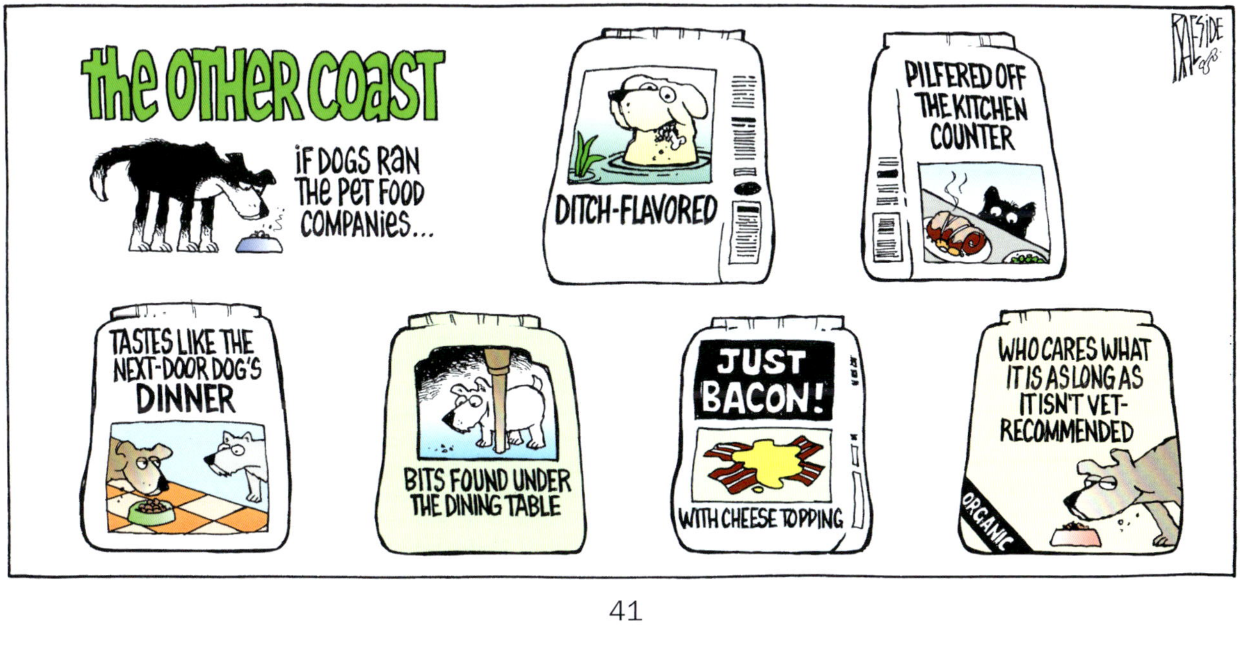
the OTHER COAST
IF DOGS RAN THE PET FOOD COMPANIES...
DITCH-FLAVORED
PILFERED OFF THE KITCHEN COUNTER
TASTES LIKE THE NEXT-DOOR DOG'S DINNER
BITS FOUND UNDER THE DINING TABLE
JUST BACON!
WITH CHEESE TOPPING
WHO CARES WHAT IT IS AS LONG AS IT ISN'T VET-RECOMMENDED
ORGANIC

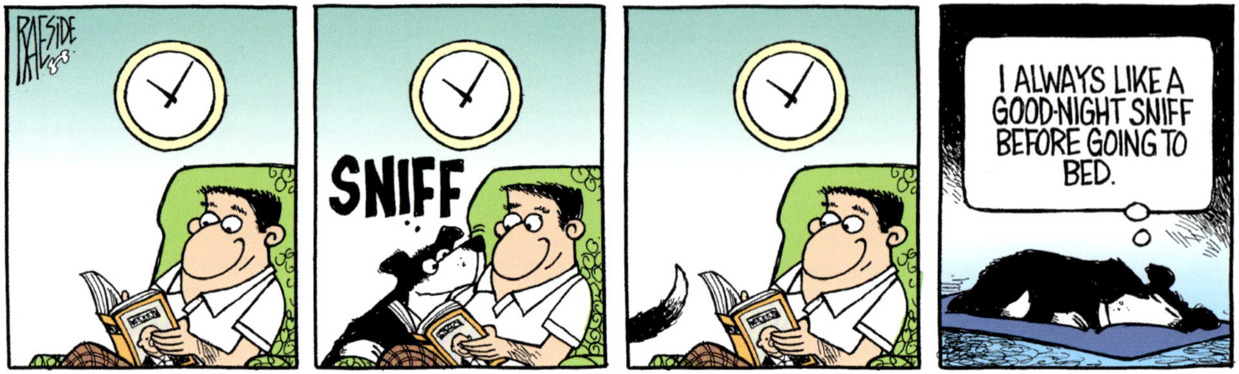
SNIFF
I ALWAYS LIKE A GOOD-NIGHT SNIFF BEFORE GOING TO BED.

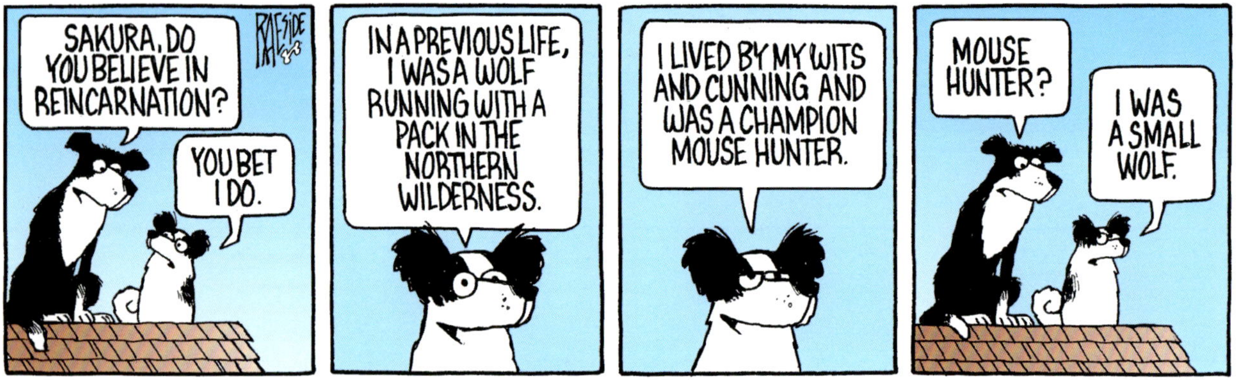
SAKURA, DO YOU BELIEVE IN REINCARNATION?
YOU BET I DO.
IN A PREVIOUS LIFE, I WAS A WOLF RUNNING WITH A PACK IN THE NORTHERN WILDERNESS.
I LIVED BY MY WITS AND CUNNING AND WAS A CHAMPION MOUSE HUNTER.
MOUSE HUNTER?
I WAS A SMALL WOLF.

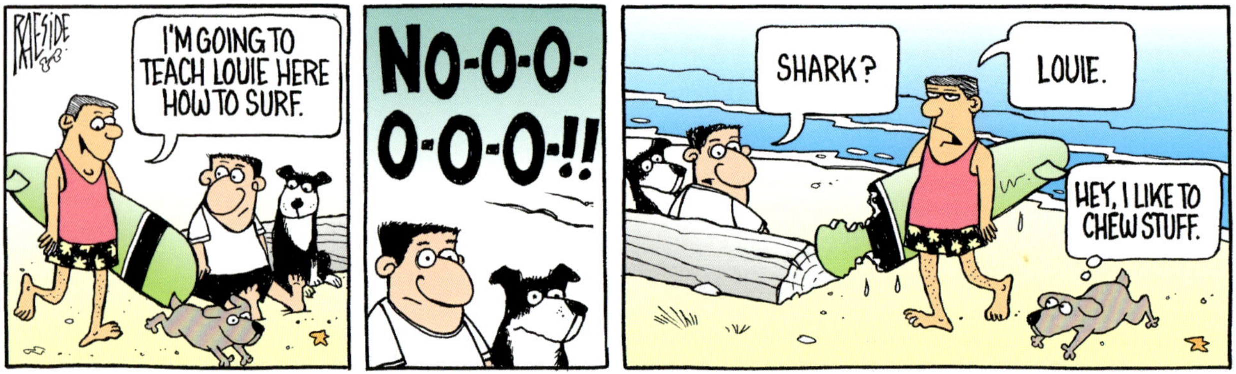
I'M GOING TO TEACH LOUIE HERE HOW TO SURF.
NO-O-O-O-O-O-!!
SHARK?
LOUIE.
HEY, I LIKE TO CHEW STUFF.

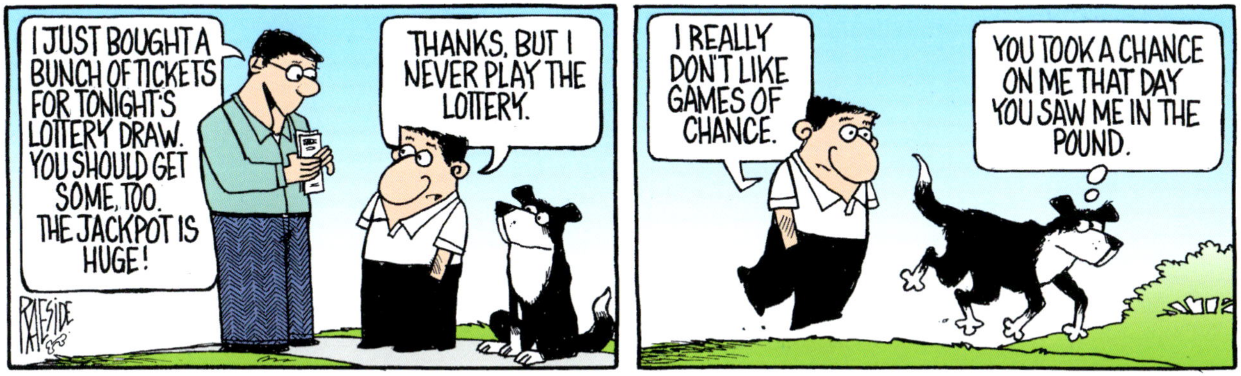
I JUST BOUGHT A BUNCH OF TICKETS FOR TONIGHT'S LOTTERY DRAW. YOU SHOULD GET SOME, TOO. THE JACKPOT IS HUGE!
THANKS, BUT I NEVER PLAY THE LOTTERY.
I REALLY DON'T LIKE GAMES OF CHANCE.
YOU TOOK A CHANCE ON ME THAT DAY YOU SAW ME IN THE POUND.

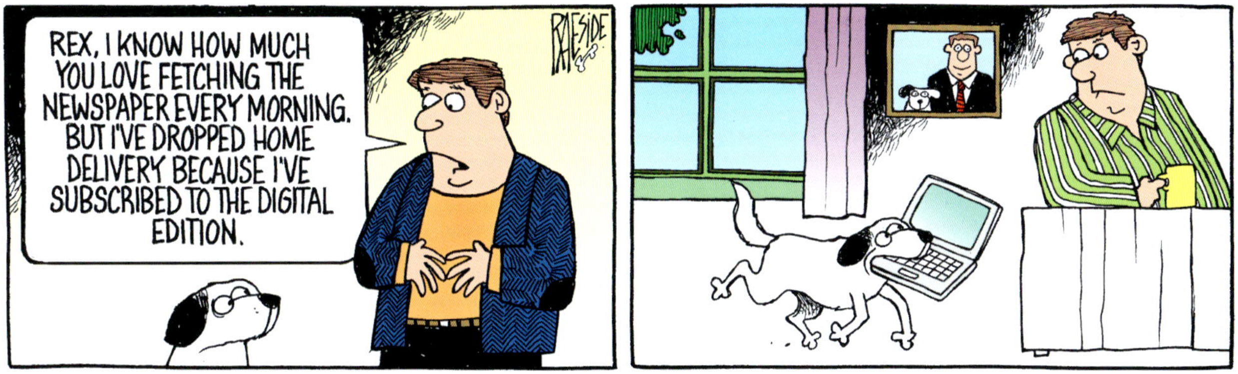
REX, I KNOW HOW MUCH YOU LOVE FETCHING THE NEWSPAPER EVERY MORNING. BUT I'VE DROPPED HOME DELIVERY BECAUSE I'VE SUBSCRIBED TO THE DIGITAL EDITION.

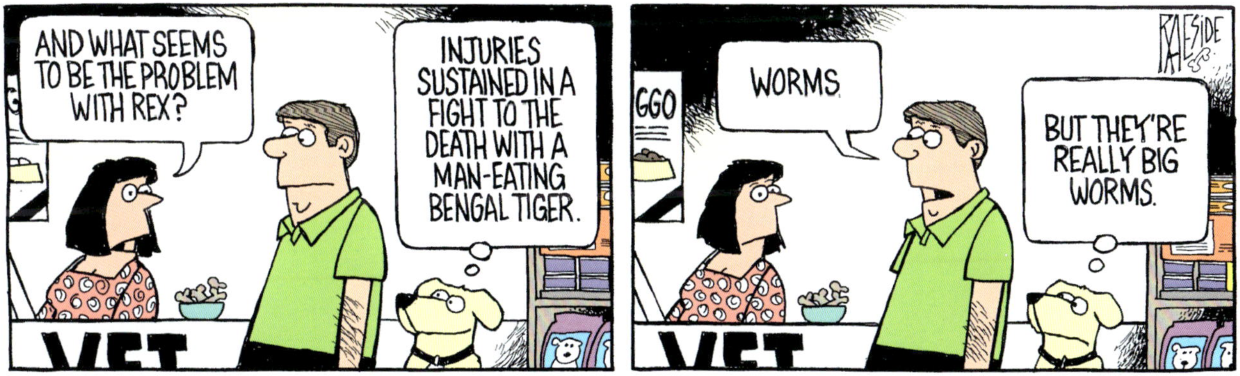
AND WHAT SEEMS TO BE THE PROBLEM WITH REX?
INJURIES SUSTAINED IN A FIGHT TO THE DEATH WITH A MAN-EATING BENGAL TIGER.
WORMS.
BUT THEY'RE REALLY BIG WORMS.

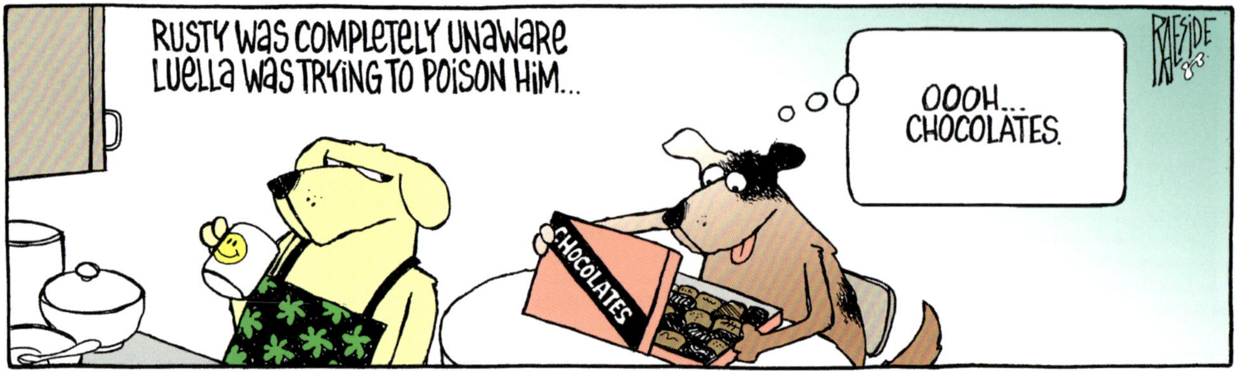
RUSTY WAS COMPLETELY UNAWARE LUELLA WAS TRYING TO POISON HIM...
OOOH... CHOCOLATES.
CHOCOLATES

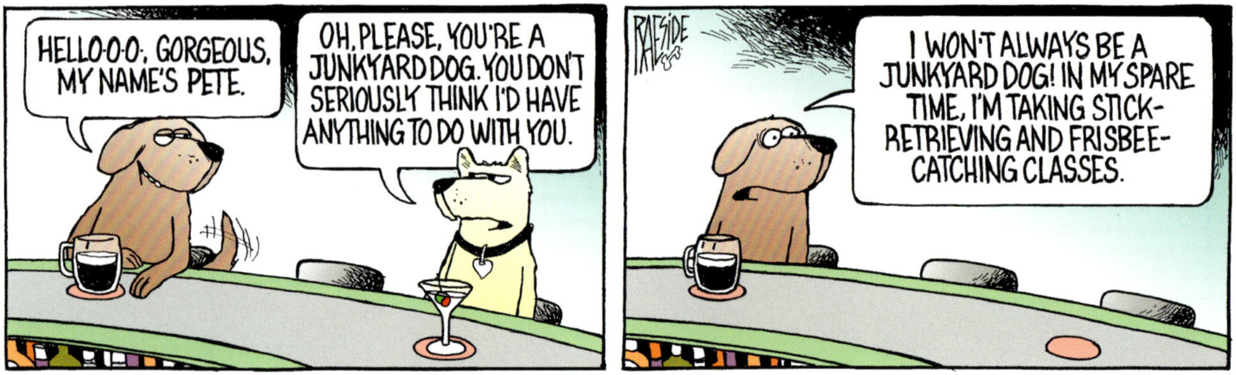
HELLO-O-O-, GORGEOUS. MY NAME'S PETE.
OH, PLEASE, YOU'RE A JUNKYARD DOG. YOU DON'T SERIOUSLY THINK I'D HAVE ANYTHING TO DO WITH YOU.
I WON'T ALWAYS BE A JUNKYARD DOG! IN MY SPARE TIME, I'M TAKING STICK-RETRIEVING AND FRISBEE-CATCHING CLASSES.

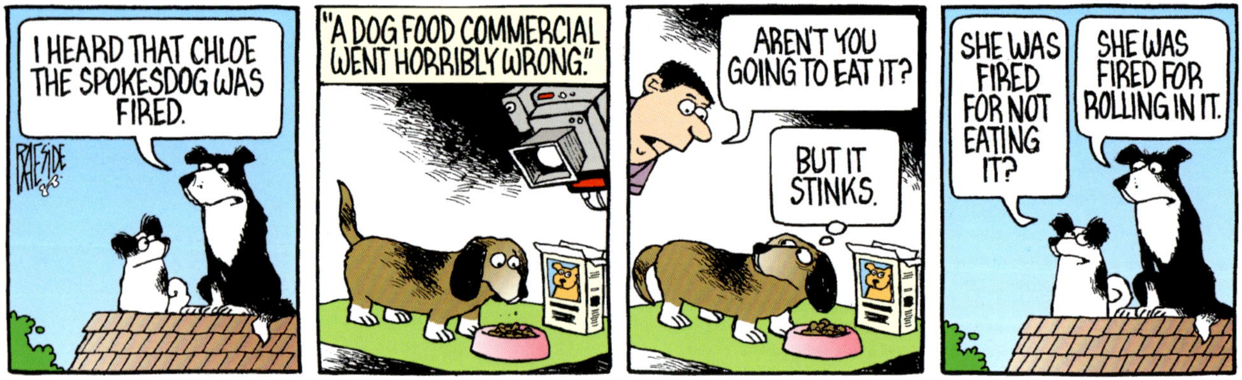
I HEARD THAT CHLOE THE SPOKESDOG WAS FIRED.
"A DOG FOOD COMMERCIAL WENT HORRIBLY WRONG."
AREN'T YOU GOING TO EAT IT?
BUT IT STINKS.
SHE WAS FIRED FOR NOT EATING IT?
SHE WAS FIRED FOR ROLLING IN IT.

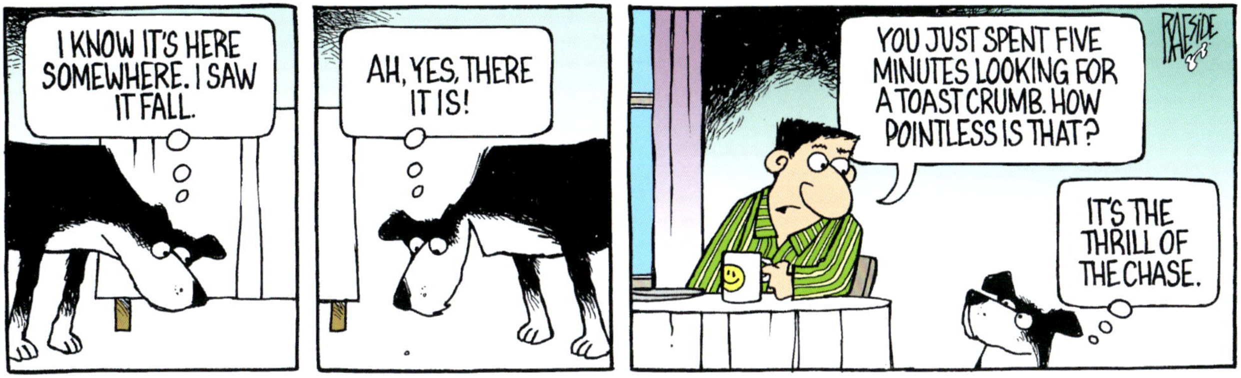
I KNOW IT'S HERE SOMEWHERE. I SAW IT FALL.
AH, YES, THERE IT IS!
YOU JUST SPENT FIVE MINUTES LOOKING FOR A TOAST CRUMB. HOW POINTLESS IS THAT?
IT'S THE THRILL OF THE CHASE.

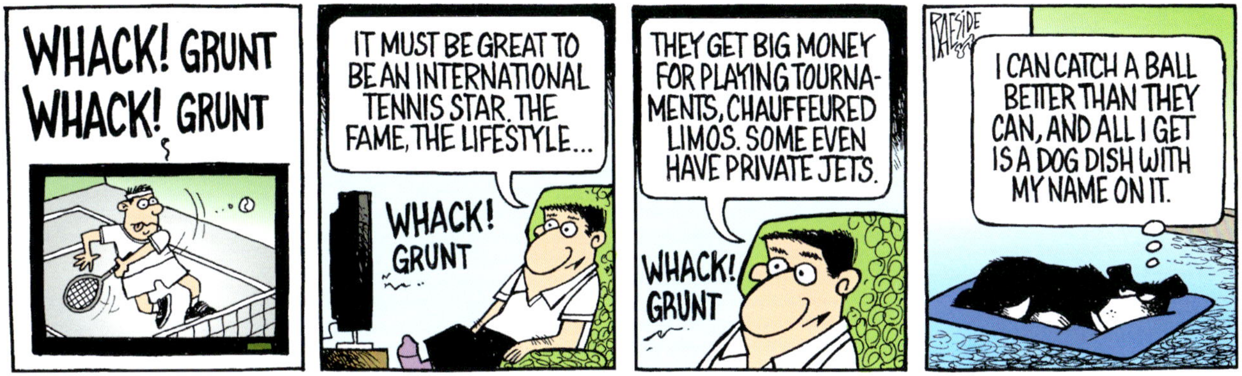
WHACK! GRUNT
WHACK! GRUNT
IT MUST BE GREAT TO BE AN INTERNATIONAL TENNIS STAR. THE FAME, THE LIFESTYLE...
WHACK! GRUNT
THEY GET BIG MONEY FOR PLAYING TOURNAMENTS, CHAUFFEURED LIMOS. SOME EVEN HAVE PRIVATE JETS.
WHACK! GRUNT
I CAN CATCH A BALL BETTER THAN THEY CAN, AND ALL I GET IS A DOG DISH WITH MY NAME ON IT.

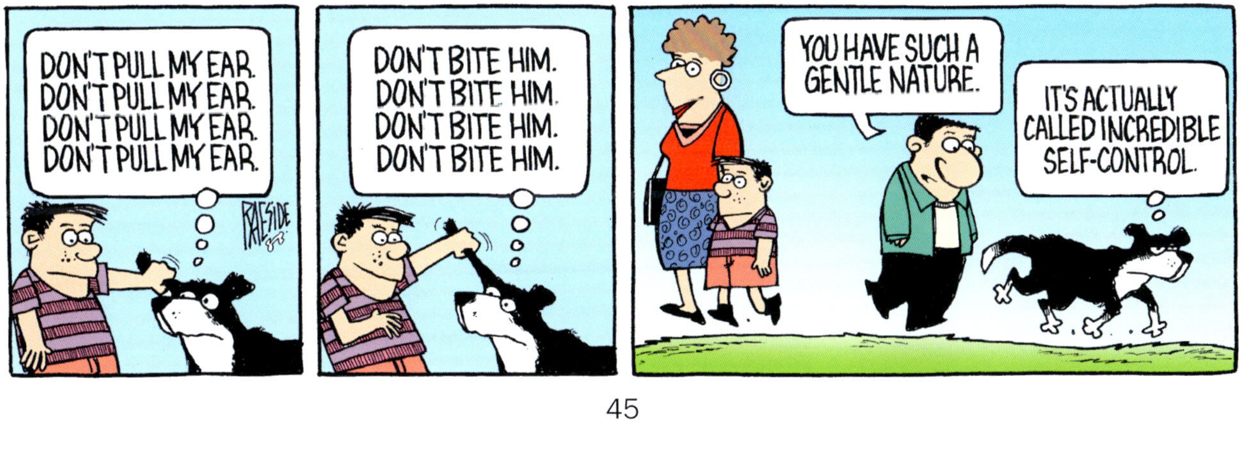
DON'T PULL MY EAR. DON'T PULL MY EAR. DON'T PULL MY EAR. DON'T PULL MY EAR.
DON'T BITE HIM. DON'T BITE HIM. DON'T BITE HIM. DON'T BITE HIM.
YOU HAVE SUCH A GENTLE NATURE.
IT'S ACTUALLY CALLED INCREDIBLE SELF-CONTROL.

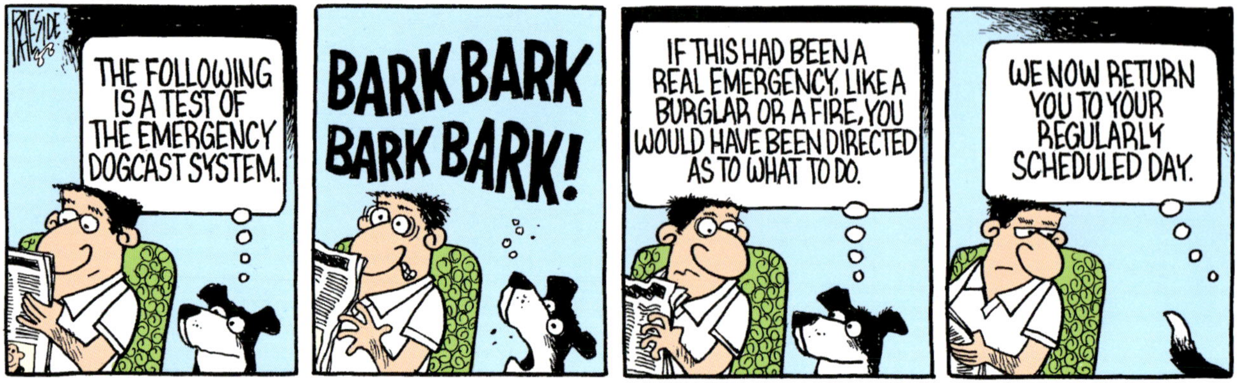
THE FOLLOWING IS A TEST OF THE EMERGENCY DOGCAST SYSTEM.
BARK BARK BARK BARK!
IF THIS HAD BEEN A REAL EMERGENCY, LIKE A BURGLAR OR A FIRE, YOU WOULD HAVE BEEN DIRECTED AS TO WHAT TO DO.
WE NOW RETURN YOU TO YOUR REGULARLY SCHEDULED DAY.

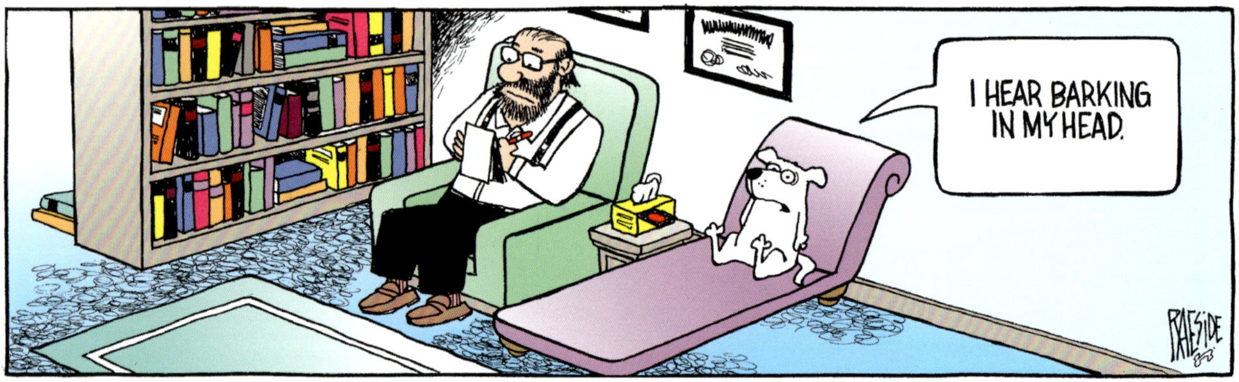
I HEAR BARKING IN MY HEAD.

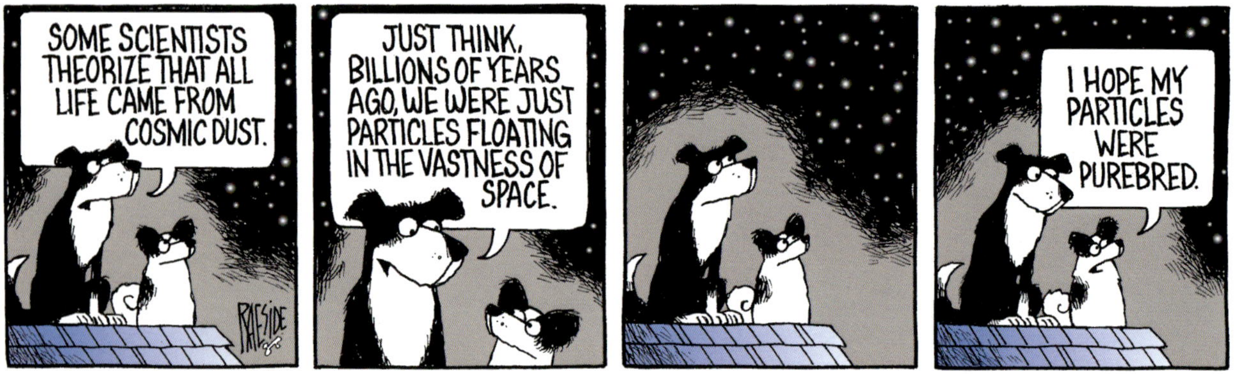
SOME SCIENTISTS THEORIZE THAT ALL LIFE CAME FROM COSMIC DUST.
JUST THINK, BILLIONS OF YEARS AGO, WE WERE JUST PARTICLES FLOATING IN THE VASTNESS OF SPACE.
I HOPE MY PARTICLES WERE PUREBRED.

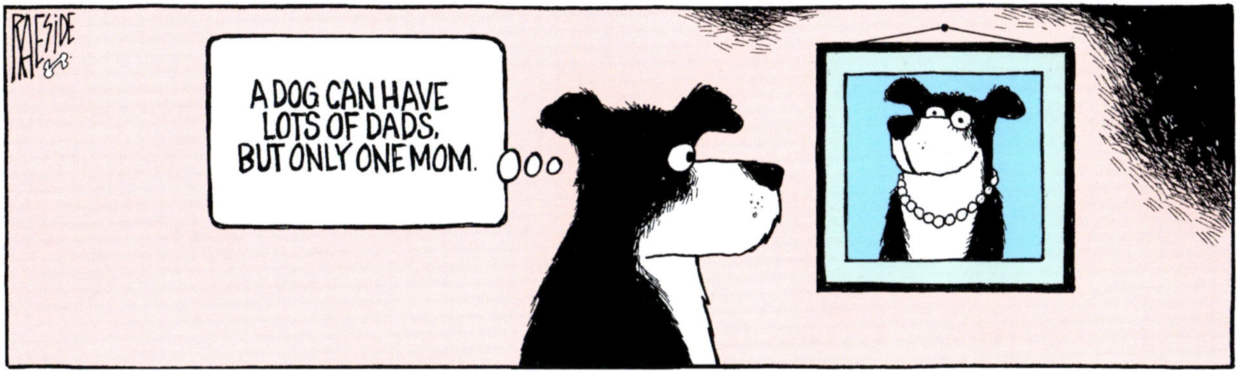
A DOG CAN HAVE LOTS OF DADS, BUT ONLY ONE MOM.

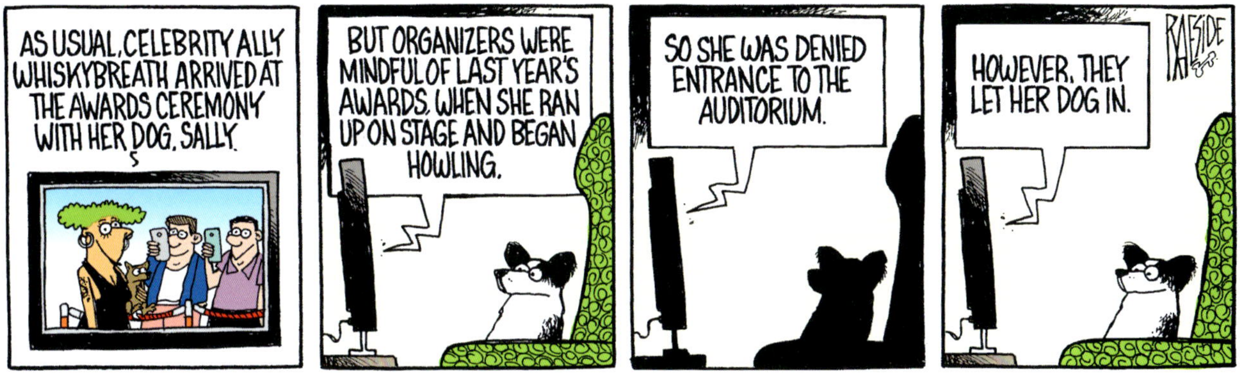
AS USUAL, CELEBRITY ALLY WHISKYBREATH ARRIVED AT THE AWARDS CEREMONY WITH HER DOG, SALLY.
BUT ORGANIZERS WERE MINDFUL OF LAST YEAR'S AWARDS, WHEN SHE RAN UP ON STAGE AND BEGAN HOWLING.
SO SHE WAS DENIED ENTRANCE TO THE AUDITORIUM.
HOWEVER, THEY LET HER DOG IN.

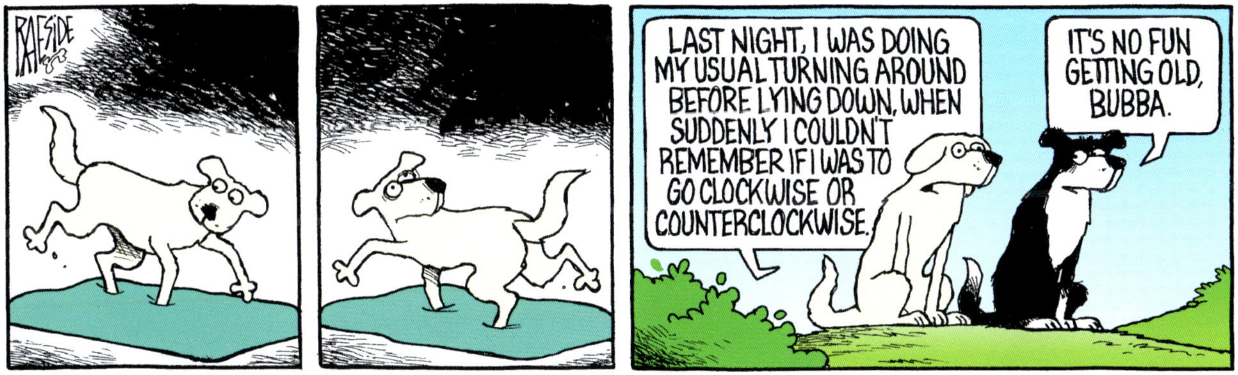
LAST NIGHT, I WAS DOING MY USUAL TURNING AROUND BEFORE LYING DOWN, WHEN SUDDENLY I COULDN'T REMEMBER IF I WAS TO GO CLOCKWISE OR COUNTERCLOCKWISE.
IT'S NO FUN GETTING OLD, BUBBA.

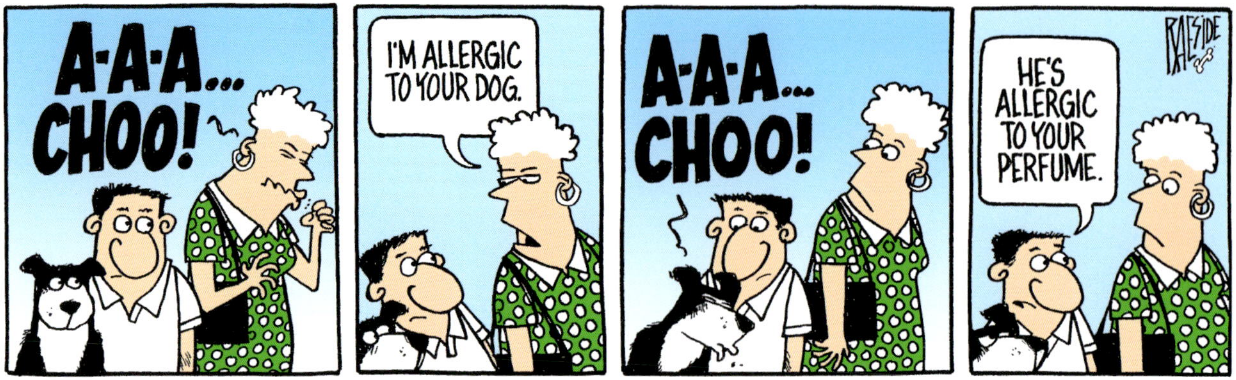
A-A-A... CHOO!
I'M ALLERGIC TO YOUR DOG.
A-A-A... CHOO!
HE'S ALLERGIC TO YOUR PERFUME.

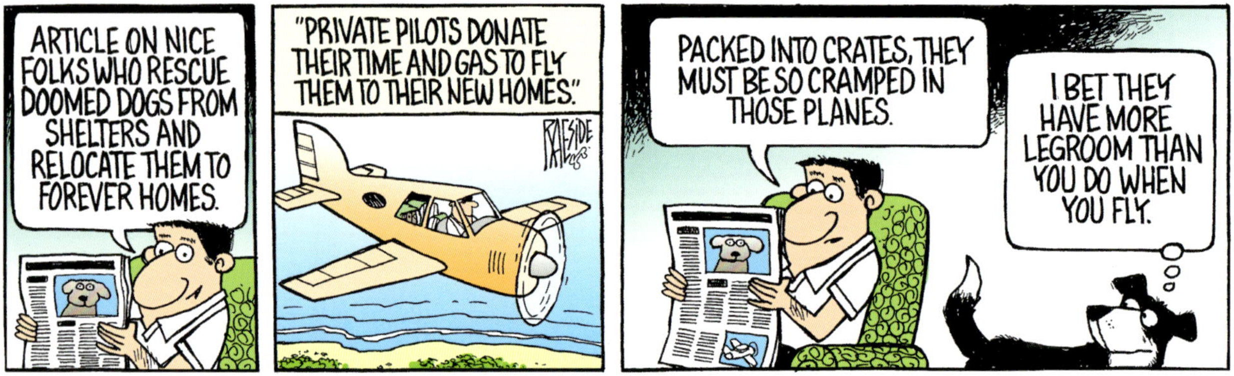
ARTICLE ON NICE FOLKS WHO RESCUE DOOMED DOGS FROM SHELTERS AND RELOCATE THEM TO FOREVER HOMES.
"PRIVATE PILOTS DONATE THEIR TIME AND GAS TO FLY THEM TO THEIR NEW HOMES."
PACKED INTO CRATES, THEY MUST BE SO CRAMPED IN THOSE PLANES.
I BET THEY HAVE MORE LEGROOM THAN YOU DO WHEN YOU FLY.

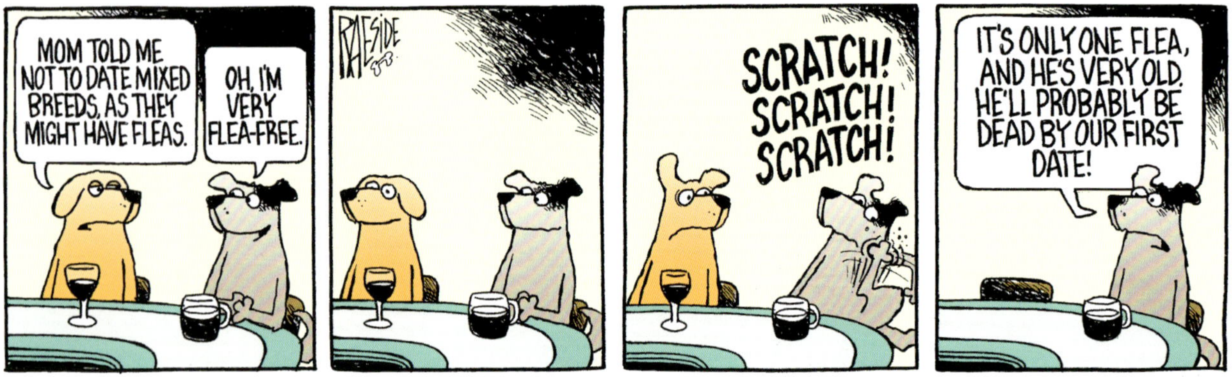
MOM TOLD ME NOT TO DATE MIXED BREEDS, AS THEY MIGHT HAVE FLEAS.
OH, I'M VERY FLEA-FREE.
SCRATCH! SCRATCH! SCRATCH!
IT'S ONLY ONE FLEA, AND HE'S VERY OLD. HE'LL PROBABLY BE DEAD BY OUR FIRST DATE!

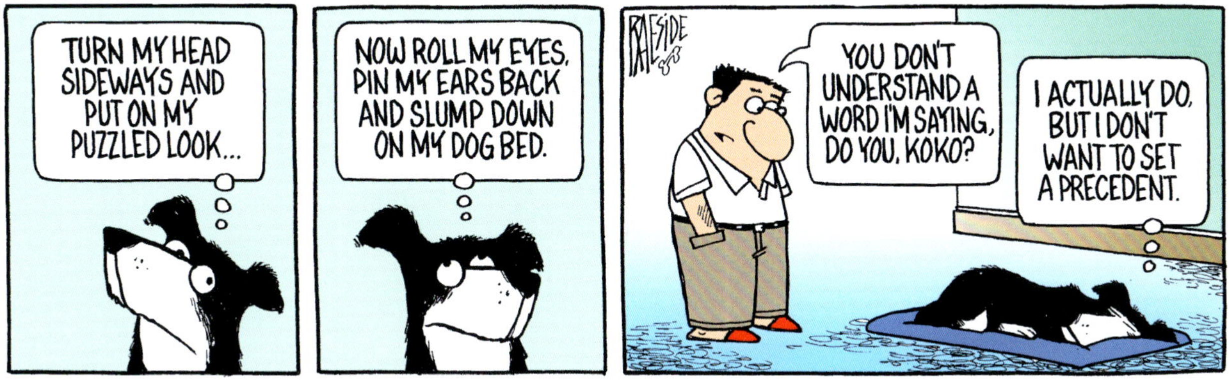
TURN MY HEAD SIDEWAYS AND PUT ON MY PUZZLED LOOK...
NOW ROLL MY EYES, PIN MY EARS BACK AND SLUMP DOWN ON MY DOG BED.
RAESIDE
YOU DON'T UNDERSTAND A WORD I'M SAYING, DO YOU, KOKO?
I ACTUALLY DO, BUT I DON'T WANT TO SET A PRECEDENT.

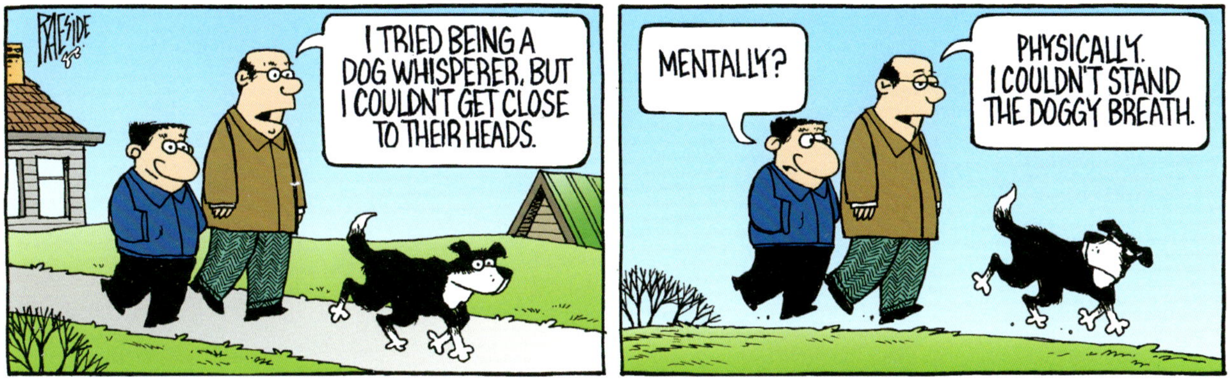
RAESIDE
I TRIED BEING A DOG WHISPERER, BUT I COULDN'T GET CLOSE TO THEIR HEADS.
MENTALLY?
PHYSICALLY. I COULDN'T STAND THE DOGGY BREATH.

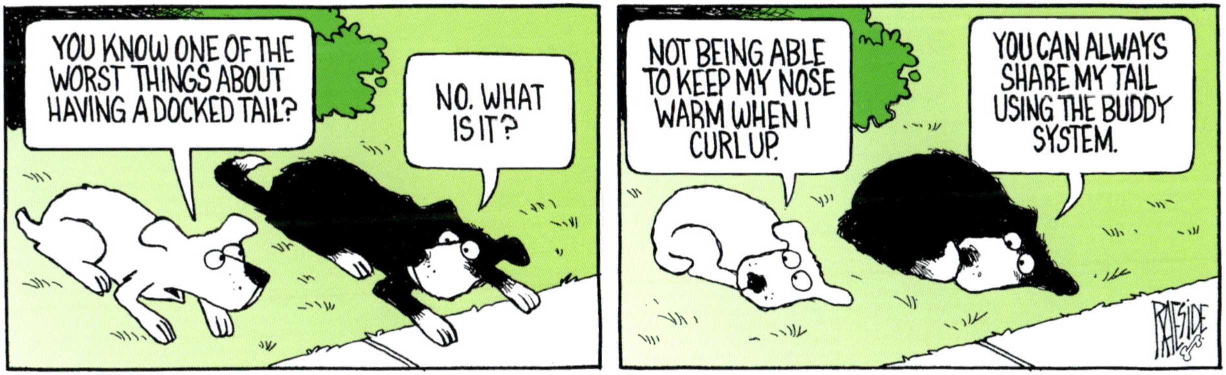
YOU KNOW ONE OF THE WORST THINGS ABOUT HAVING A DOCKED TAIL?
NO. WHAT IS IT?
NOT BEING ABLE TO KEEP MY NOSE WARM WHEN I CURL UP.
YOU CAN ALWAYS SHARE MY TAIL USING THE BUDDY SYSTEM.
RAESIDE

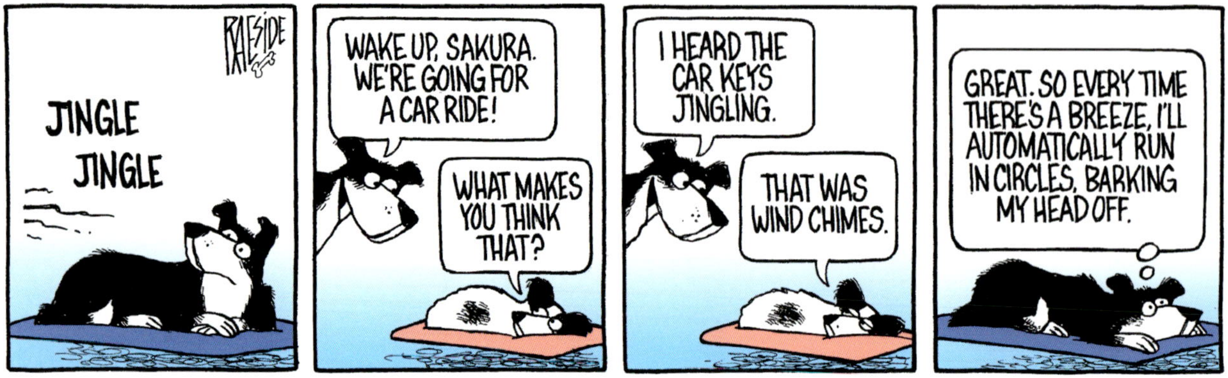
JINGLE
JINGLE
WAKE UP, SAKURA. WE'RE GOING FOR A CAR RIDE!
WHAT MAKES YOU THINK THAT?
I HEARD THE CAR KEYS JINGLING.
THAT WAS WIND CHIMES.
GREAT. SO EVERY TIME THERE'S A BREEZE, I'LL AUTOMATICALLY RUN IN CIRCLES, BARKING MY HEAD OFF.

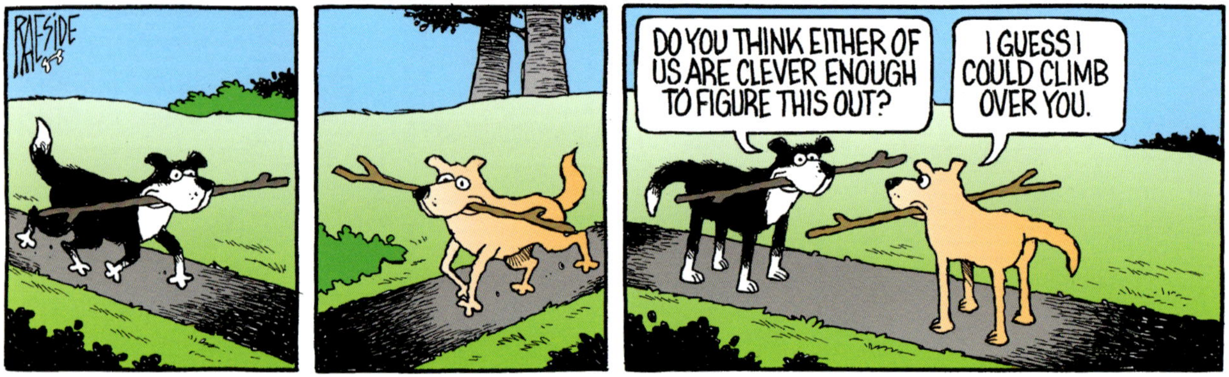
DO YOU THINK EITHER OF US ARE CLEVER ENOUGH TO FIGURE THIS OUT?
I GUESS I COULD CLIMB OVER YOU.

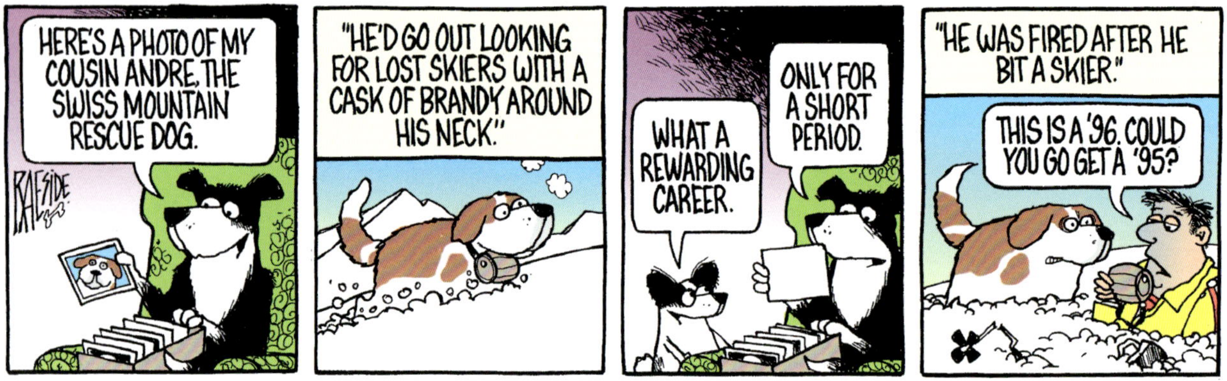
HERE'S A PHOTO OF MY COUSIN ANDRE, THE SWISS MOUNTAIN RESCUE DOG.
"HE'D GO OUT LOOKING FOR LOST SKIERS WITH A CASK OF BRANDY AROUND HIS NECK."
WHAT A REWARDING CAREER.
ONLY FOR A SHORT PERIOD.
"HE WAS FIRED AFTER HE BIT A SKIER."
THIS IS A '96. COULD YOU GO GET A '95?

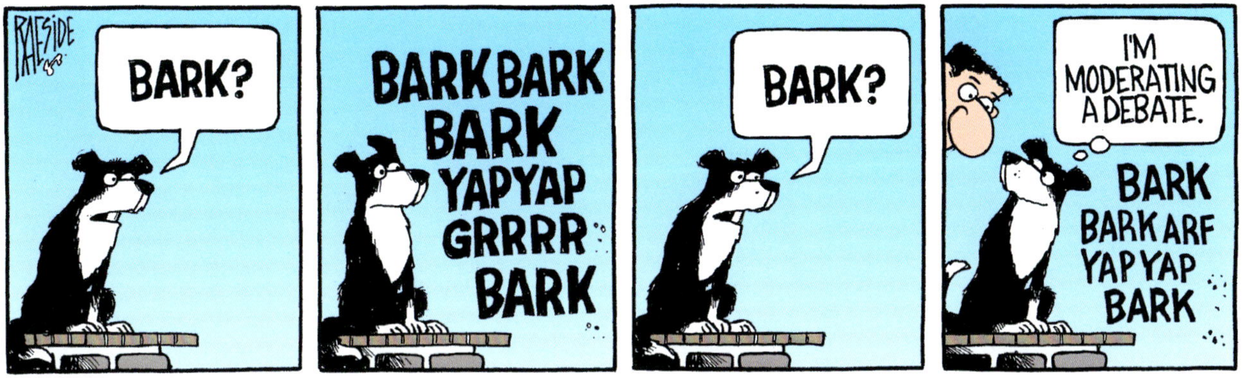
BARK?
BARK BARK BARK YAP YAP GRRRR BARK
BARK?
I'M MODERATING A DEBATE.
BARK BARK ARF YAP YAP BARK

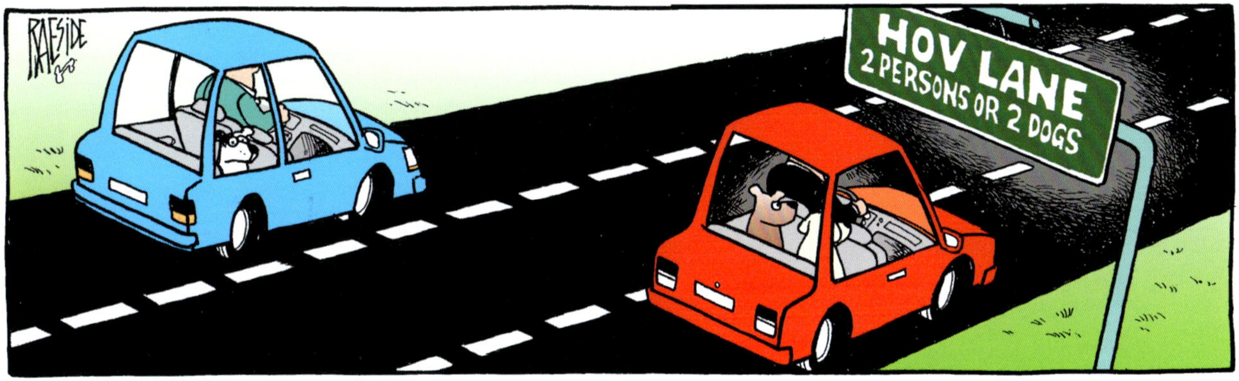
HOV LANE
2 PERSONS OR 2 DOGS

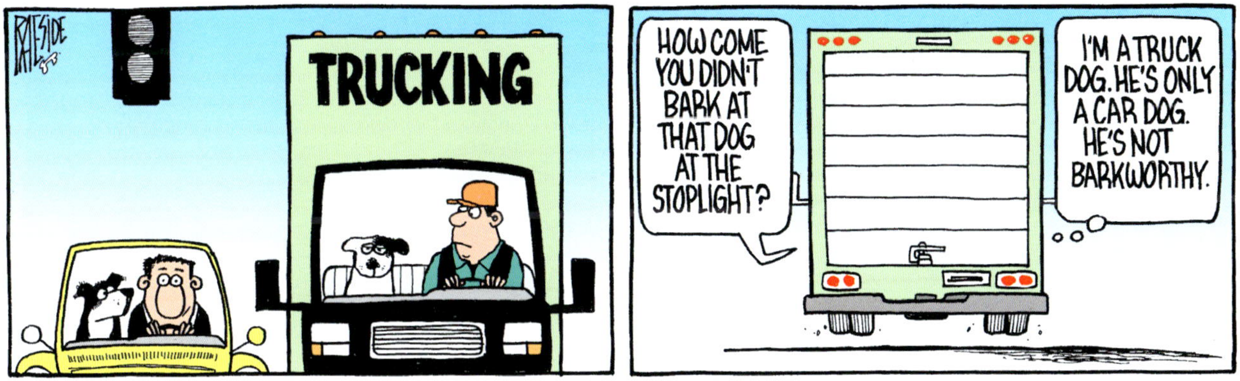
TRUCKING
HOW COME YOU DIDN'T BARK AT THAT DOG AT THE STOPLIGHT?
I'M A TRUCK DOG. HE'S ONLY A CAR DOG. HE'S NOT BARKWORTHY.

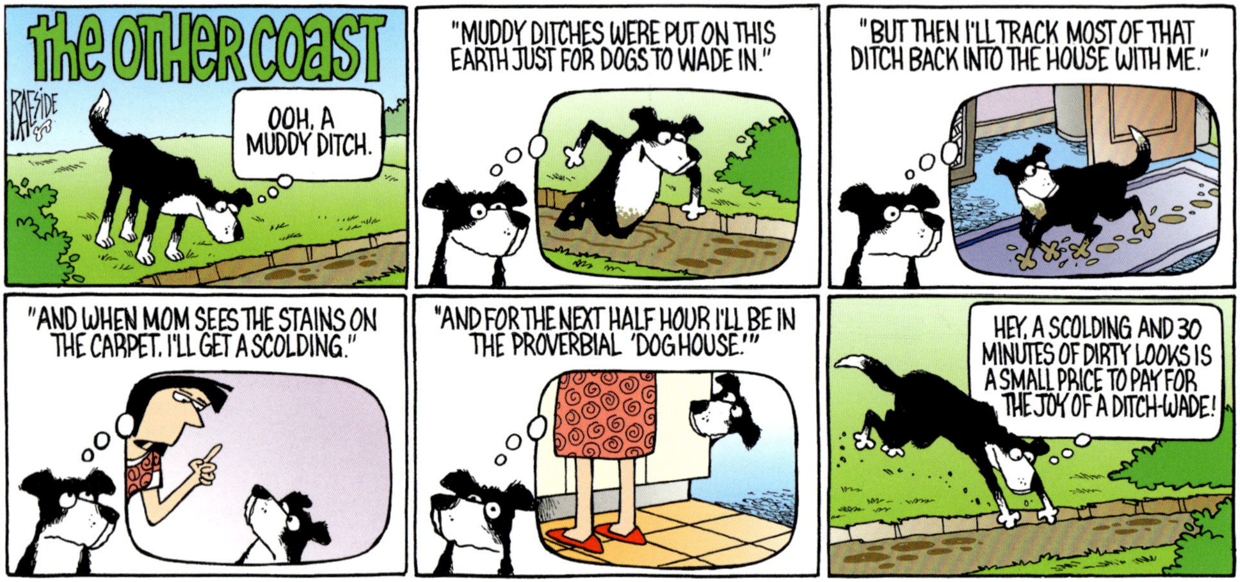
the OTHER COAST
RAESIDE
OOH, A MUDDY DITCH.
"MUDDY DITCHES WERE PUT ON THIS EARTH JUST FOR DOGS TO WADE IN."
"BUT THEN I'LL TRACK MOST OF THAT DITCH BACK INTO THE HOUSE WITH ME."
"AND WHEN MOM SEES THE STAINS ON THE CARPET, I'LL GET A SCOLDING."
"AND FOR THE NEXT HALF HOUR I'LL BE IN THE PROVERBIAL 'DOGHOUSE.'"
HEY, A SCOLDING AND 30 MINUTES OF DIRTY LOOKS IS A SMALL PRICE TO PAY FOR THE JOY OF A DITCH-WADE!

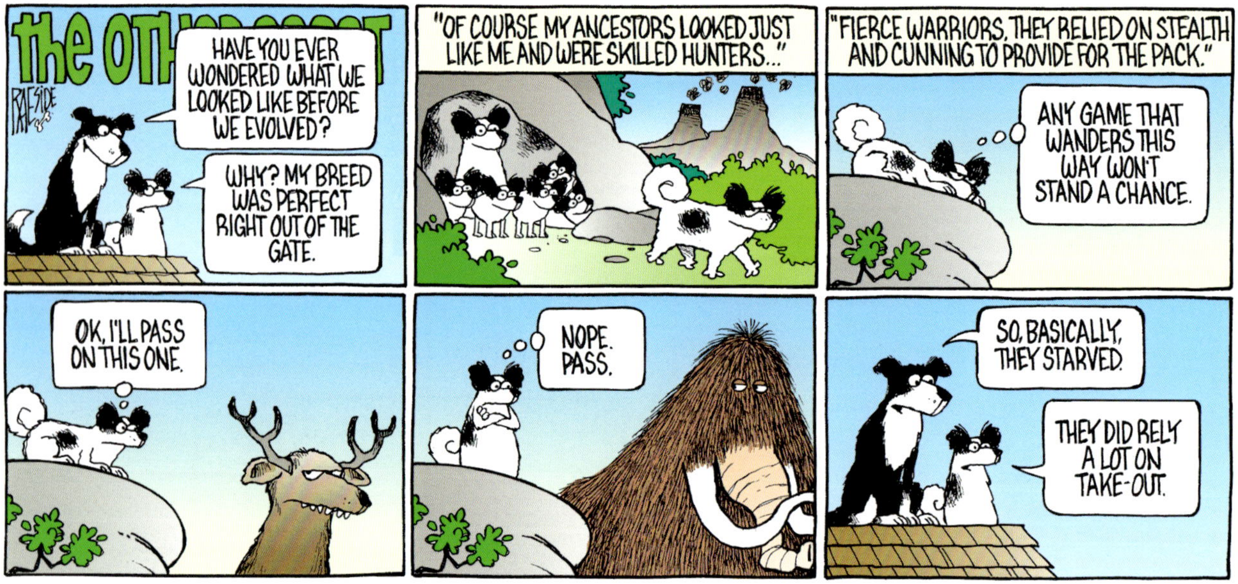
the OTHER COAST
RAESIDE
HAVE YOU EVER WONDERED WHAT WE LOOKED LIKE BEFORE WE EVOLVED?
WHY? MY BREED WAS PERFECT RIGHT OUT OF THE GATE.
"OF COURSE MY ANCESTORS LOOKED JUST LIKE ME AND WERE SKILLED HUNTERS..."
"FIERCE WARRIORS, THEY RELIED ON STEALTH AND CUNNING TO PROVIDE FOR THE PACK."
ANY GAME THAT WANDERS THIS WAY WON'T STAND A CHANCE.
OK, I'LL PASS ON THIS ONE.
NOPE. PASS.
SO, BASICALLY, THEY STARVED.
THEY DID RELY A LOT ON TAKE-OUT.

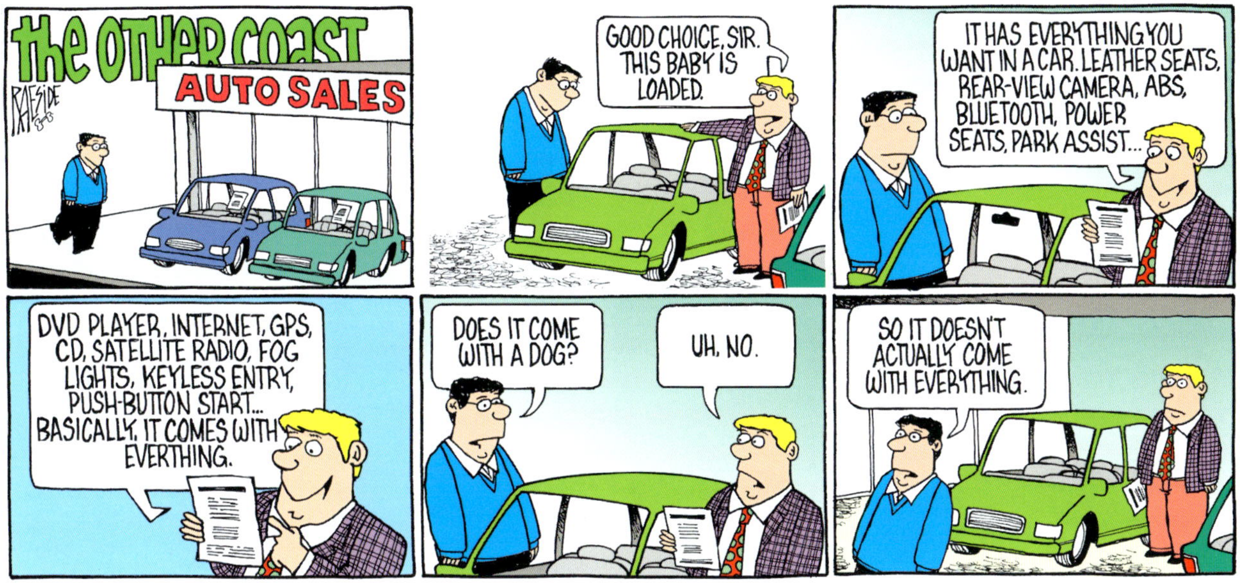
the OTHER COAST
AUTO SALES
RAESIDE
GOOD CHOICE, SIR. THIS BABY IS LOADED.
IT HAS EVERYTHING YOU WANT IN A CAR. LEATHER SEATS, REAR-VIEW CAMERA, ABS, BLUETOOTH, POWER SEATS, PARK ASSIST...
DVD PLAYER, INTERNET, GPS, CD, SATELLITE RADIO, FOG LIGHTS, KEYLESS ENTRY, PUSH-BUTTON START... BASICALLY, IT COMES WITH EVERTHING.
DOES IT COME WITH A DOG?
UH, NO.
SO IT DOESN'T ACTUALLY COME WITH EVERYTHING.

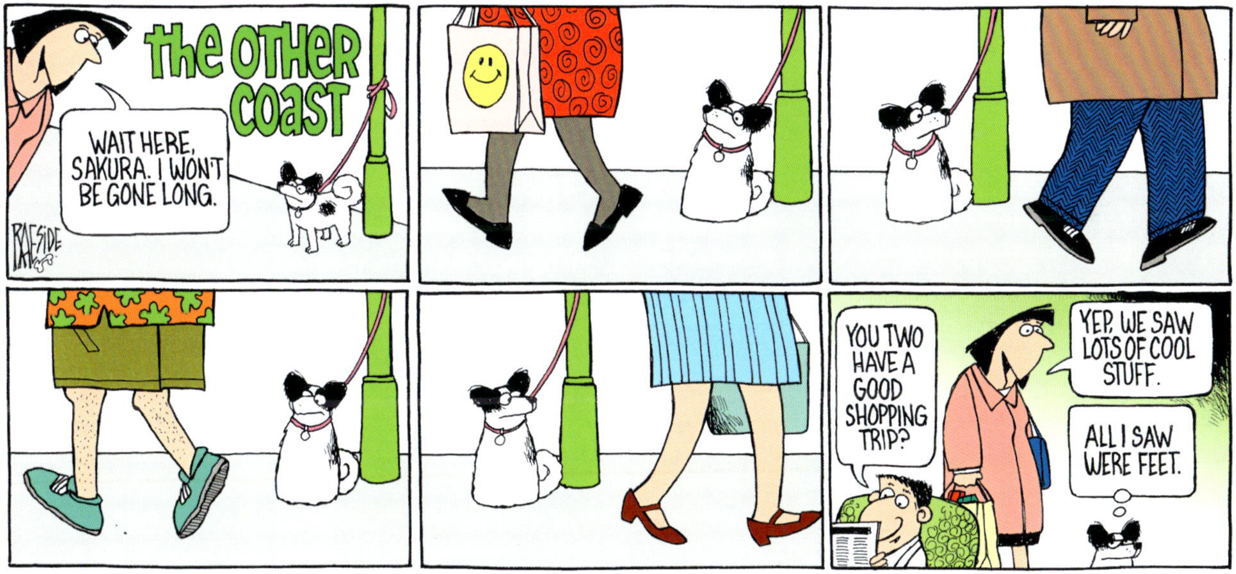
the OTHER COAST
WAIT HERE, SAKURA. I WON'T BE GONE LONG.
RAESIDE
YOU TWO HAVE A GOOD SHOPPING TRIP?
YEP, WE SAW LOTS OF COOL STUFF.
ALL I SAW WERE FEET.

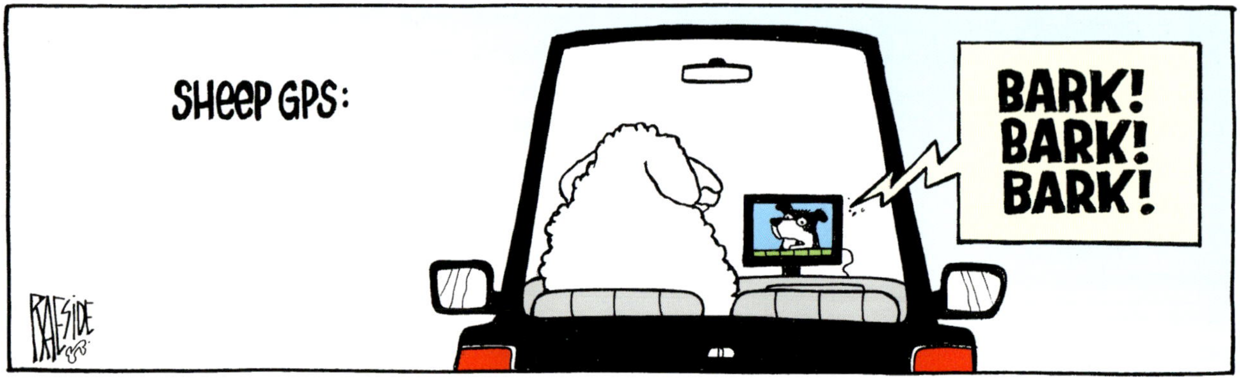
SHEEP GPS:
BARK! BARK! BARK!

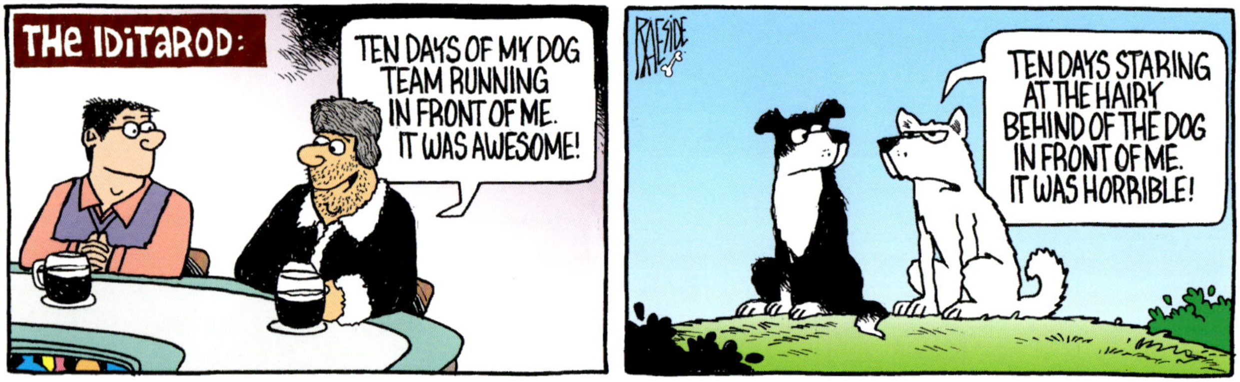
THE IDITAROD:
TEN DAYS OF MY DOG TEAM RUNNING IN FRONT OF ME. IT WAS AWESOME!
TEN DAYS STARING AT THE HAIRY BEHIND OF THE DOG IN FRONT OF ME. IT WAS HORRIBLE!

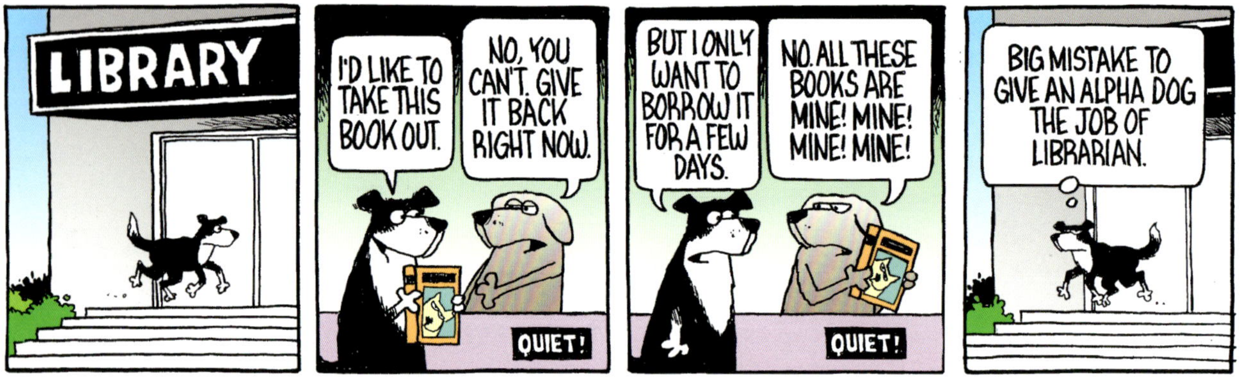
LIBRARY
I'D LIKE TO TAKE THIS BOOK OUT.
NO, YOU CAN'T. GIVE IT BACK RIGHT NOW.
QUIET!
BUT I ONLY WANT TO BORROW IT FOR A FEW DAYS.
NO. ALL THESE BOOKS ARE MINE! MINE! MINE! MINE!
QUIET!
BIG MISTAKE TO GIVE AN ALPHA DOG THE JOB OF LIBRARIAN.

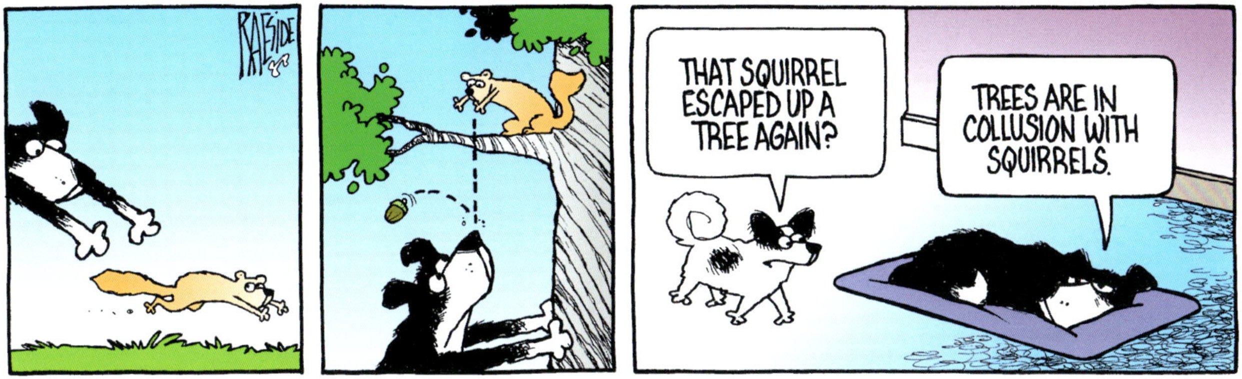
THAT SQUIRREL ESCAPED UP A TREE AGAIN?
TREES ARE IN COLLUSION WITH SQUIRRELS.

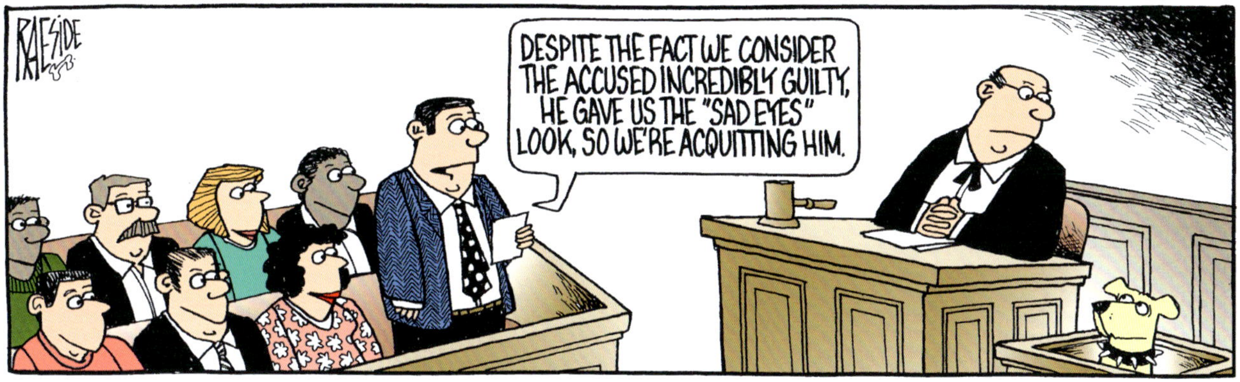
DESPITE THE FACT WE CONSIDER THE ACCUSED INCREDIBLY GUILTY, HE GAVE US THE "SAD EYES" LOOK, SO WE'RE ACQUITTING HIM.

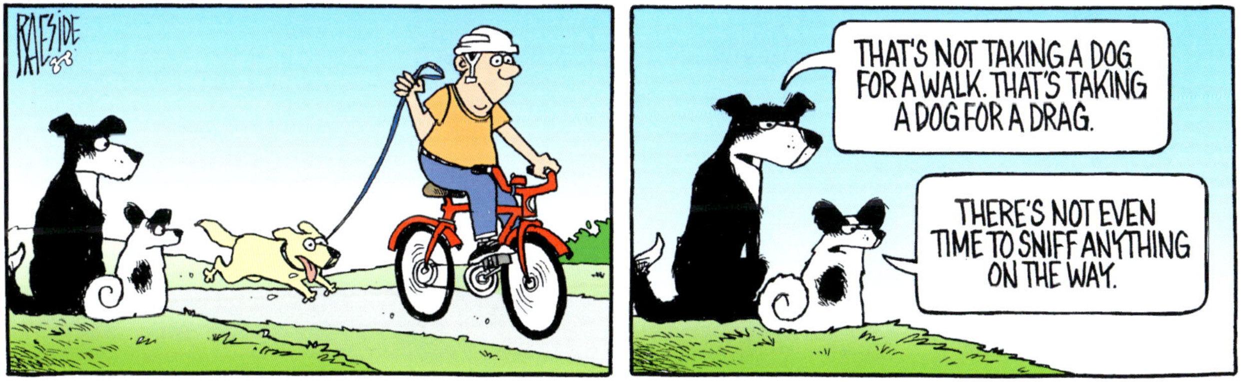
THAT'S NOT TAKING A DOG FOR A WALK. THAT'S TAKING A DOG FOR A DRAG.
THERE'S NOT EVEN TIME TO SNIFF ANYTHING ON THE WAY.

59

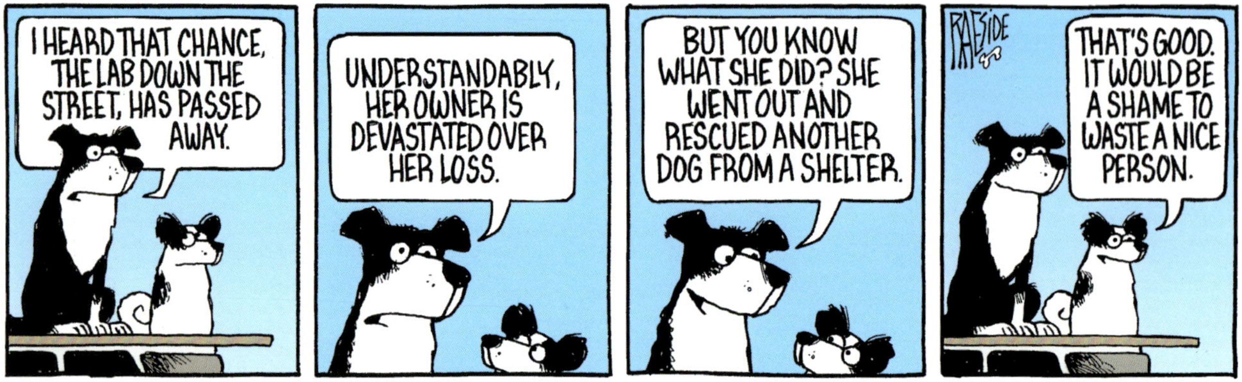
I HEARD THAT CHANCE, THE LAB DOWN THE STREET, HAS PASSED AWAY.
UNDERSTANDABLY, HER OWNER IS DEVASTATED OVER HER LOSS.
BUT YOU KNOW WHAT SHE DID? SHE WENT OUT AND RESCUED ANOTHER DOG FROM A SHELTER.
THAT'S GOOD. IT WOULD BE A SHAME TO WASTE A NICE PERSON.

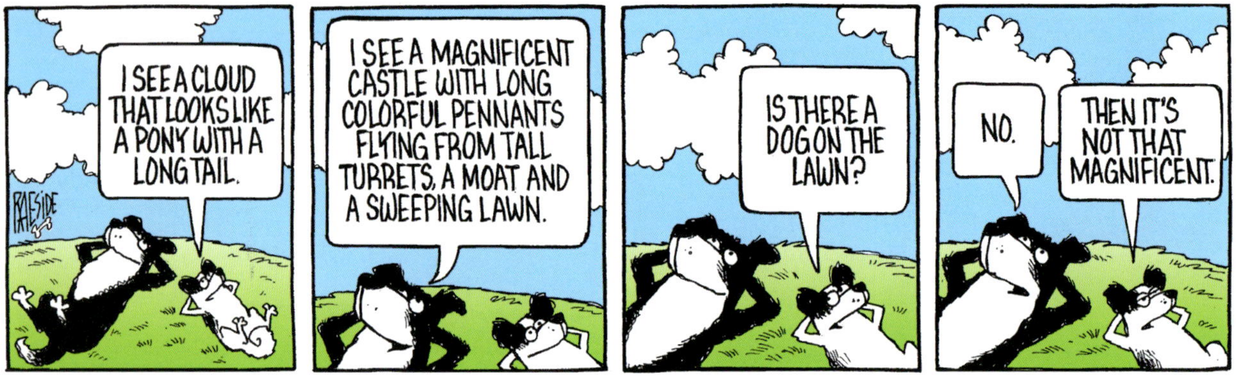
I SEE A CLOUD THAT LOOKS LIKE A PONY WITH A LONG TAIL.
I SEE A MAGNIFICENT CASTLE WITH LONG COLORFUL PENNANTS FLYING FROM TALL TURRETS, A MOAT AND A SWEEPING LAWN.
IS THERE A DOG ON THE LAWN?
NO.
THEN IT'S NOT THAT MAGNIFICENT.

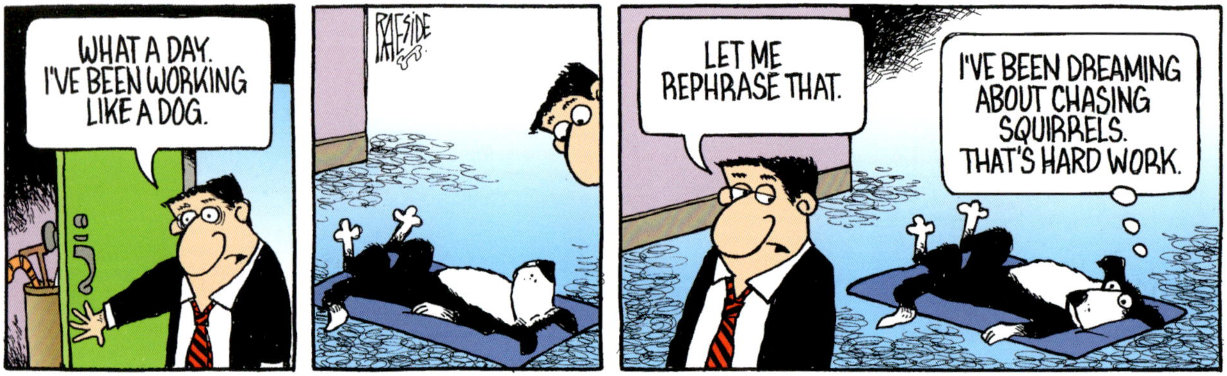
WHAT A DAY. I'VE BEEN WORKING LIKE A DOG.
LET ME REPHRASE THAT.
I'VE BEEN DREAMING ABOUT CHASING SQUIRRELS. THAT'S HARD WORK.

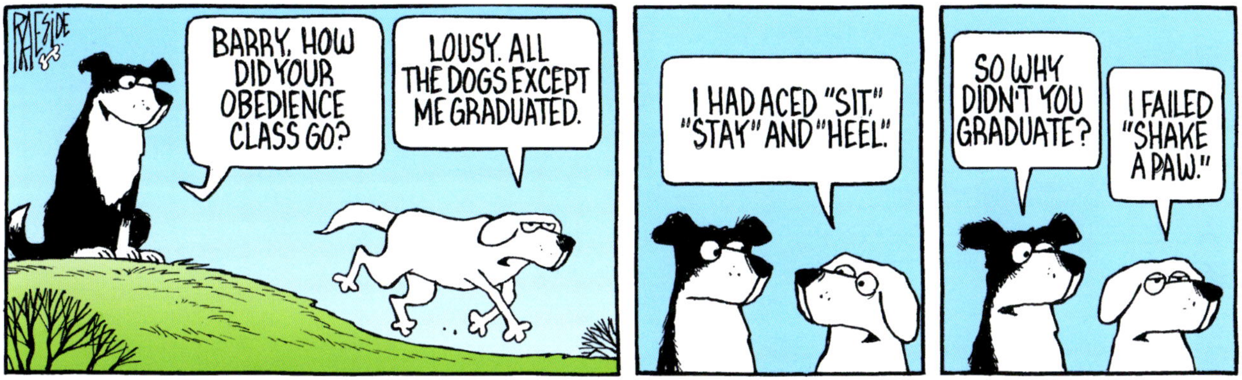
BARRY, HOW DID YOUR OBEDIENCE CLASS GO?
LOUSY. ALL THE DOGS EXCEPT ME GRADUATED.
I HAD ACED "SIT," "STAY" AND "HEEL."
SO WHY DIDN'T YOU GRADUATE?
I FAILED "SHAKE A PAW."

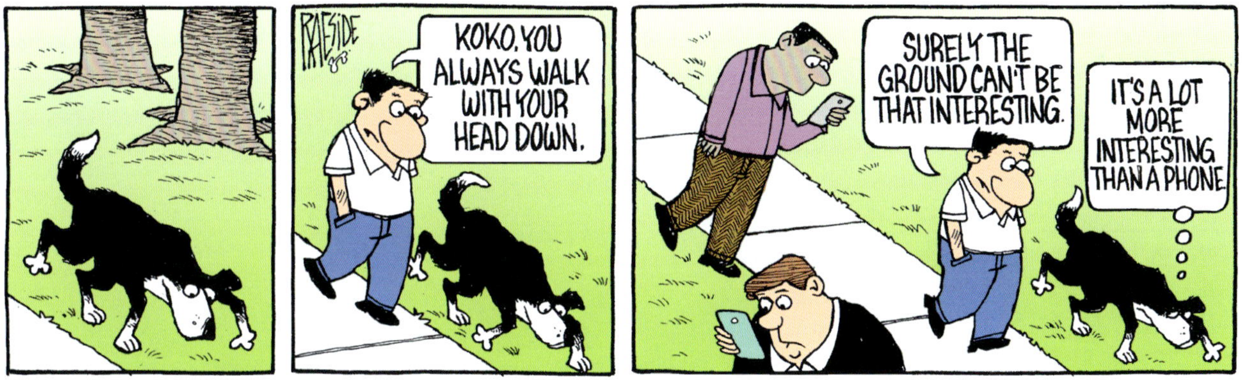
KOKO, YOU ALWAYS WALK WITH YOUR HEAD DOWN.
SURELY THE GROUND CAN'T BE THAT INTERESTING.
IT'S A LOT MORE INTERESTING THAN A PHONE.

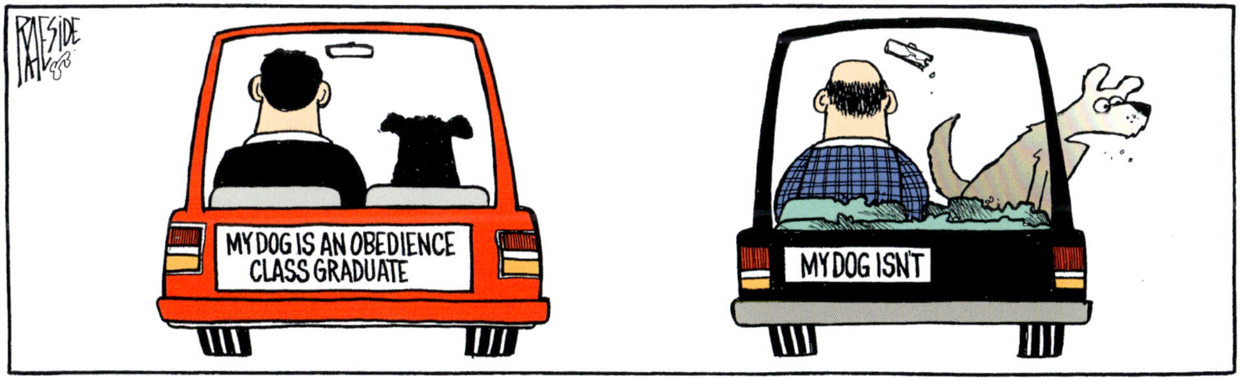
MY DOG IS AN OBEDIENCE CLASS GRADUATE
MY DOG ISN'T

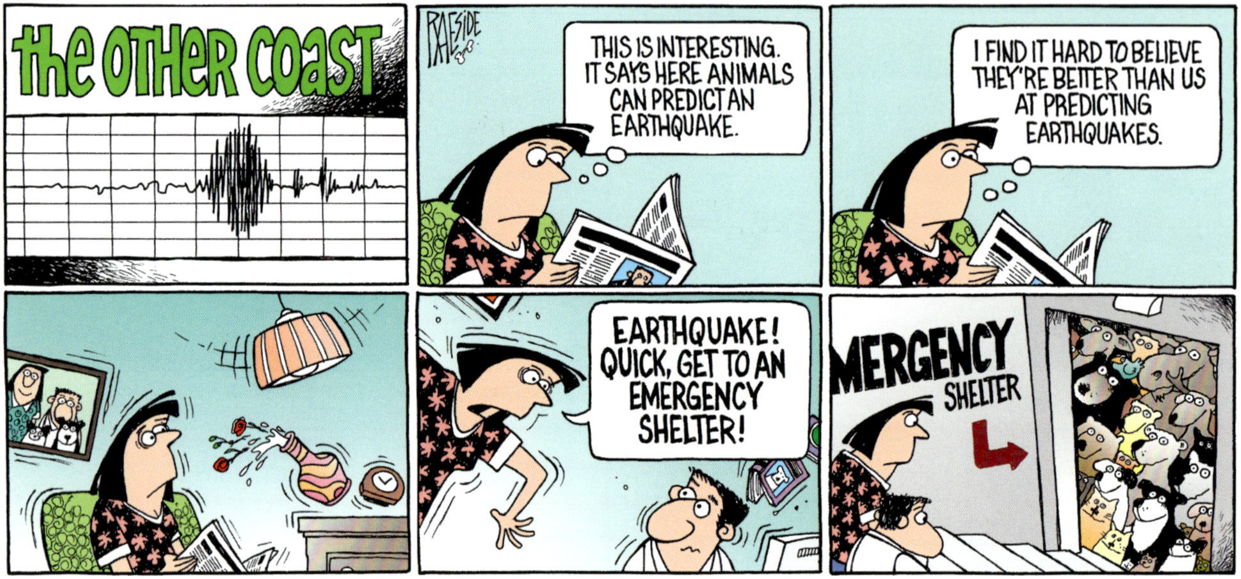
the OTHER COAST
RAESIDE
THIS IS INTERESTING. IT SAYS HERE ANIMALS CAN PREDICT AN EARTHQUAKE.
I FIND IT HARD TO BELIEVE THEY'RE BETTER THAN US AT PREDICTING EARTHQUAKES.
EARTHQUAKE! QUICK, GET TO AN EMERGENCY SHELTER!
MERGENCY
SHELTER

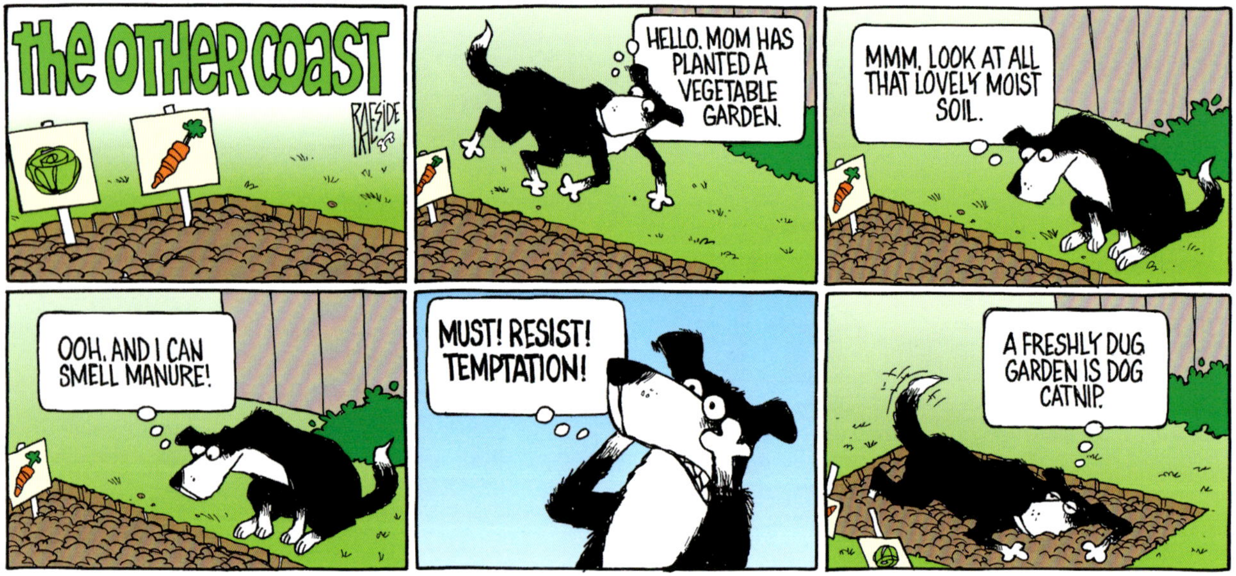
the OTHER COAST
RAESIDE
HELLO. MOM HAS PLANTED A VEGETABLE GARDEN.
MMM, LOOK AT ALL THAT LOVELY MOIST SOIL.
OOH, AND I CAN SMELL MANURE!
MUST! RESIST! TEMPTATION!
A FRESHLY DUG GARDEN IS DOG CATNIP.

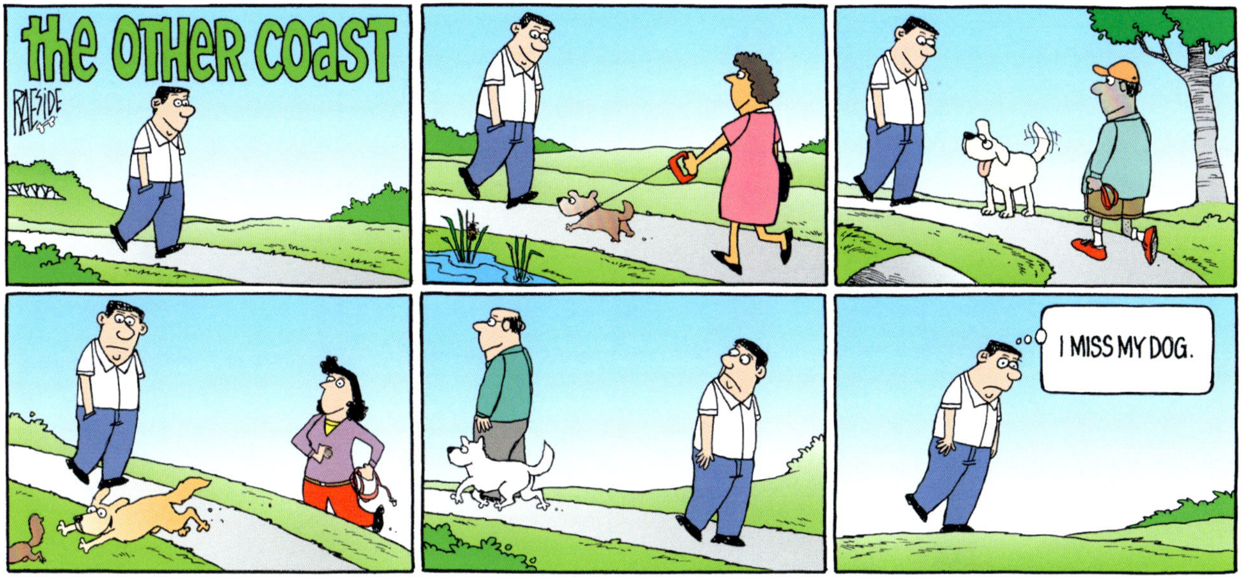
the OTHER COAST
RAESIDE
I MISS MY DOG.

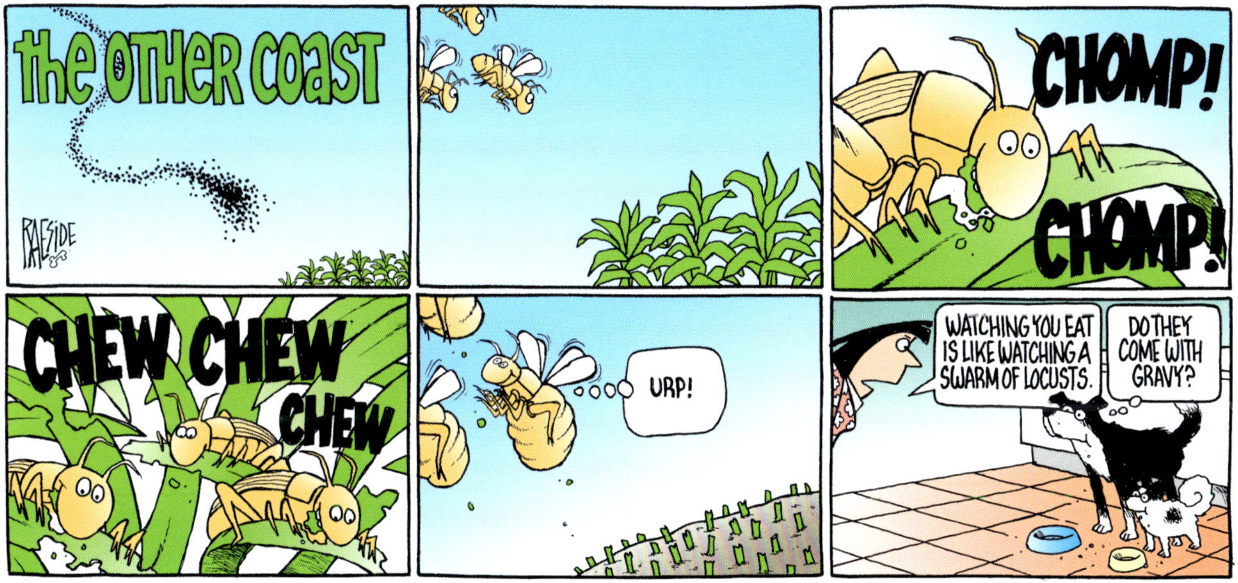
the OTHER COAST
RAESIDE
CHOMP!
CHOMP!
CHEW CHEW
CHEW
URP!
WATCHING YOU EAT IS LIKE WATCHING A SWARM OF LOCUSTS.
DO THEY COME WITH GRAVY?

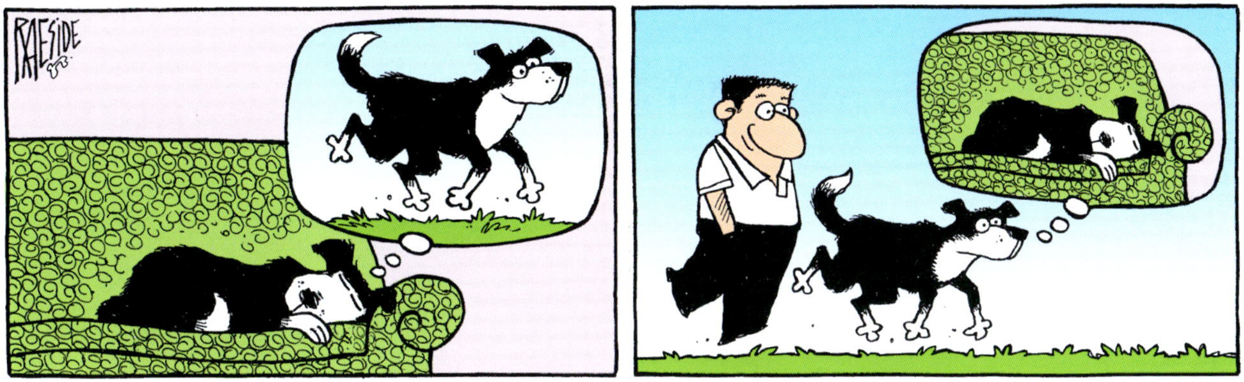
RAESIDE

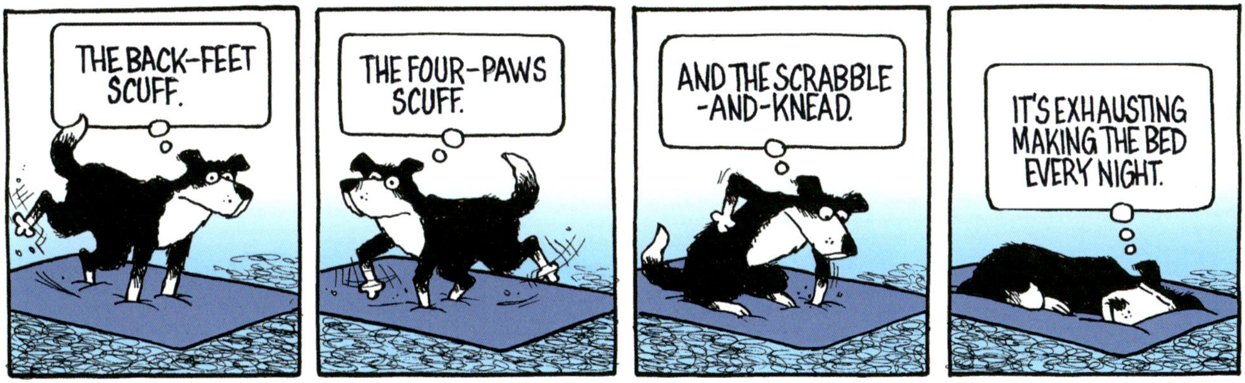
THE BACK-FEET SCUFF.
THE FOUR-PAWS SCUFF.
AND THE SCRABBLE -AND-KNEAD.
IT'S EXHAUSTING MAKING THE BED EVERY NIGHT.

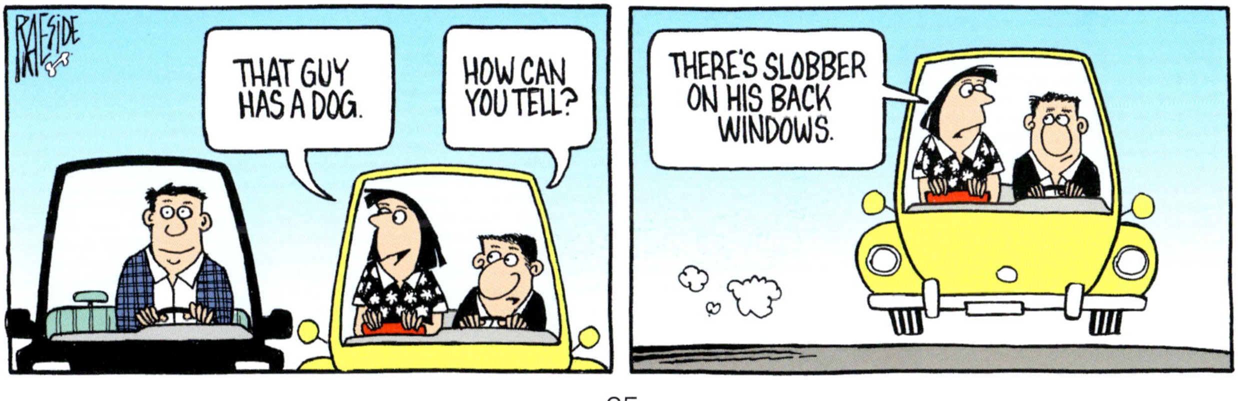
RAESIDE
THAT GUY HAS A DOG.
HOW CAN YOU TELL?
THERE'S SLOBBER ON HIS BACK WINDOWS.

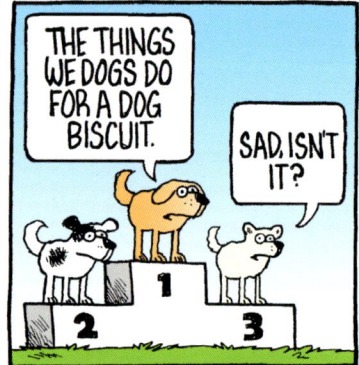

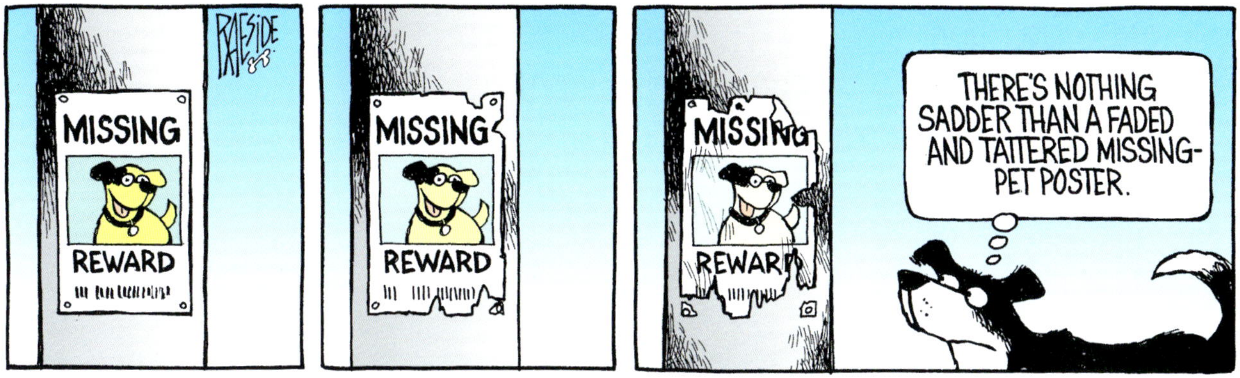
MISSING
REWARD
MISSING
REWARD
THERE'S NOTHING SADDER THAN A FADED AND TATTERED MISSING-PET POSTER.

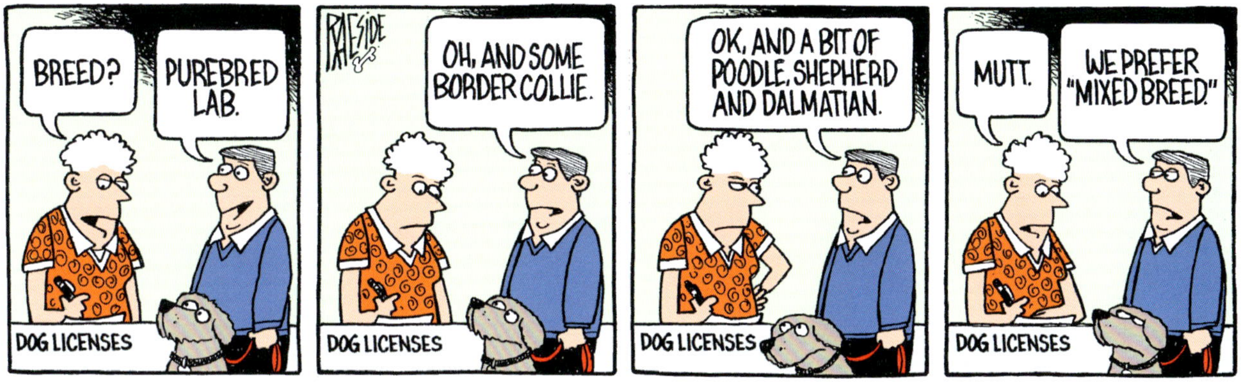
BREED?
PUREBRED LAB.
DOG LICENSES
OH, AND SOME BORDER COLLIE.
DOG LICENSES
OK, AND A BIT OF POODLE, SHEPHERD AND DALMATIAN.
DOG LICENSES
MUTT.
WE PREFER "MIXED BREED."
DOG LICENSES

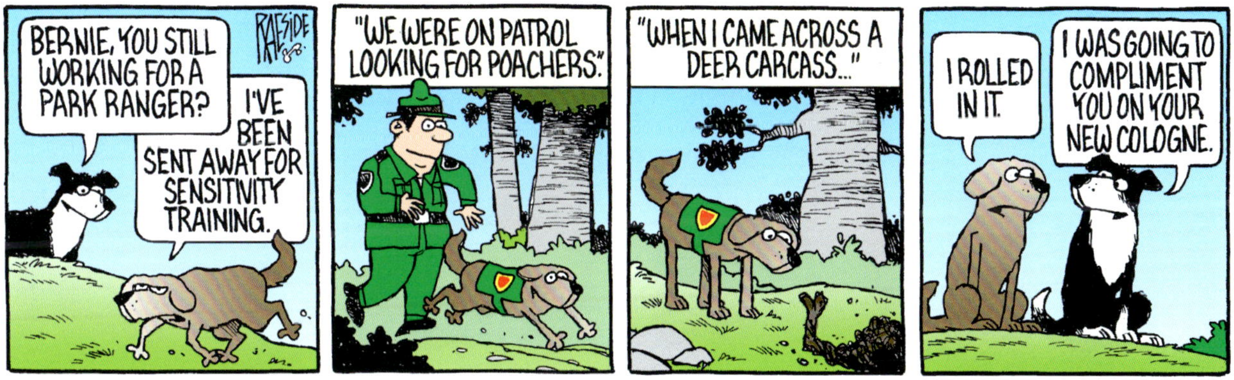
BERNIE, YOU STILL WORKING FOR A PARK RANGER?
I'VE BEEN SENT AWAY FOR SENSITIVITY TRAINING.
"WE WERE ON PATROL LOOKING FOR POACHERS."
"WHEN I CAME ACROSS A DEER CARCASS..."
I ROLLED IN IT.
I WAS GOING TO COMPLIMENT YOU ON YOUR NEW COLOGNE.

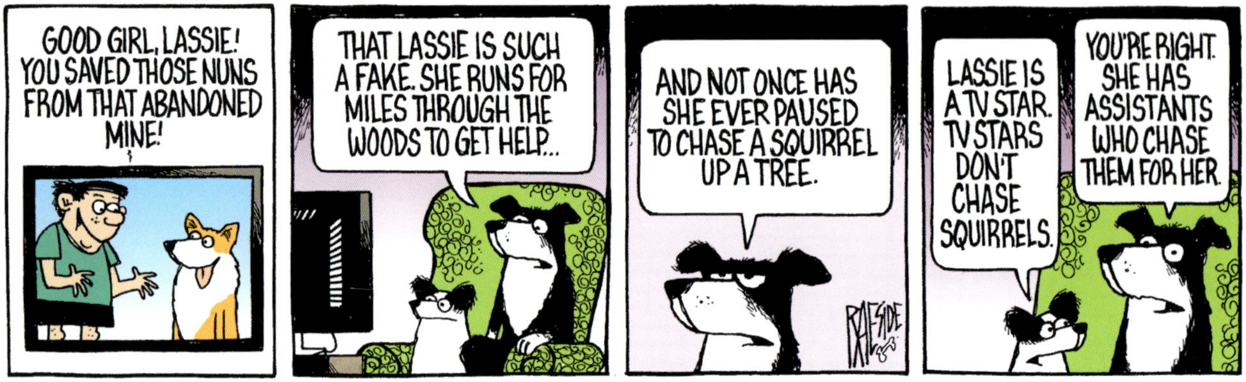
GOOD GIRL, LASSIE! YOU SAVED THOSE NUNS FROM THAT ABANDONED MINE!
THAT LASSIE IS SUCH A FAKE. SHE RUNS FOR MILES THROUGH THE WOODS TO GET HELP...
AND NOT ONCE HAS SHE EVER PAUSED TO CHASE A SQUIRREL UP A TREE.
LASSIE IS A TV STAR. TV STARS DON'T CHASE SQUIRRELS.
YOU'RE RIGHT. SHE HAS ASSISTANTS WHO CHASE THEM FOR HER.

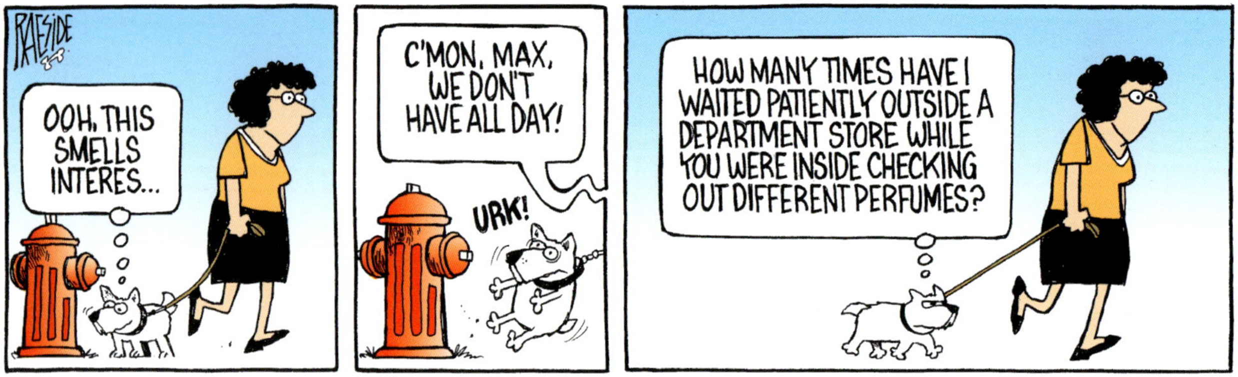
OOH, THIS SMELLS INTERES...
C'MON, MAX, WE DON'T HAVE ALL DAY!
URK!
HOW MANY TIMES HAVE I WAITED PATIENTLY OUTSIDE A DEPARTMENT STORE WHILE YOU WERE INSIDE CHECKING OUT DIFFERENT PERFUMES?

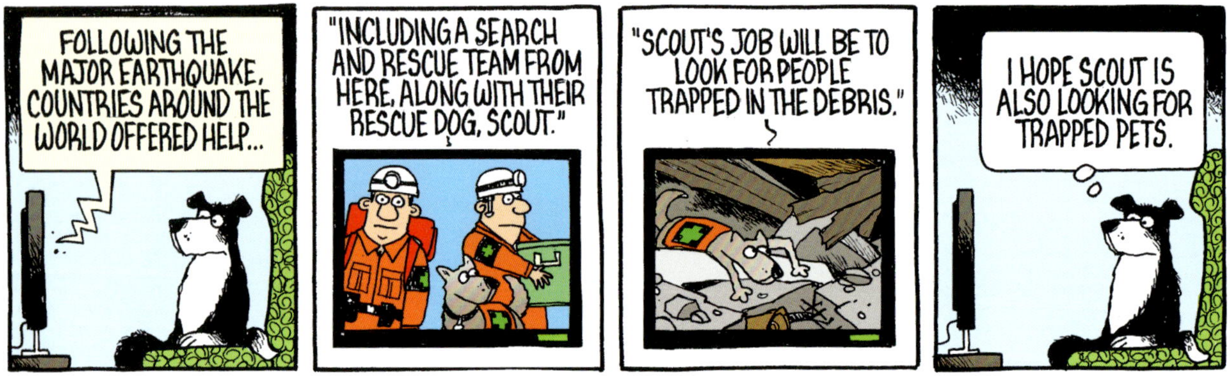
FOLLOWING THE MAJOR EARTHQUAKE, COUNTRIES AROUND THE WORLD OFFERED HELP...
"INCLUDING A SEARCH AND RESCUE TEAM FROM HERE, ALONG WITH THEIR RESCUE DOG, SCOUT."
"SCOUT'S JOB WILL BE TO LOOK FOR PEOPLE TRAPPED IN THE DEBRIS."
I HOPE SCOUT IS ALSO LOOKING FOR TRAPPED PETS.

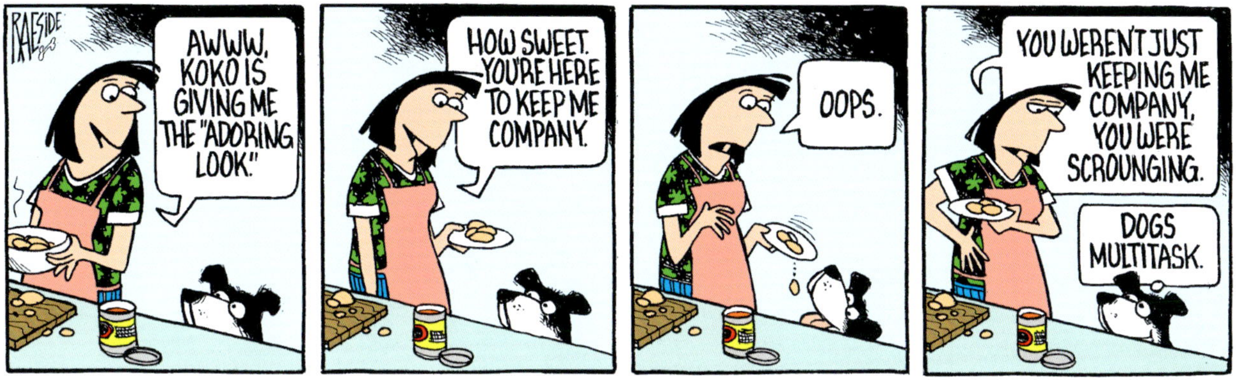
RAESIDE
AWWW, KOKO IS GIVING ME THE "ADORING LOOK."
HOW SWEET. YOU'RE HERE TO KEEP ME COMPANY.
OOPS.
YOU WEREN'T JUST KEEPING ME COMPANY, YOU WERE SCROUNGING.
DOGS MULTITASK.

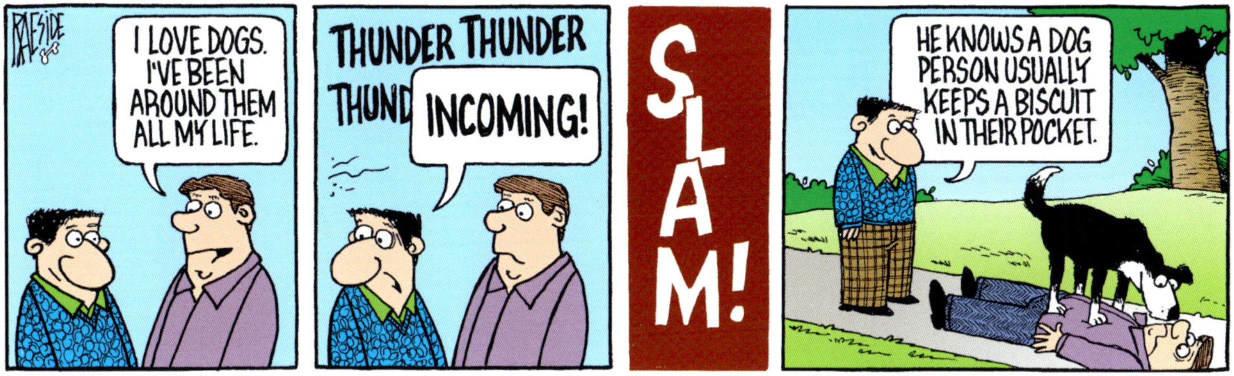
RAESIDE
I LOVE DOGS. I'VE BEEN AROUND THEM ALL MY LIFE.
THUNDER THUNDER
THUND
INCOMING!
SLAM!
HE KNOWS A DOG PERSON USUALLY KEEPS A BISCUIT IN THEIR POCKET.

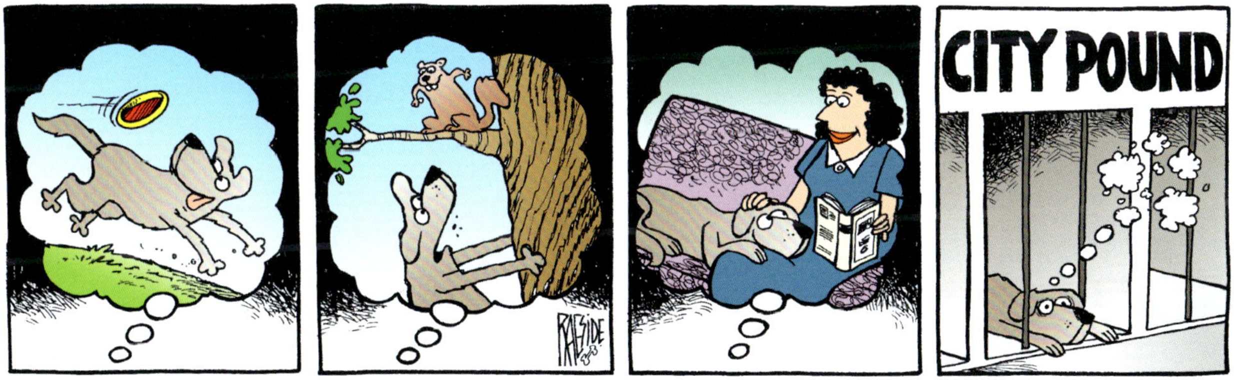
RAESIDE
CITY POUND

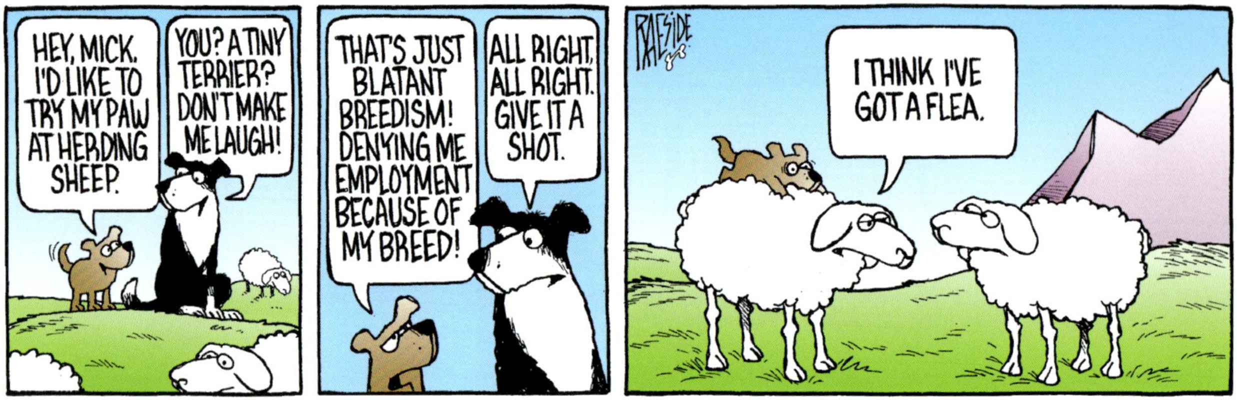
HEY, MICK. I'D LIKE TO TRY MY PAW AT HERDING SHEEP.
YOU? A TINY TERRIER? DON'T MAKE ME LAUGH!
THAT'S JUST BLATANT BREEDISM! DENYING ME EMPLOYMENT BECAUSE OF MY BREED!
ALL RIGHT, ALL RIGHT. GIVE IT A SHOT.
I THINK I'VE GOT A FLEA.

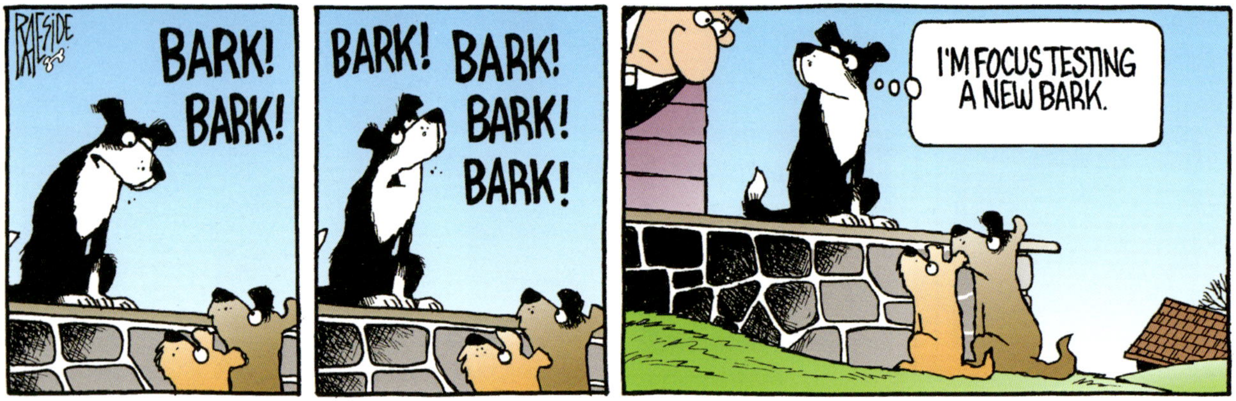
BARK! BARK!
BARK! BARK! BARK! BARK!
I'M FOCUS TESTING A NEW BARK.

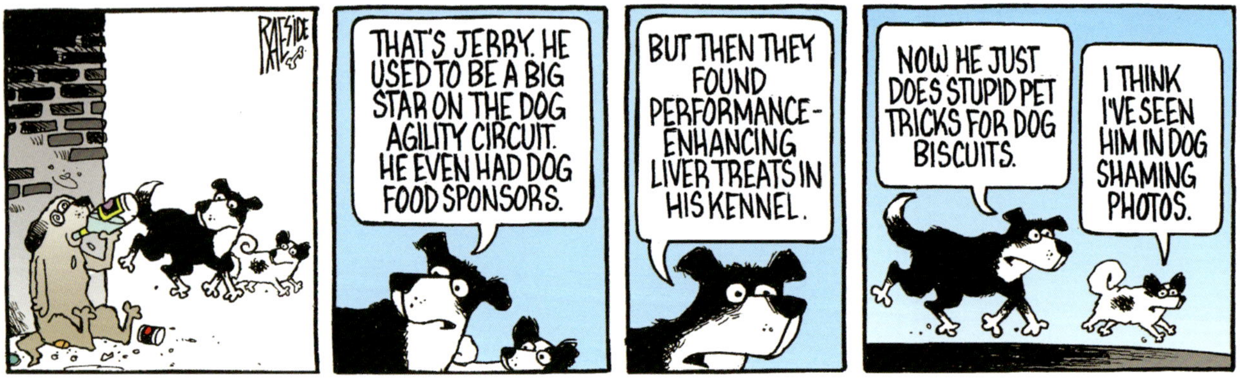
THAT'S JERRY. HE USED TO BE A BIG STAR ON THE DOG AGILITY CIRCUIT. HE EVEN HAD DOG FOOD SPONSORS.
BUT THEN THEY FOUND PERFORMANCE-ENHANCING LIVER TREATS IN HIS KENNEL.
NOW HE JUST DOES STUPID PET TRICKS FOR DOG BISCUITS.
I THINK I'VE SEEN HIM IN DOG SHAMING PHOTOS.

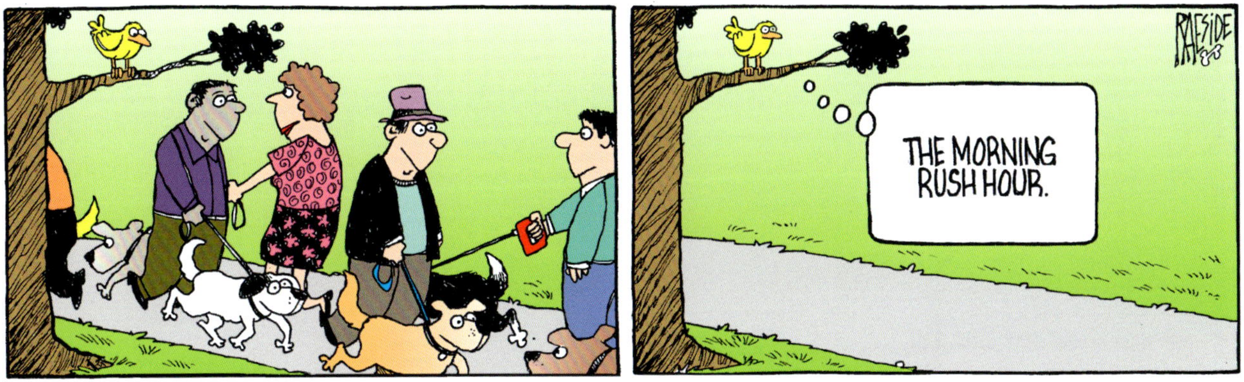
THE MORNING RUSH HOUR.

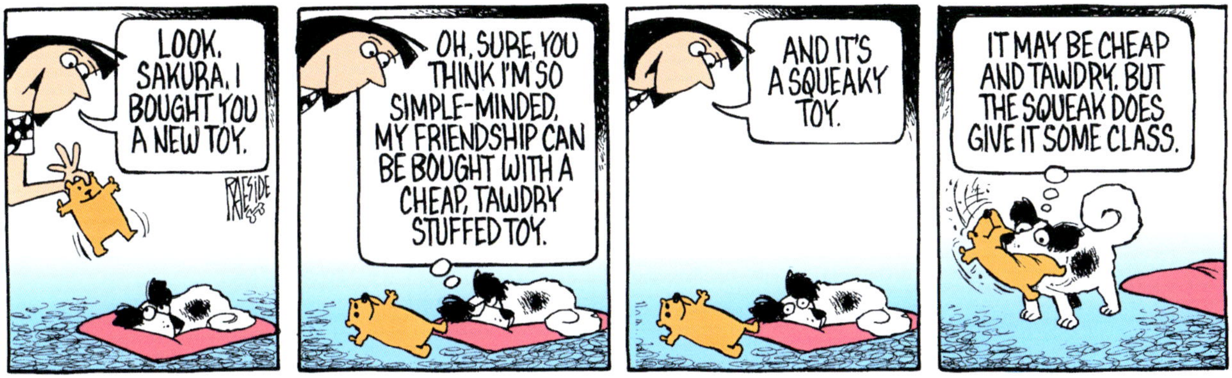
LOOK, SAKURA, I BOUGHT YOU A NEW TOY.
OH, SURE, YOU THINK I'M SO SIMPLE-MINDED, MY FRIENDSHIP CAN BE BOUGHT WITH A CHEAP, TAWDRY STUFFED TOY.
AND IT'S A SQUEAKY TOY.
IT MAY BE CHEAP AND TAWDRY, BUT THE SQUEAK DOES GIVE IT SOME CLASS.

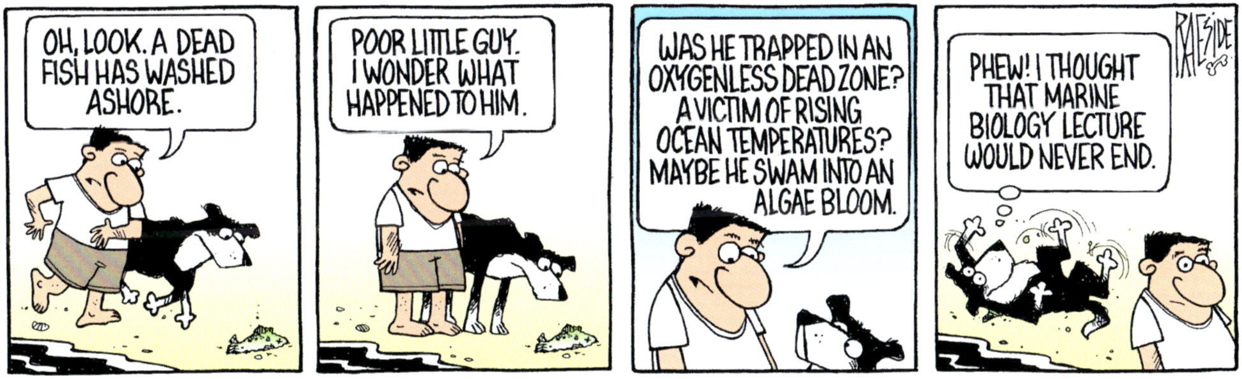
OH, LOOK. A DEAD FISH HAS WASHED ASHORE.
POOR LITTLE GUY. I WONDER WHAT HAPPENED TO HIM.
WAS HE TRAPPED IN AN OXYGENLESS DEAD ZONE? A VICTIM OF RISING OCEAN TEMPERATURES? MAYBE HE SWAM INTO AN ALGAE BLOOM.
PHEW! I THOUGHT THAT MARINE BIOLOGY LECTURE WOULD NEVER END.

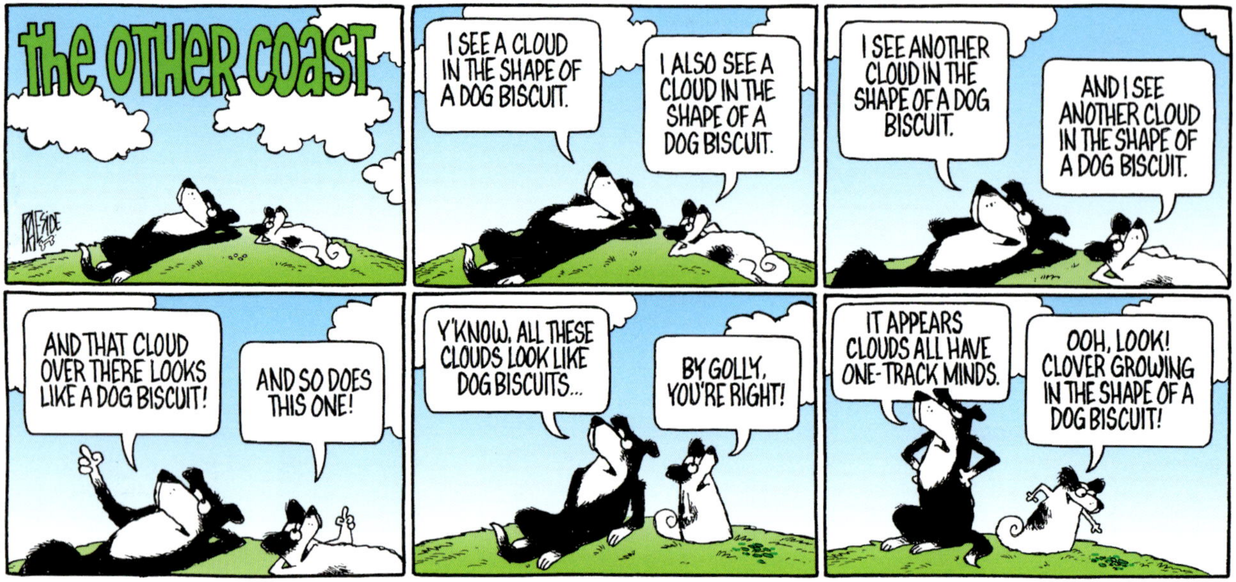
the OTHER COAST
RAESIDE
I SEE A CLOUD IN THE SHAPE OF A DOG BISCUIT.
I ALSO SEE A CLOUD IN THE SHAPE OF A DOG BISCUIT.
I SEE ANOTHER CLOUD IN THE SHAPE OF A DOG BISCUIT.
AND I SEE ANOTHER CLOUD IN THE SHAPE OF A DOG BISCUIT.
AND THAT CLOUD OVER THERE LOOKS LIKE A DOG BISCUIT!
AND SO DOES THIS ONE!
Y'KNOW, ALL THESE CLOUDS LOOK LIKE DOG BISCUITS...
BY GOLLY, YOU'RE RIGHT!
IT APPEARS CLOUDS ALL HAVE ONE-TRACK MINDS.
OOH, LOOK! CLOVER GROWING IN THE SHAPE OF A DOG BISCUIT!

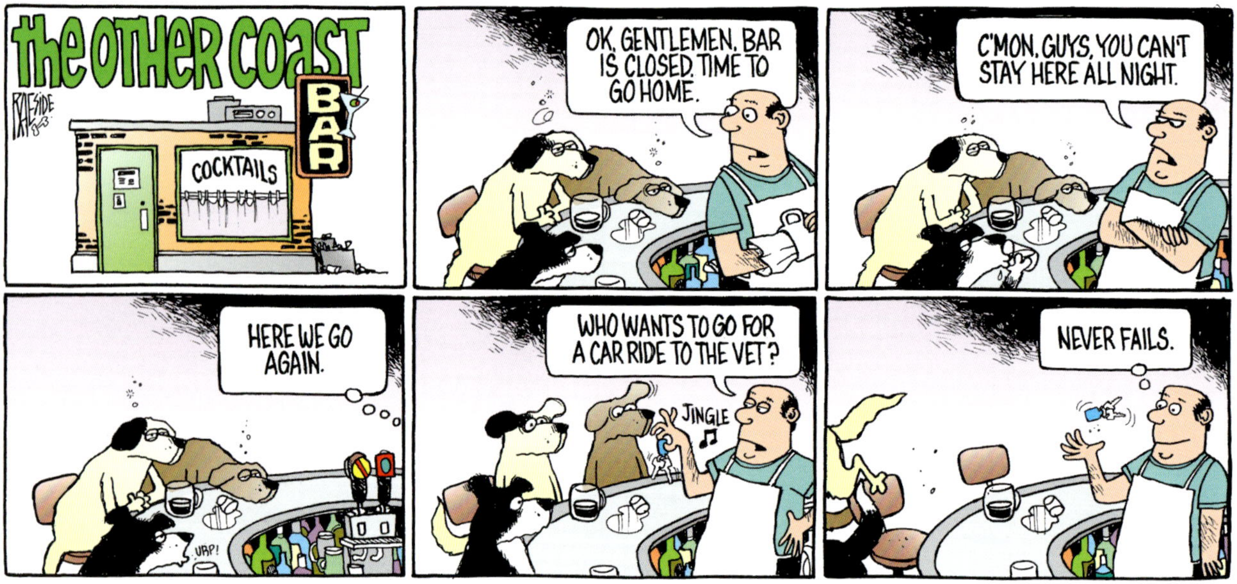
the OTHER COAST
RAESIDE
BAR
COCKTAILS
OK, GENTLEMEN, BAR IS CLOSED. TIME TO GO HOME.
C'MON, GUYS, YOU CAN'T STAY HERE ALL NIGHT.
HERE WE GO AGAIN.
URP!
WHO WANTS TO GO FOR A CAR RIDE TO THE VET?
JINGLE
NEVER FAILS.

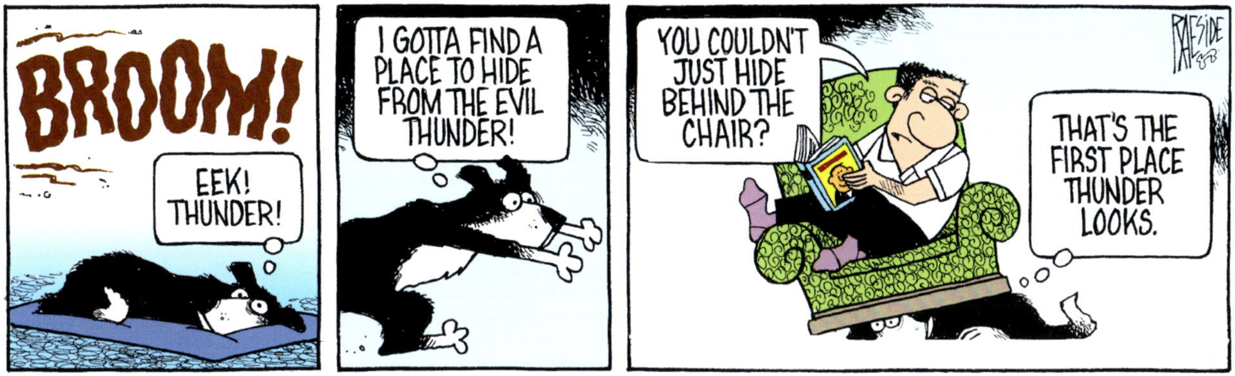
BROOM!
EEK! THUNDER!
I GOTTA FIND A PLACE TO HIDE FROM THE EVIL THUNDER!
YOU COULDN'T JUST HIDE BEHIND THE CHAIR?
RAESIDE
THAT'S THE FIRST PLACE THUNDER LOOKS.

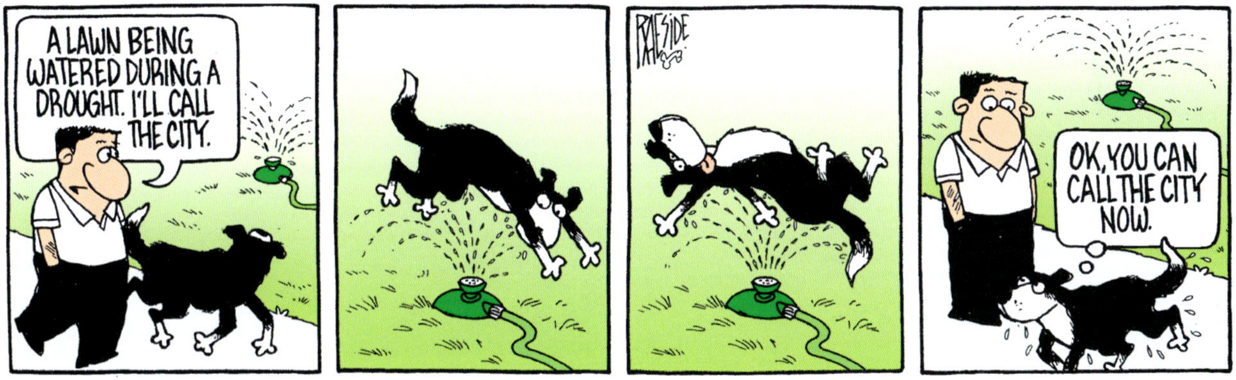
A LAWN BEING WATERED DURING A DROUGHT. I'LL CALL THE CITY.
RAESIDE
OK, YOU CAN CALL THE CITY NOW.

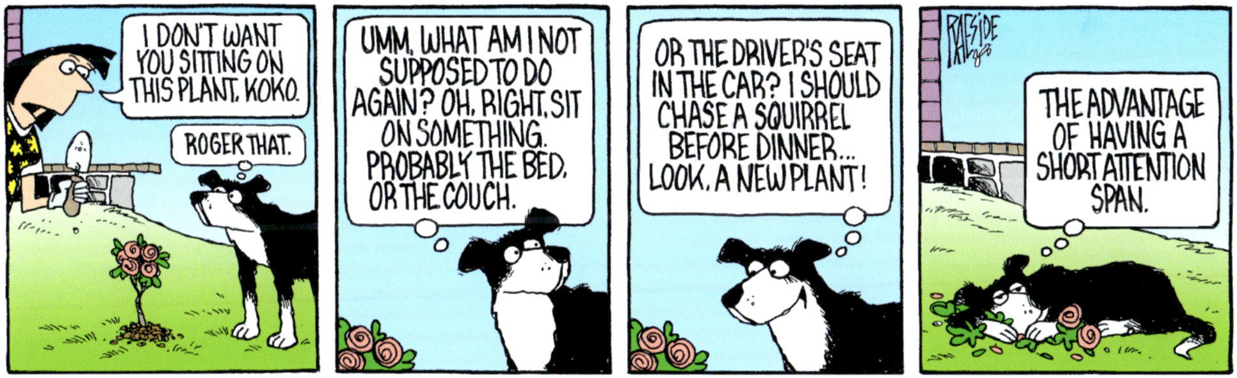
I DON'T WANT YOU SITTING ON THIS PLANT, KOKO.
ROGER THAT.
UMM, WHAT AM I NOT SUPPOSED TO DO AGAIN? OH, RIGHT, SIT ON SOMETHING. PROBABLY THE BED. OR THE COUCH.
OR THE DRIVER'S SEAT IN THE CAR? I SHOULD CHASE A SQUIRREL BEFORE DINNER... LOOK, A NEW PLANT!
RAESIDE
THE ADVANTAGE OF HAVING A SHORT ATTENTION SPAN.

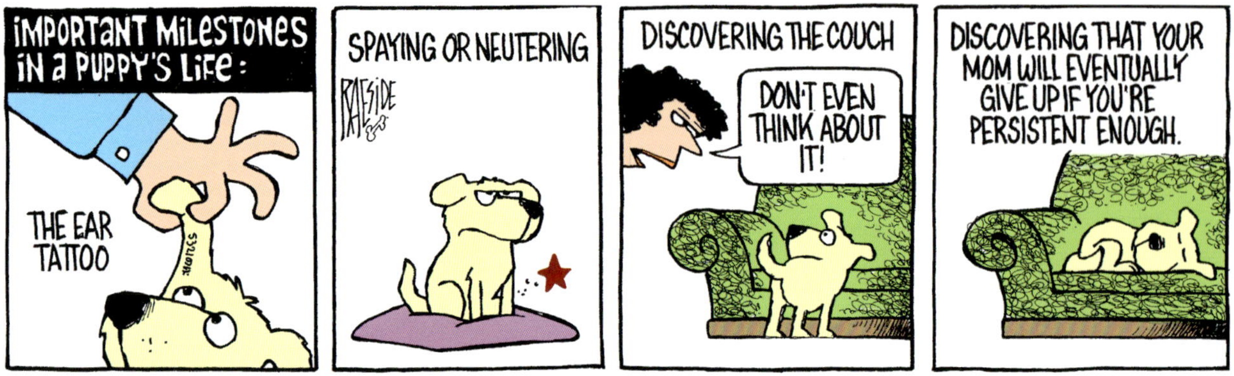
IMPORTANT MILESTONES IN A PUPPY'S LIFE:
THE EAR TATTOO
SPAYING OR NEUTERING
DISCOVERING THE COUCH
DON'T EVEN THINK ABOUT IT!
DISCOVERING THAT YOUR MOM WILL EVENTUALLY GIVE UP IF YOU'RE PERSISTENT ENOUGH.

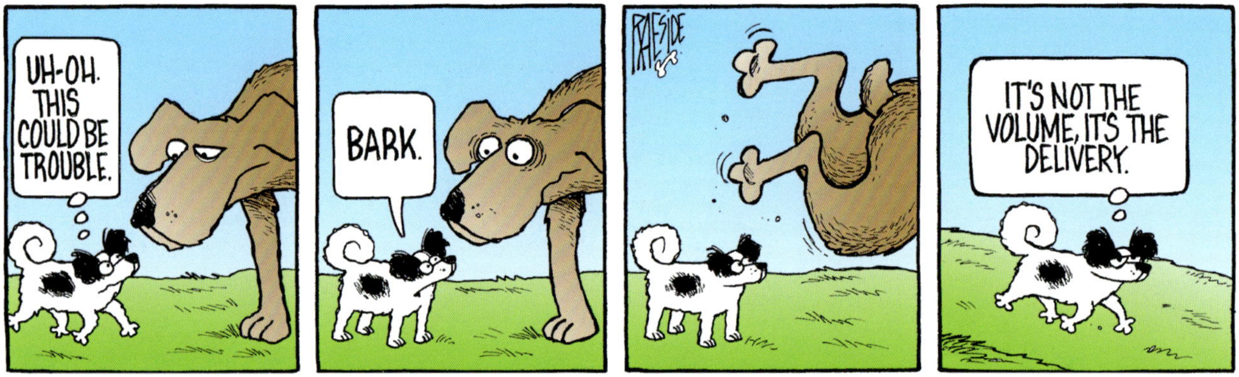
UH-OH. THIS COULD BE TROUBLE.
BARK.
IT'S NOT THE VOLUME, IT'S THE DELIVERY.

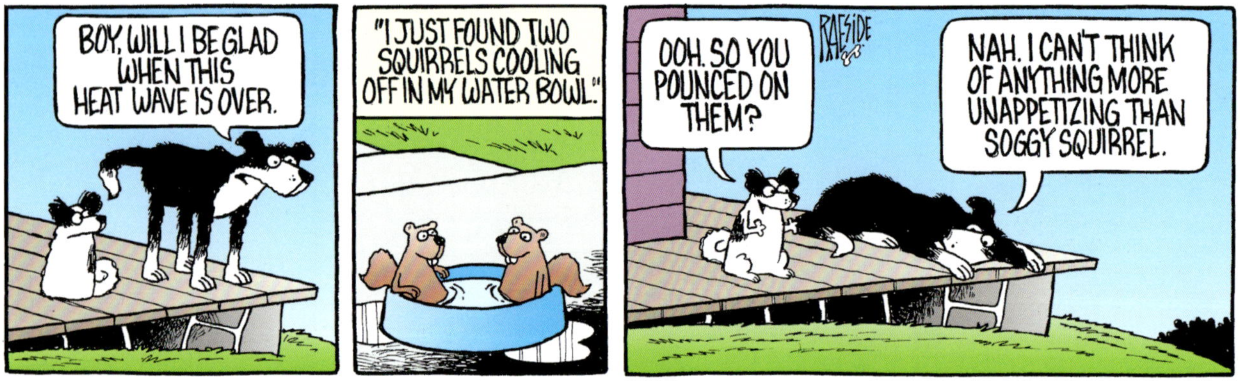
BOY, WILL I BE GLAD WHEN THIS HEAT WAVE IS OVER.
"I JUST FOUND TWO SQUIRRELS COOLING OFF IN MY WATER BOWL."
OOH. SO YOU POUNCED ON THEM?
NAH. I CAN'T THINK OF ANYTHING MORE UNAPPETIZING THAN SOGGY SQUIRREL.

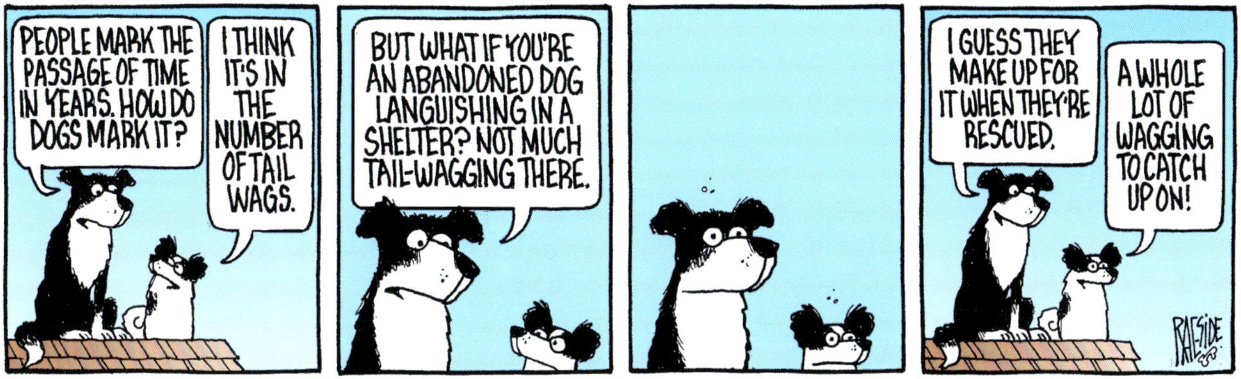
PEOPLE MARK THE PASSAGE OF TIME IN YEARS. HOW DO DOGS MARK IT?
I THINK IT'S IN THE NUMBER OF TAIL WAGS.
BUT WHAT IF YOU'RE AN ABANDONED DOG LANGUISHING IN A SHELTER? NOT MUCH TAIL-WAGGING THERE.
I GUESS THEY MAKE UP FOR IT WHEN THEY'RE RESCUED.
A WHOLE LOT OF WAGGING TO CATCH UP ON!
RAESIDE

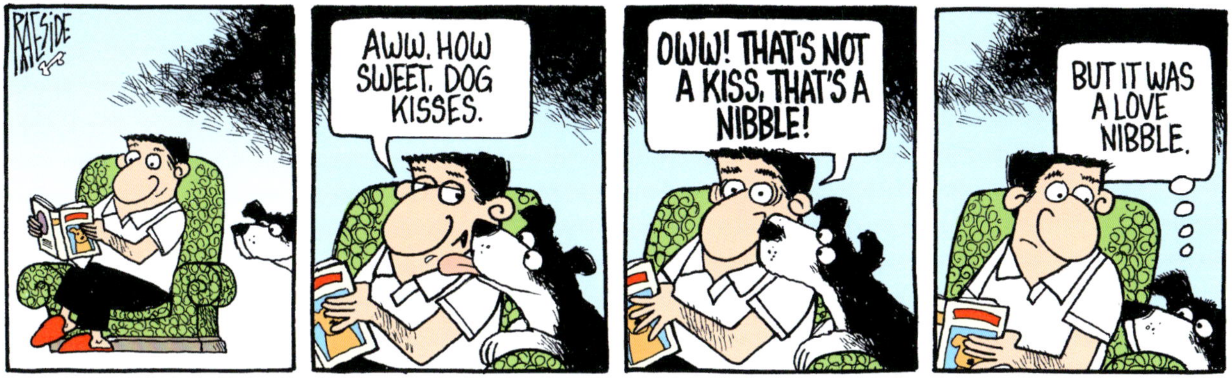
RAESIDE
AWW. HOW SWEET. DOG KISSES.
OWW! THAT'S NOT A KISS, THAT'S A NIBBLE!
BUT IT WAS A LOVE NIBBLE.

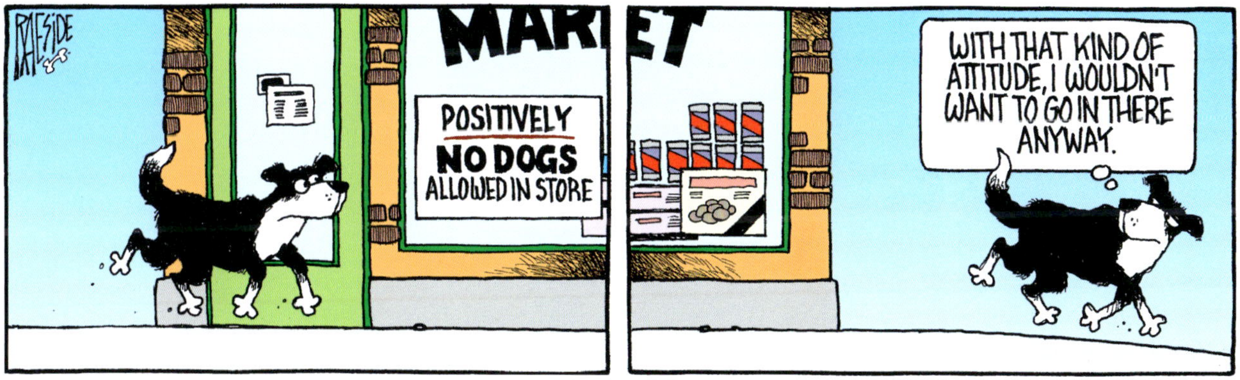
RAESIDE
MAR ET
POSITIVELY
NO DOGS
ALLOWED IN STORE
WITH THAT KIND OF ATTITUDE, I WOULDN'T WANT TO GO IN THERE ANYWAY.

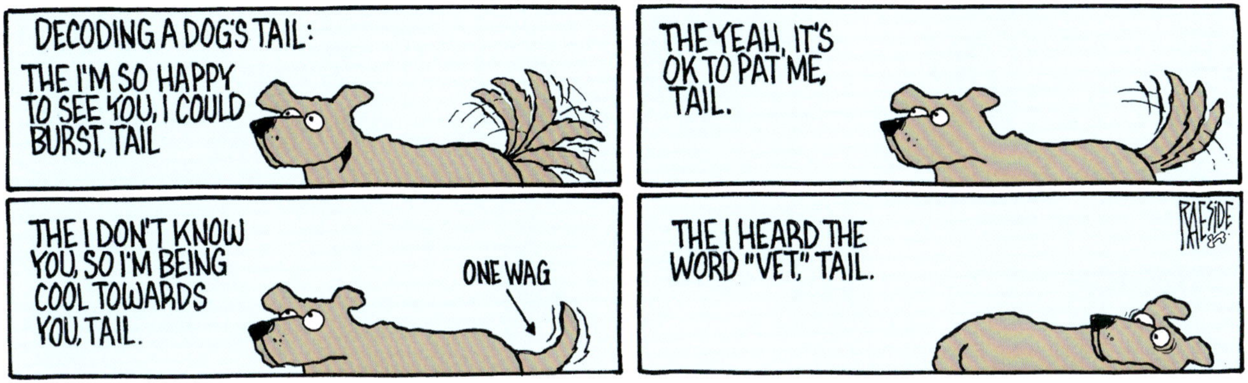
DECODING A DOG'S TAIL:
THE I'M SO HAPPY TO SEE YOU, I COULD BURST, TAIL
THE YEAH, IT'S OK TO PAT ME, TAIL.
THE I DON'T KNOW YOU, SO I'M BEING COOL TOWARDS YOU, TAIL.
ONE WAG
THE I HEARD THE WORD "VET," TAIL.

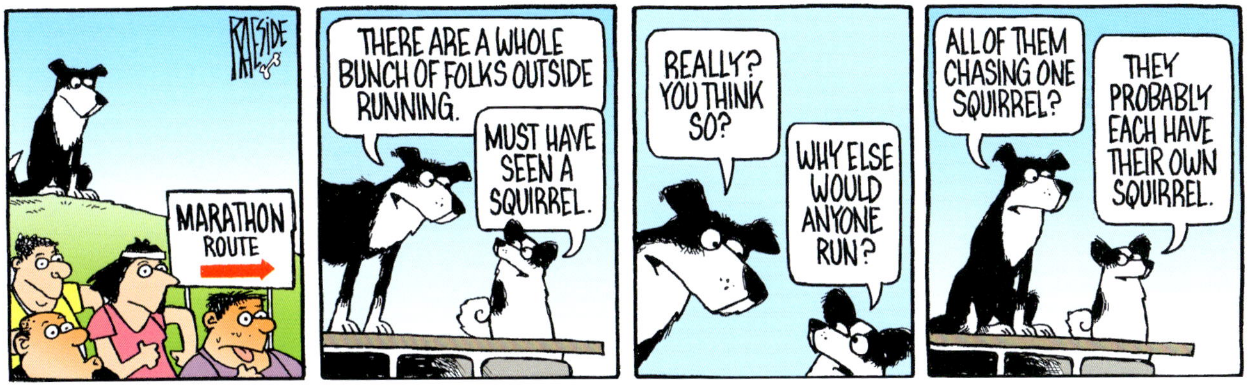
MARATHON ROUTE
THERE ARE A WHOLE BUNCH OF FOLKS OUTSIDE RUNNING.
MUST HAVE SEEN A SQUIRREL.
REALLY? YOU THINK SO?
WHY ELSE WOULD ANYONE RUN?
ALL OF THEM CHASING ONE SQUIRREL?
THEY PROBABLY EACH HAVE THEIR OWN SQUIRREL.

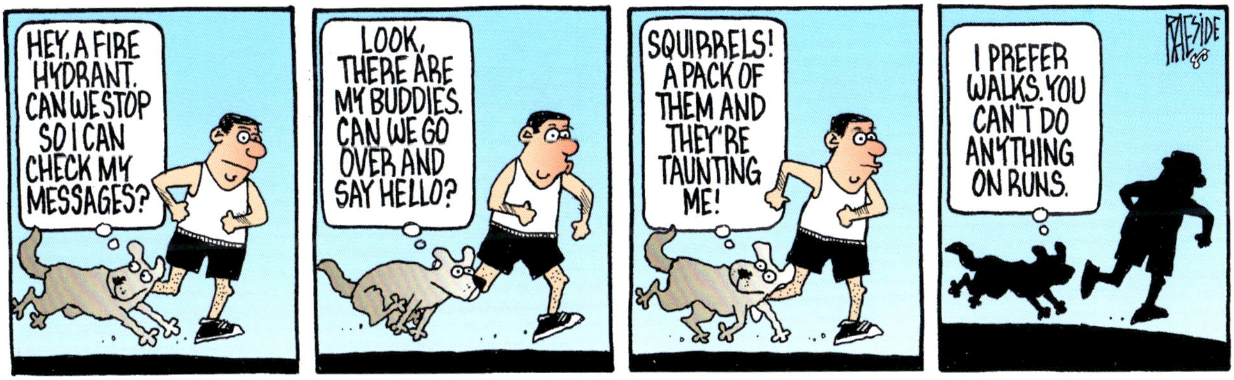
HEY, A FIRE HYDRANT. CAN WE STOP SO I CAN CHECK MY MESSAGES?
LOOK, THERE ARE MY BUDDIES. CAN WE GO OVER AND SAY HELLO?
SQUIRRELS! A PACK OF THEM AND THEY'RE TAUNTING ME!
I PREFER WALKS. YOU CAN'T DO ANYTHING ON RUNS.

83

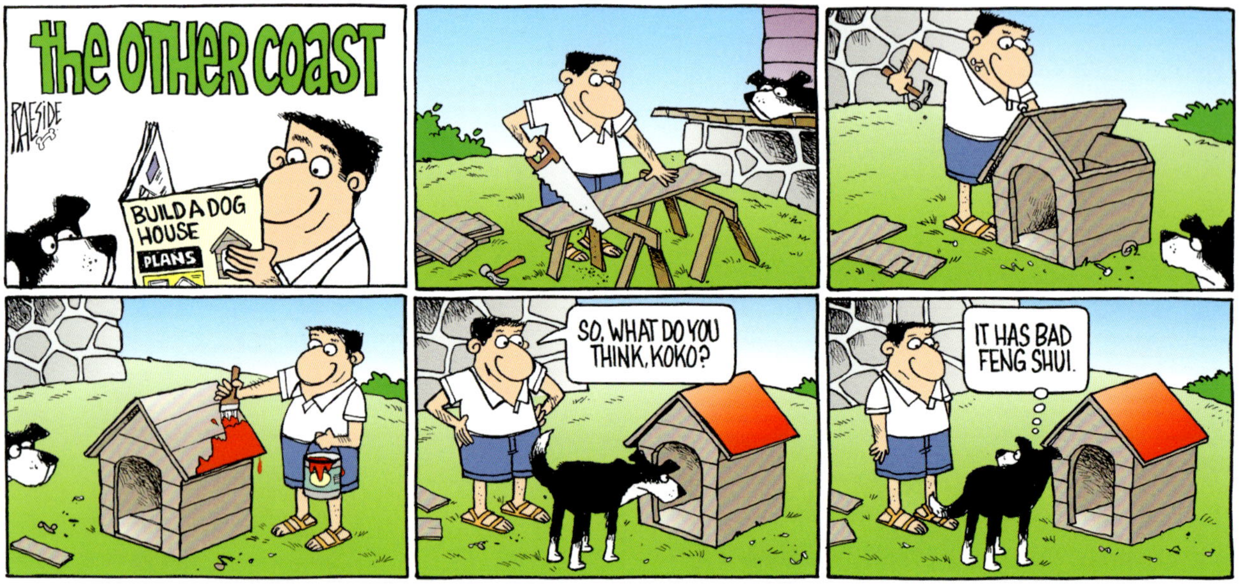
the OTHER COAST
RAESIDE
BUILD A DOG HOUSE
PLANS
SO, WHAT DO YOU THINK, KOKO?
IT HAS BAD FENG SHUI.

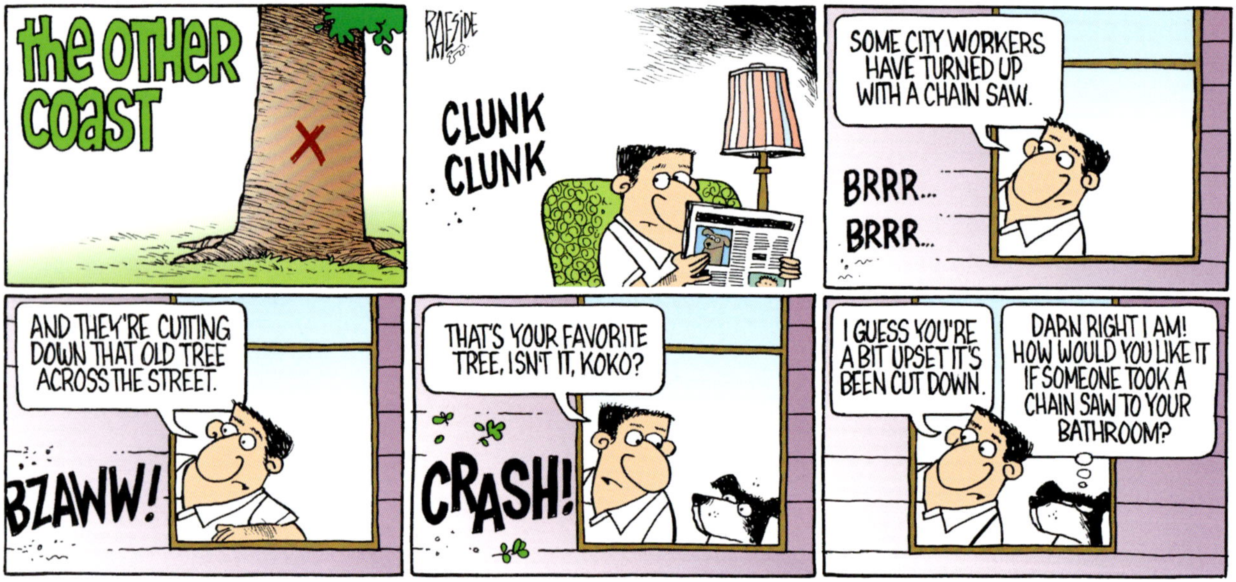
the OTHER COAST
RAESIDE
CLUNK
CLUNK
SOME CITY WORKERS HAVE TURNED UP WITH A CHAIN SAW.
BRRR...
BRRR...
AND THEY'RE CUTTING DOWN THAT OLD TREE ACROSS THE STREET.
BZAWW!
THAT'S YOUR FAVORITE TREE, ISN'T IT, KOKO?
CRASH!
I GUESS YOU'RE A BIT UPSET IT'S BEEN CUT DOWN.
DARN RIGHT I AM! HOW WOULD YOU LIKE IT IF SOMEONE TOOK A CHAIN SAW TO YOUR BATHROOM?

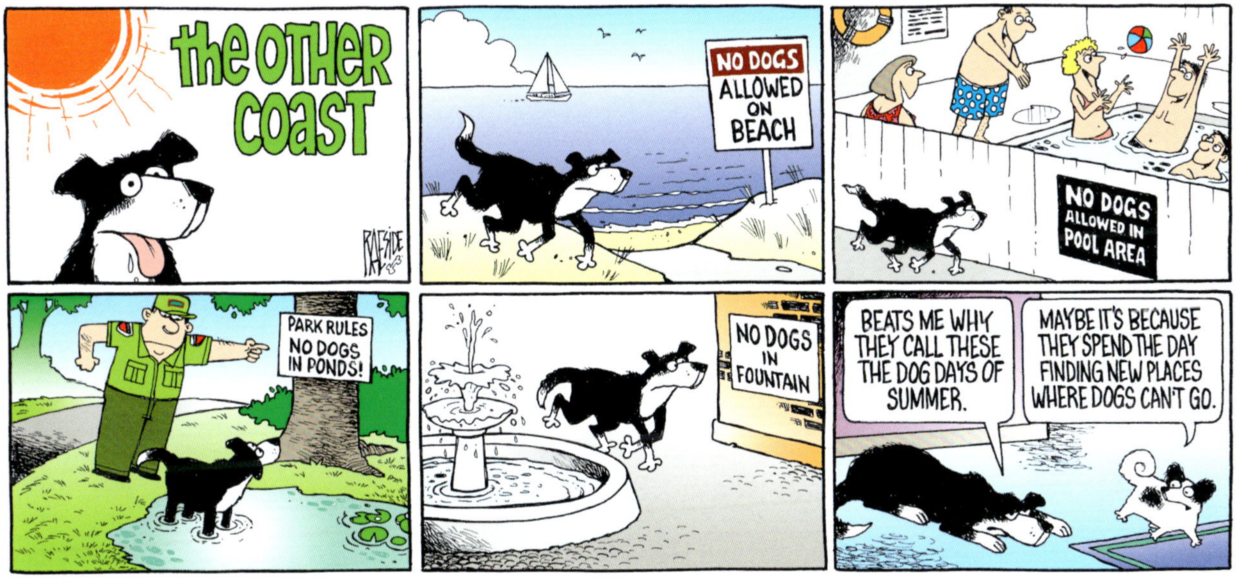

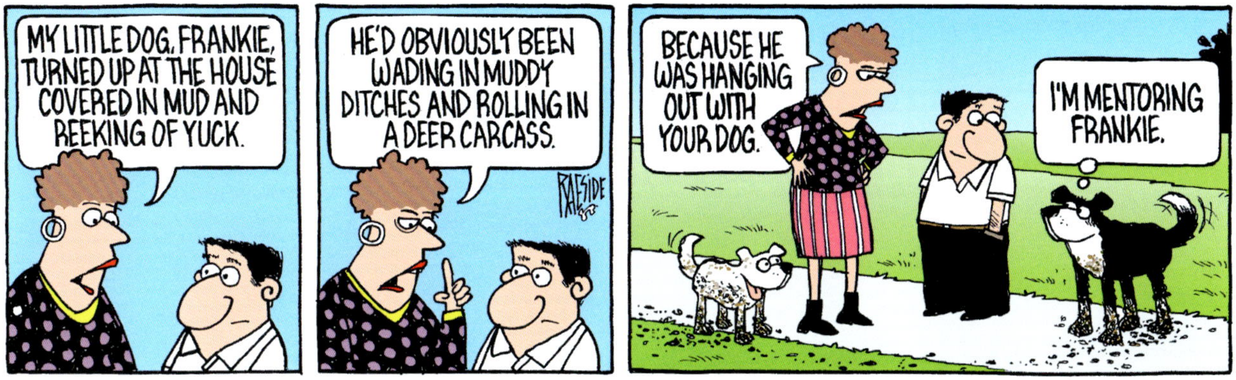
MY LITTLE DOG, FRANKIE, TURNED UP AT THE HOUSE COVERED IN MUD AND REEKING OF YUCK.
HE'D OBVIOUSLY BEEN WADING IN MUDDY DITCHES AND ROLLING IN A DEER CARCASS.
BECAUSE HE WAS HANGING OUT WITH YOUR DOG.
I'M MENTORING FRANKIE.

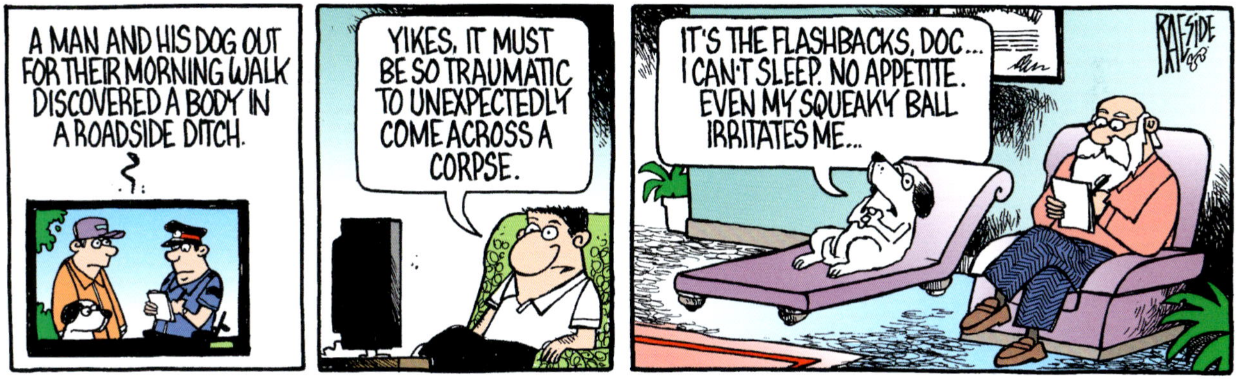
A MAN AND HIS DOG OUT FOR THEIR MORNING WALK DISCOVERED A BODY IN A ROADSIDE DITCH.
YIKES, IT MUST BE SO TRAUMATIC TO UNEXPECTEDLY COME ACROSS A CORPSE.
IT'S THE FLASHBACKS, DOC... I CAN'T SLEEP. NO APPETITE. EVEN MY SQUEAKY BALL IRRITATES ME...

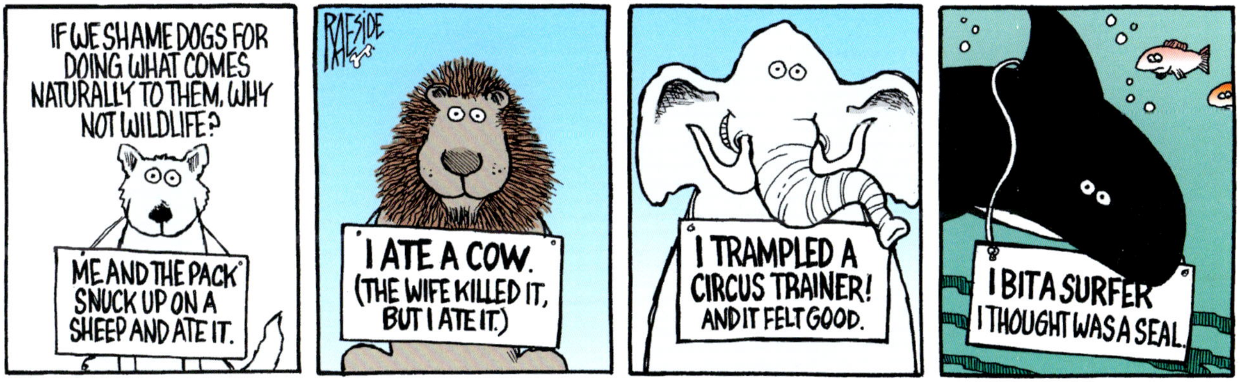
IF WE SHAME DOGS FOR DOING WHAT COMES NATURALLY TO THEM, WHY NOT WILDLIFE?
ME AND THE PACK SNUCK UP ON A SHEEP AND ATE IT.
I ATE A COW. (THE WIFE KILLED IT, BUT I ATE IT.)
I TRAMPLED A CIRCUS TRAINER! AND IT FELT GOOD.
I BIT A SURFER I THOUGHT WAS A SEAL.

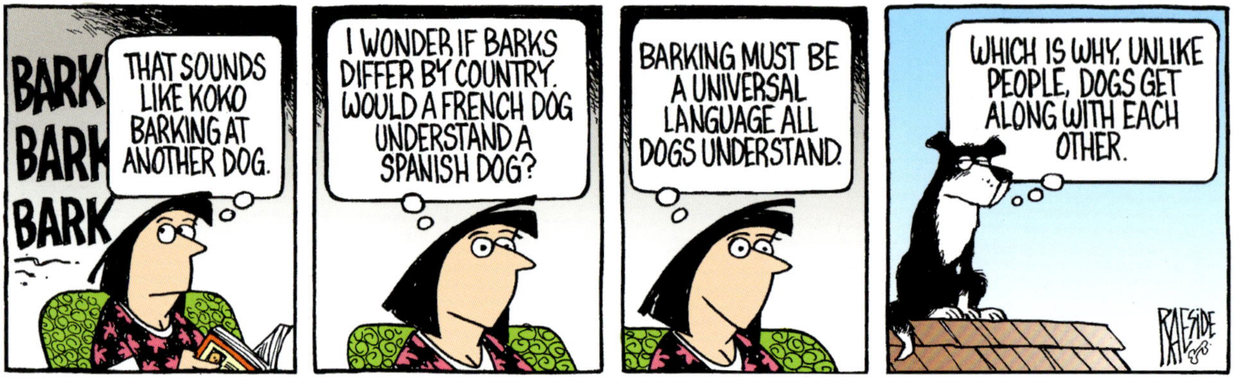
BARK BARK BARK
THAT SOUNDS LIKE KOKO BARKING AT ANOTHER DOG.
I WONDER IF BARKS DIFFER BY COUNTRY. WOULD A FRENCH DOG UNDERSTAND A SPANISH DOG?
BARKING MUST BE A UNIVERSAL LANGUAGE ALL DOGS UNDERSTAND.
WHICH IS WHY, UNLIKE PEOPLE, DOGS GET ALONG WITH EACH OTHER.
RAESIDE

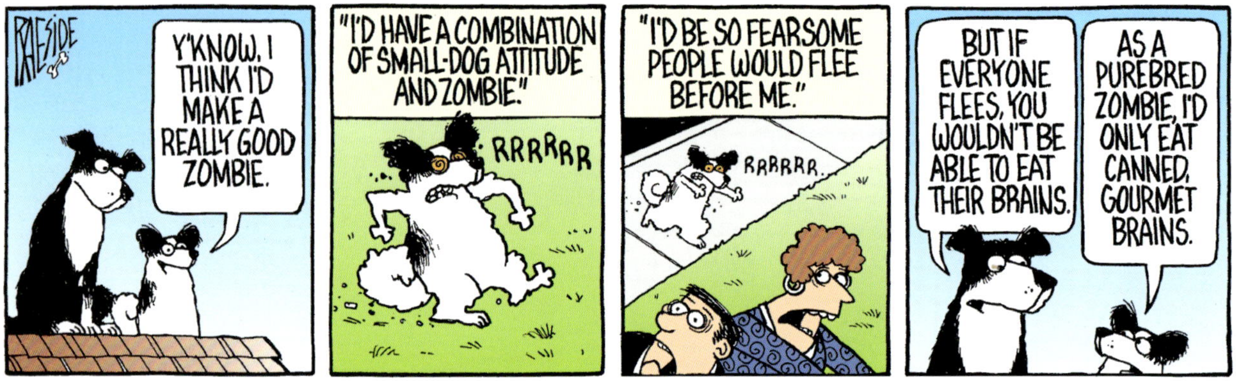
RAESIDE
Y'KNOW, I THINK I'D MAKE A REALLY GOOD ZOMBIE.
"I'D HAVE A COMBINATION OF SMALL-DOG ATTITUDE AND ZOMBIE."
RRRRRR
"I'D BE SO FEARSOME PEOPLE WOULD FLEE BEFORE ME."
RRRRRR..
BUT IF EVERYONE FLEES, YOU WOULDN'T BE ABLE TO EAT THEIR BRAINS.
AS A PUREBRED ZOMBIE, I'D ONLY EAT CANNED, GOURMET BRAINS.

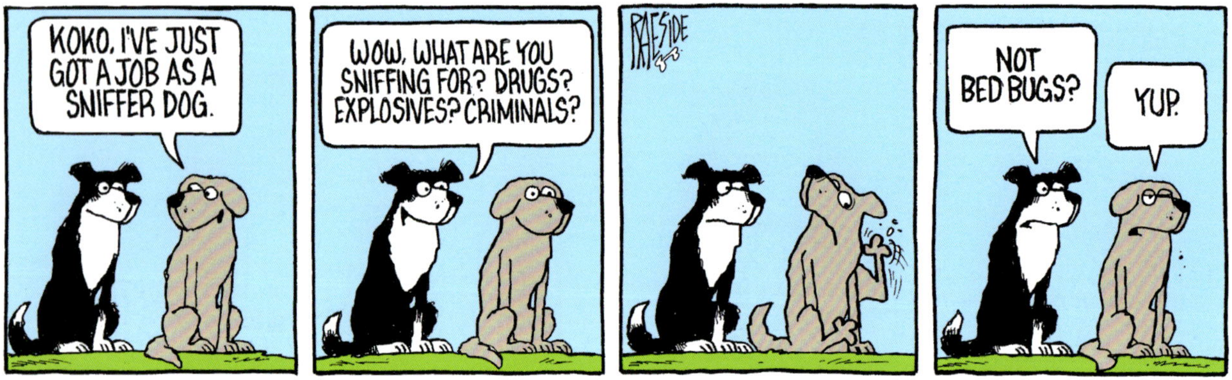
KOKO, I'VE JUST GOT A JOB AS A SNIFFER DOG.
WOW, WHAT ARE YOU SNIFFING FOR? DRUGS? EXPLOSIVES? CRIMINALS?
RAESIDE
NOT BED BUGS?
YUP.

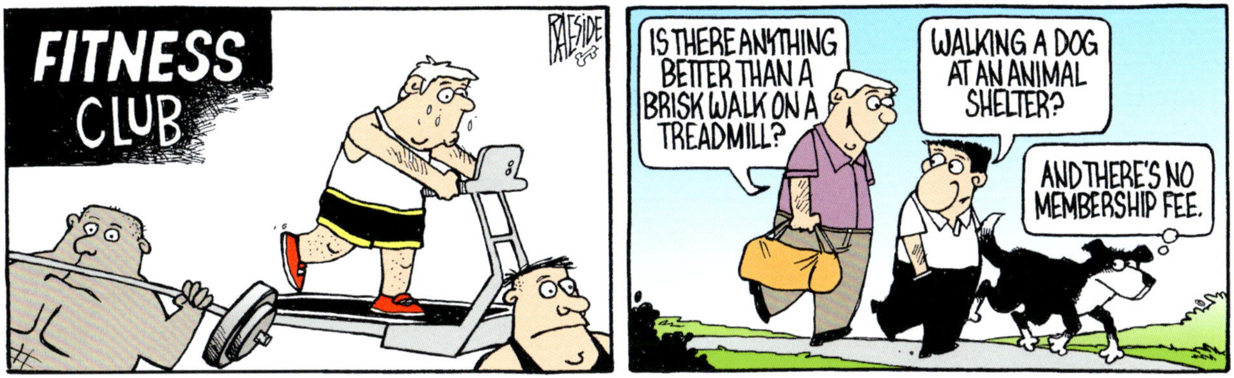
FITNESS CLUB
RAESIDE
IS THERE ANYTHING BETTER THAN A BRISK WALK ON A TREADMILL?
WALKING A DOG AT AN ANIMAL SHELTER?
AND THERE'S NO MEMBERSHIP FEE.

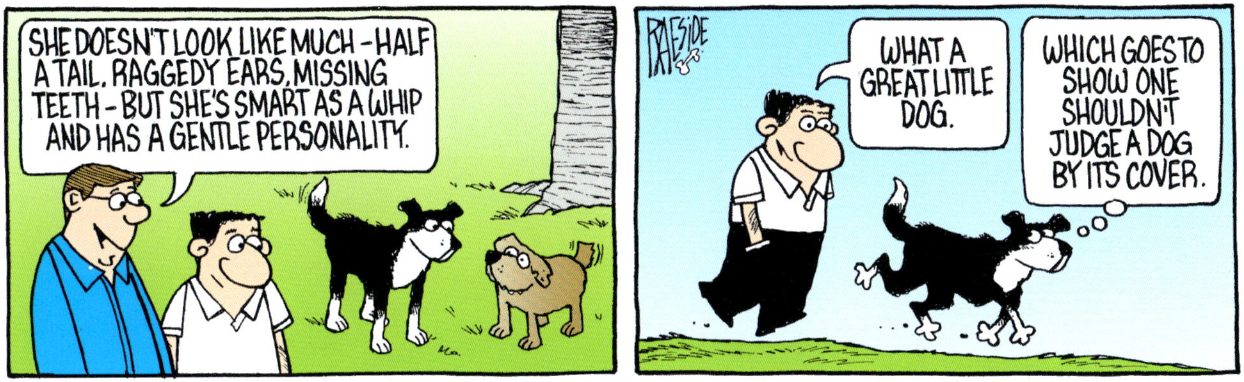
SHE DOESN'T LOOK LIKE MUCH - HALF A TAIL, RAGGEDY EARS, MISSING TEETH - BUT SHE'S SMART AS A WHIP AND HAS A GENTLE PERSONALITY.
RAESIDE
WHAT A GREAT LITTLE DOG.
WHICH GOES TO SHOW ONE SHOULDN'T JUDGE A DOG BY ITS COVER.

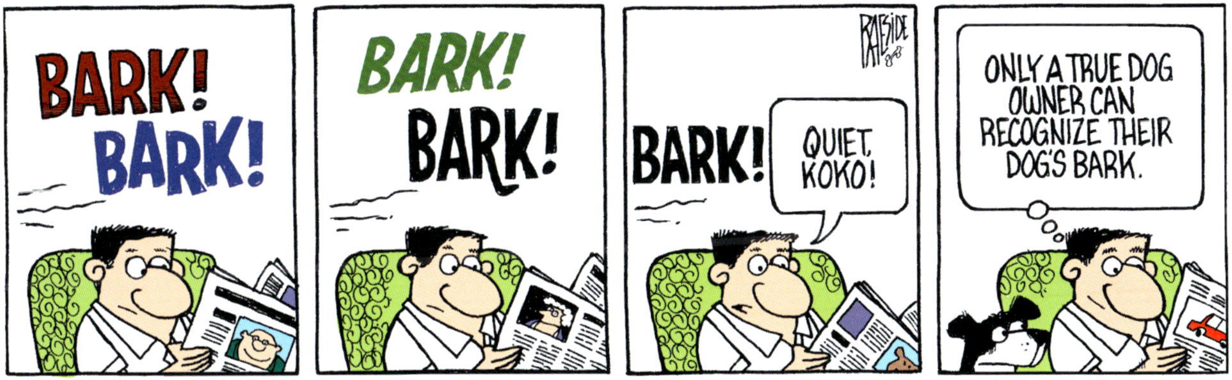
BARK!
BARK!
BARK!
BARK!
RAESIDE
BARK!
QUIET, KOKO!
ONLY A TRUE DOG OWNER CAN RECOGNIZE THEIR DOG'S BARK.

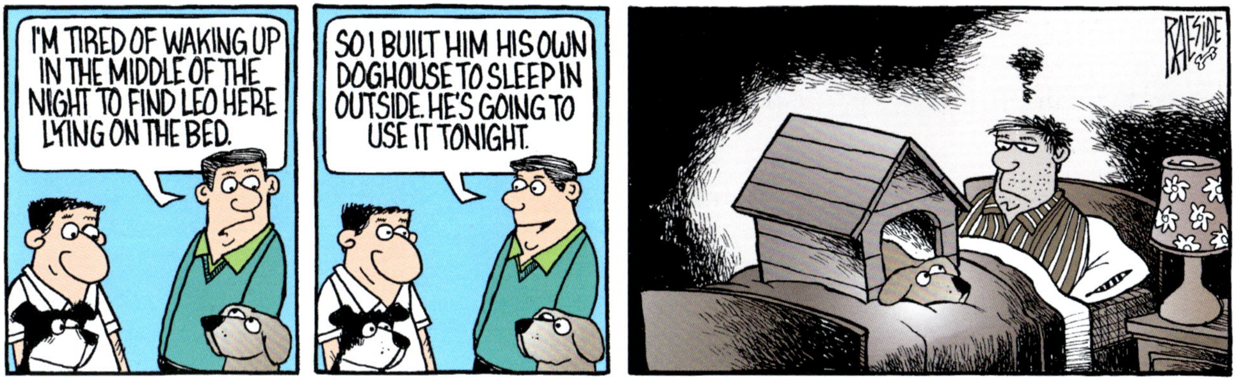
I'M TIRED OF WAKING UP IN THE MIDDLE OF THE NIGHT TO FIND LEO HERE LYING ON THE BED.
SO I BUILT HIM HIS OWN DOGHOUSE TO SLEEP IN OUTSIDE. HE'S GOING TO USE IT TONIGHT.

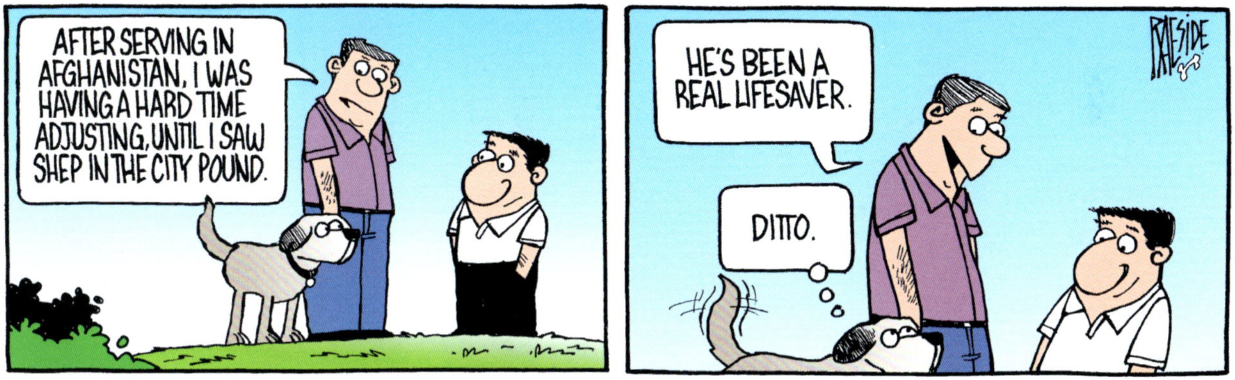
AFTER SERVING IN AFGHANISTAN, I WAS HAVING A HARD TIME ADJUSTING, UNTIL I SAW SHEP IN THE CITY POUND.
HE'S BEEN A REAL LIFESAVER.
DITTO.

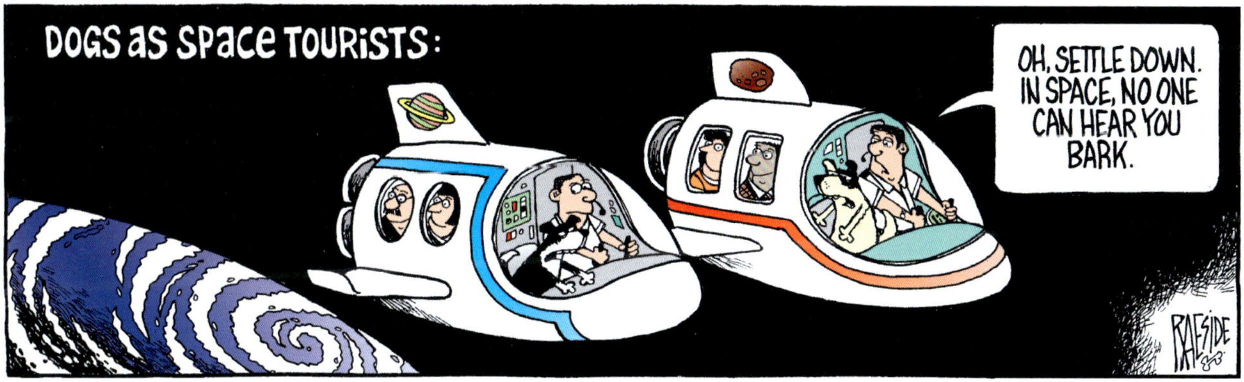
DOGS AS SPACE TOURISTS:
OH, SETTLE DOWN. IN SPACE, NO ONE CAN HEAR YOU BARK.

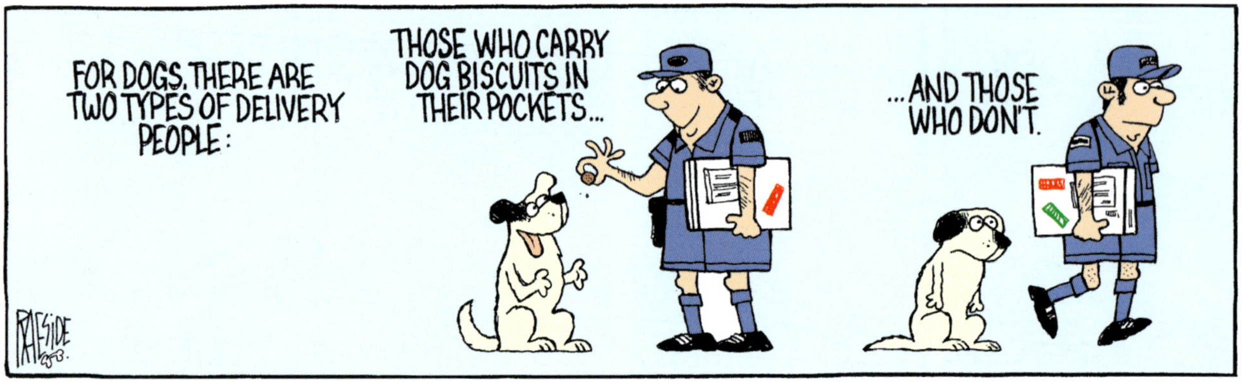
FOR DOGS, THERE ARE TWO TYPES OF DELIVERY PEOPLE:
THOSE WHO CARRY DOG BISCUITS IN THEIR POCKETS...
...AND THOSE WHO DON'T.

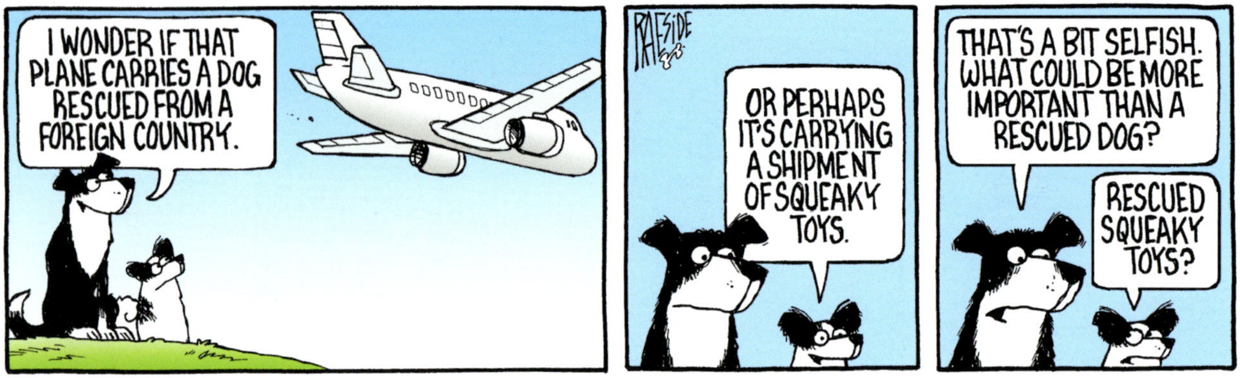
I WONDER IF THAT PLANE CARRIES A DOG RESCUED FROM A FOREIGN COUNTRY.
OR PERHAPS IT'S CARRYING A SHIPMENT OF SQUEAKY TOYS.
THAT'S A BIT SELFISH. WHAT COULD BE MORE IMPORTANT THAN A RESCUED DOG?
RESCUED SQUEAKY TOYS?

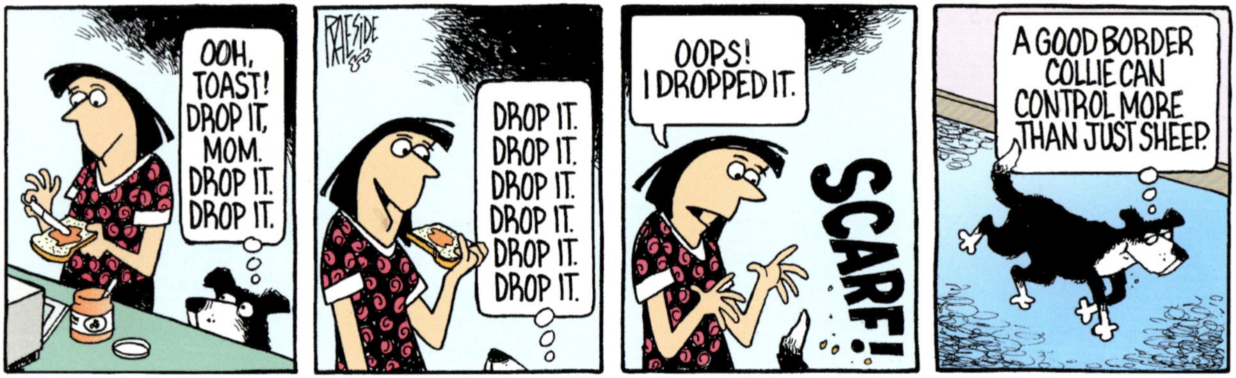
OOH, TOAST!
DROP IT, MOM. DROP IT. DROP IT.
DROP IT. DROP IT. DROP IT. DROP IT. DROP IT. DROP IT.
OOPS! I DROPPED IT.
SCARF!
A GOOD BORDER COLLIE CAN CONTROL MORE THAN JUST SHEEP.

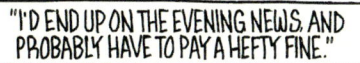

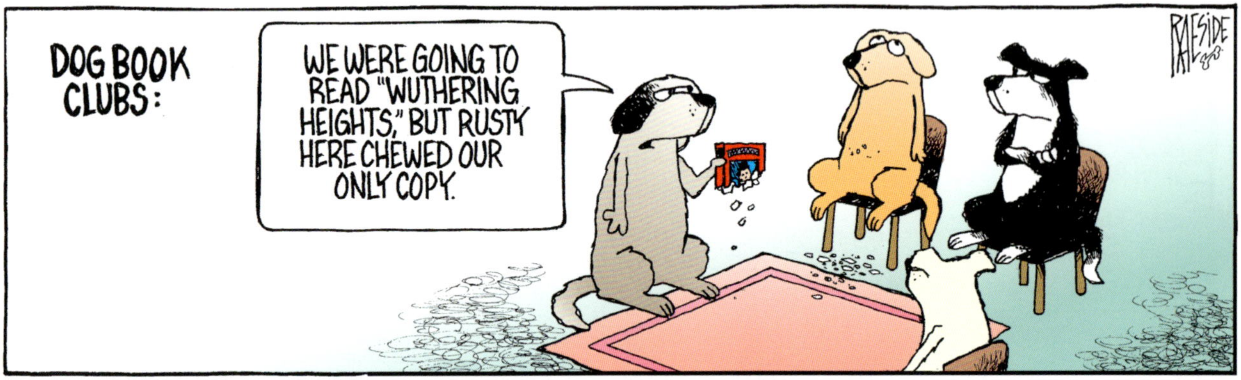
DOG BOOK CLUBS:
WE WERE GOING TO READ "WUTHERING HEIGHTS," BUT RUSTY HERE CHEWED OUR ONLY COPY.

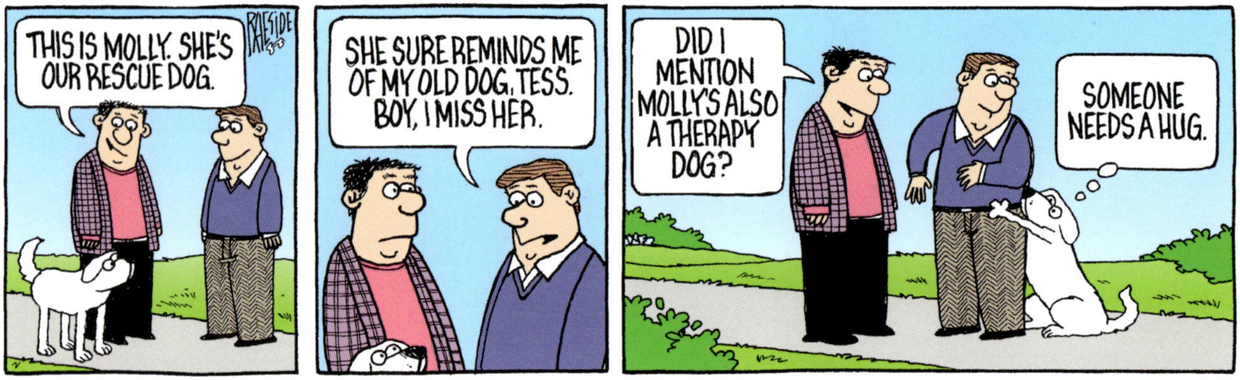
THIS IS MOLLY. SHE'S OUR RESCUE DOG.
SHE SURE REMINDS ME OF MY OLD DOG, TESS. BOY, I MISS HER.
DID I MENTION MOLLY'S ALSO A THERAPY DOG?
SOMEONE NEEDS A HUG.

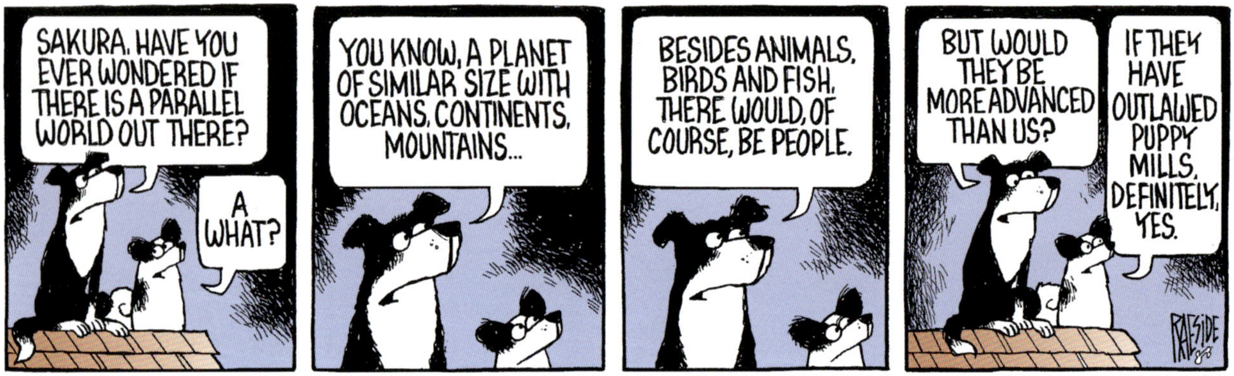
SAKURA, HAVE YOU EVER WONDERED IF THERE IS A PARALLEL WORLD OUT THERE?
A WHAT?
YOU KNOW, A PLANET OF SIMILAR SIZE WITH OCEANS, CONTINENTS, MOUNTAINS...
BESIDES ANIMALS, BIRDS AND FISH, THERE WOULD, OF COURSE, BE PEOPLE.
BUT WOULD THEY BE MORE ADVANCED THAN US?
IF THEY HAVE OUTLAWED PUPPY MILLS, DEFINITELY, YES.

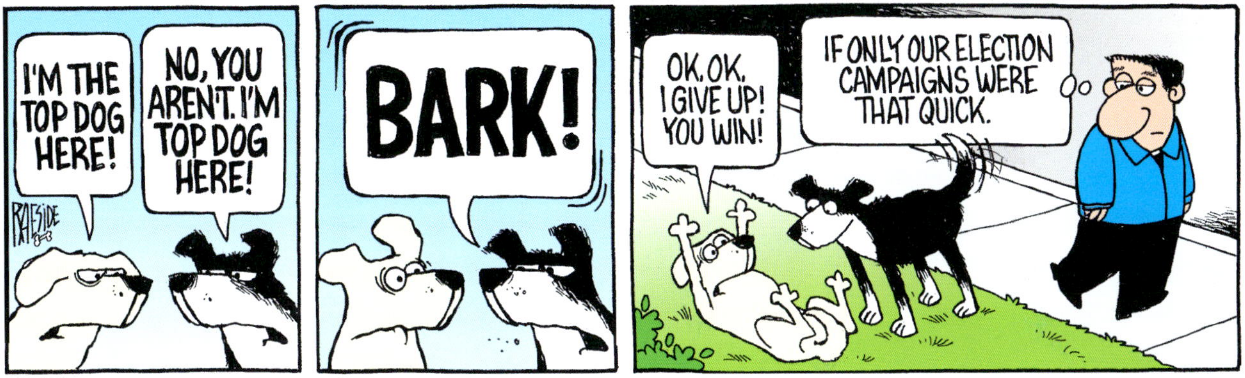
I'M THE TOP DOG HERE!
NO, YOU AREN'T. I'M TOP DOG HERE!
BARK!
OK, OK, I GIVE UP! YOU WIN!
IF ONLY OUR ELECTION CAMPAIGNS WERE THAT QUICK.

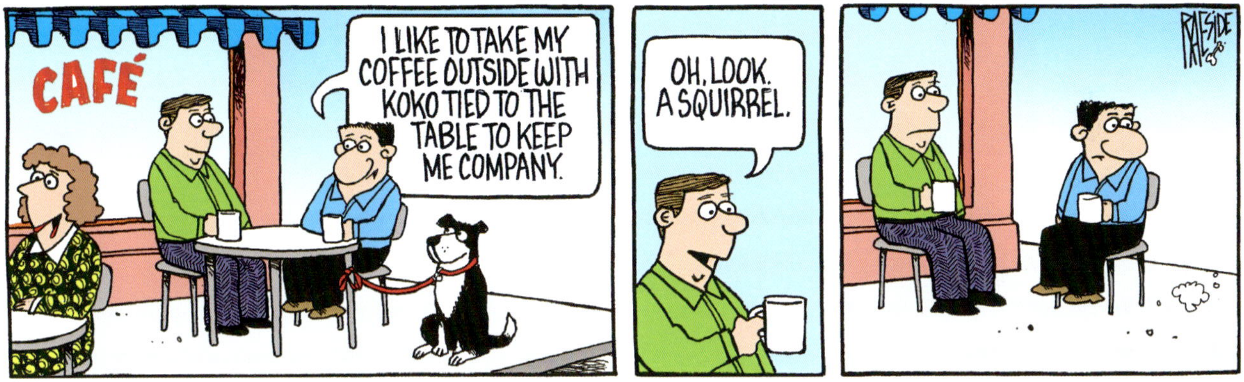
CAFÉ
I LIKE TO TAKE MY COFFEE OUTSIDE WITH KOKO TIED TO THE TABLE TO KEEP ME COMPANY.
OH, LOOK. A SQUIRREL.

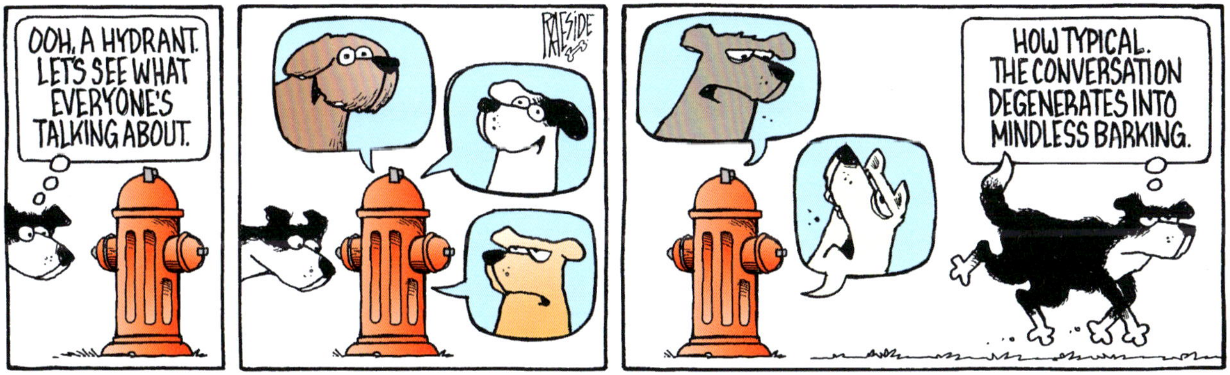
OOH, A HYDRANT. LET'S SEE WHAT EVERYONE'S TALKING ABOUT.
HOW TYPICAL. THE CONVERSATION DEGENERATES INTO MINDLESS BARKING.

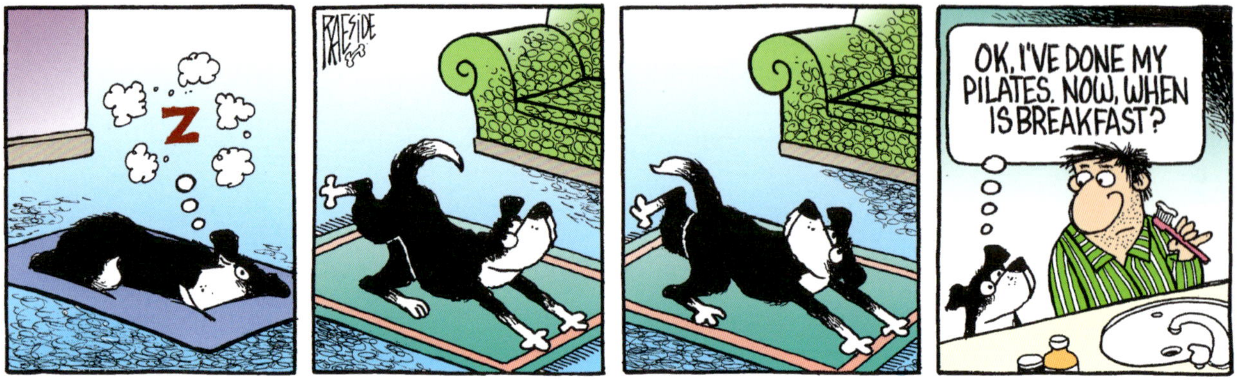
Z
OK, I'VE DONE MY PILATES. NOW, WHEN IS BREAKFAST?

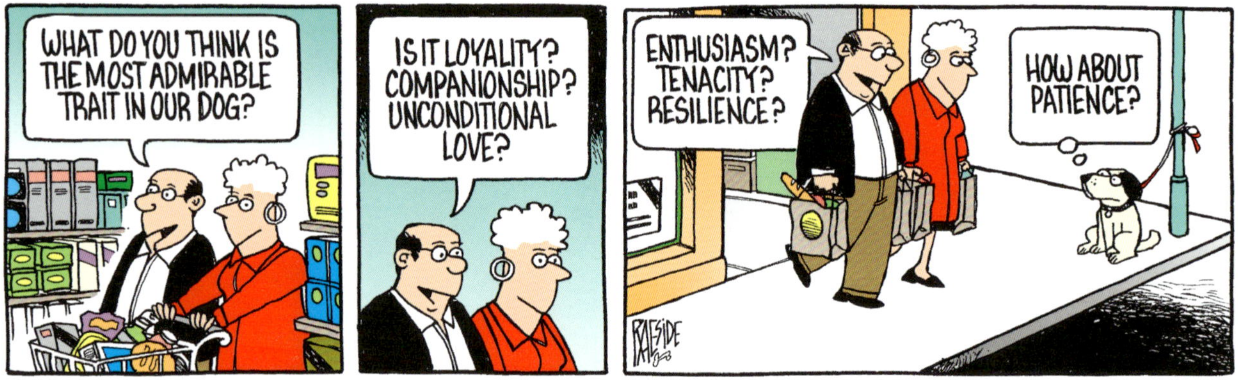
WHAT DO YOU THINK IS THE MOST ADMIRABLE TRAIT IN OUR DOG?
IS IT LOYALITY? COMPANIONSHIP? UNCONDITIONAL LOVE?
ENTHUSIASM? TENACITY? RESILIENCE?
HOW ABOUT PATIENCE?

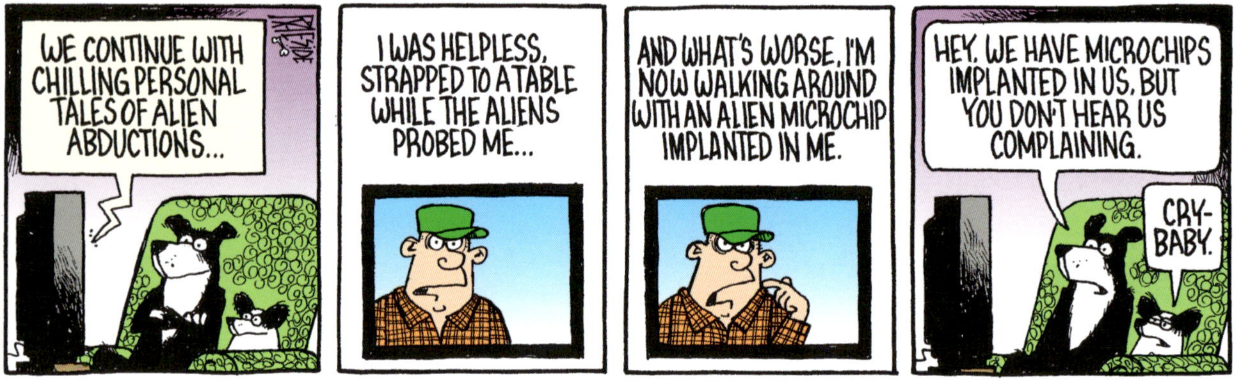
WE CONTINUE WITH CHILLING PERSONAL TALES OF ALIEN ABDUCTIONS...
I WAS HELPLESS, STRAPPED TO A TABLE WHILE THE ALIENS PROBED ME...
AND WHAT'S WORSE, I'M NOW WALKING AROUND WITH AN ALIEN MICROCHIP IMPLANTED IN ME.
HEY, WE HAVE MICROCHIPS IMPLANTED IN US, BUT YOU DON'T HEAR US COMPLAINING.
CRY-BABY.

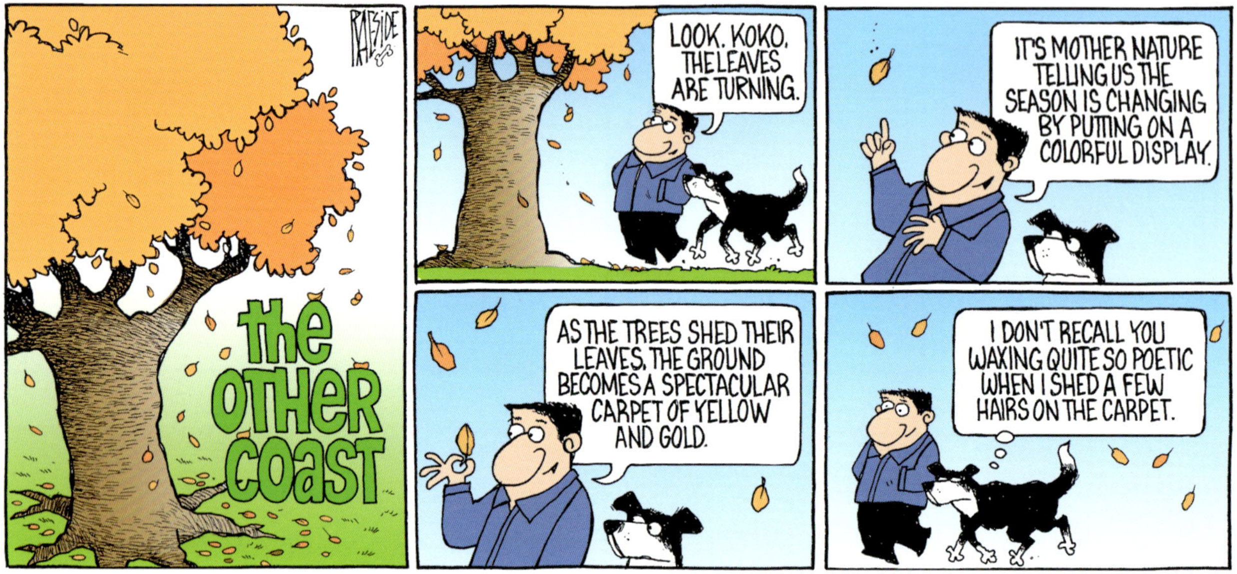
RAESIDE
the OTHER COAST
LOOK, KOKO, THE LEAVES ARE TURNING.
IT'S MOTHER NATURE TELLING US THE SEASON IS CHANGING BY PUTTING ON A COLORFUL DISPLAY.
AS THE TREES SHED THEIR LEAVES, THE GROUND BECOMES A SPECTACULAR CARPET OF YELLOW AND GOLD.
I DON'T RECALL YOU WAXING QUITE SO POETIC WHEN I SHED A FEW HAIRS ON THE CARPET.

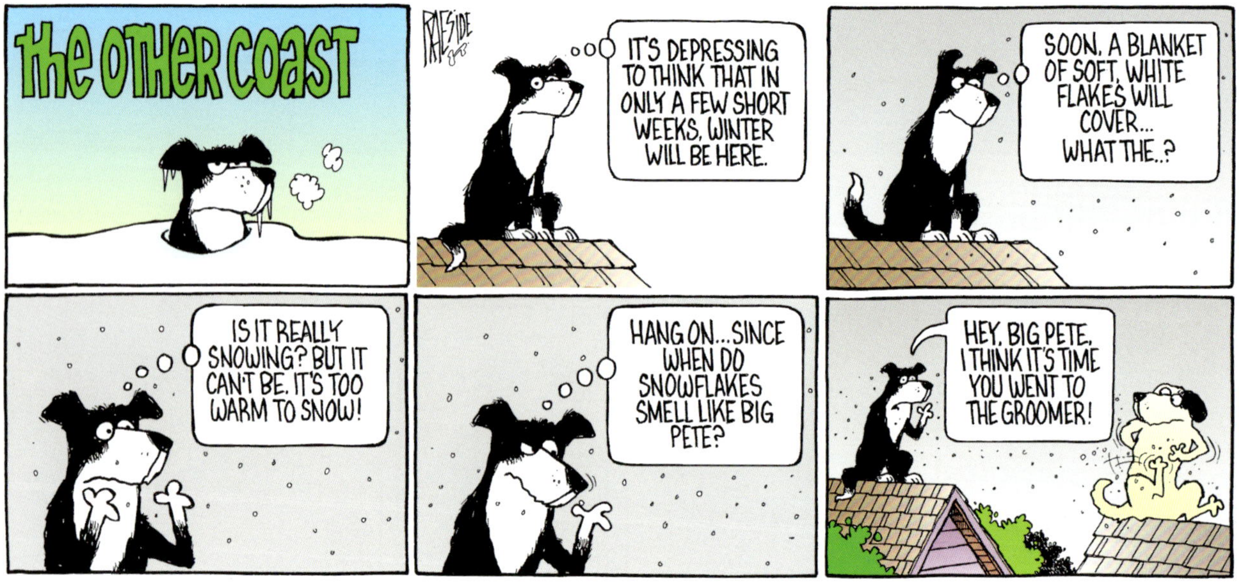
the OTHER COAST
RAESIDE
IT'S DEPRESSING TO THINK THAT IN ONLY A FEW SHORT WEEKS, WINTER WILL BE HERE.
SOON, A BLANKET OF SOFT, WHITE FLAKES WILL COVER... WHAT THE..?
IS IT REALLY SNOWING? BUT IT CAN'T BE. IT'S TOO WARM TO SNOW!
HANG ON...SINCE WHEN DO SNOWFLAKES SMELL LIKE BIG PETE?
HEY, BIG PETE, I THINK IT'S TIME YOU WENT TO THE GROOMER!

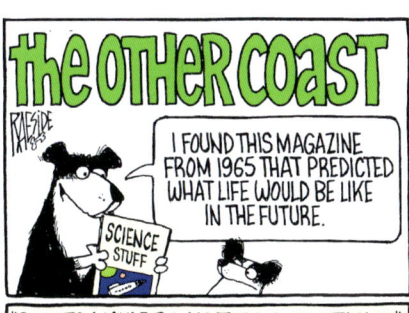

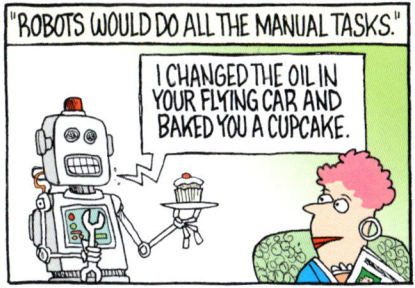

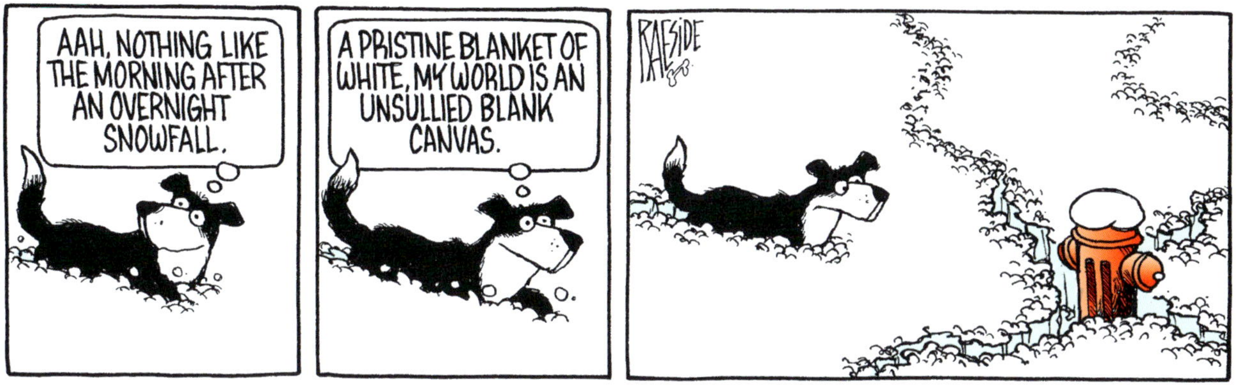
AAH, NOTHING LIKE THE MORNING AFTER AN OVERNIGHT SNOWFALL.
A PRISTINE BLANKET OF WHITE, MY WORLD IS AN UNSULLIED BLANK CANVAS.

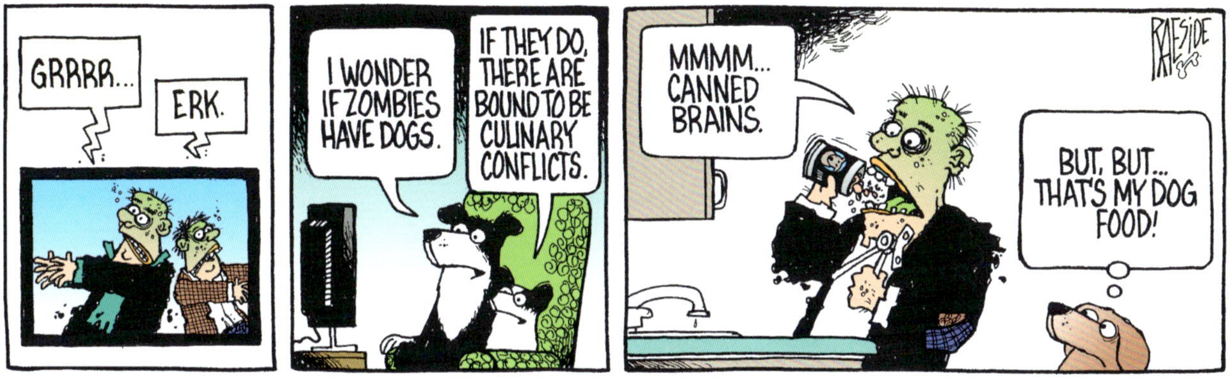
GRRRR...
ERK.
I WONDER IF ZOMBIES HAVE DOGS.
IF THEY DO, THERE ARE BOUND TO BE CULINARY CONFLICTS.
MMMM... CANNED BRAINS.
BUT, BUT... THAT'S MY DOG FOOD!

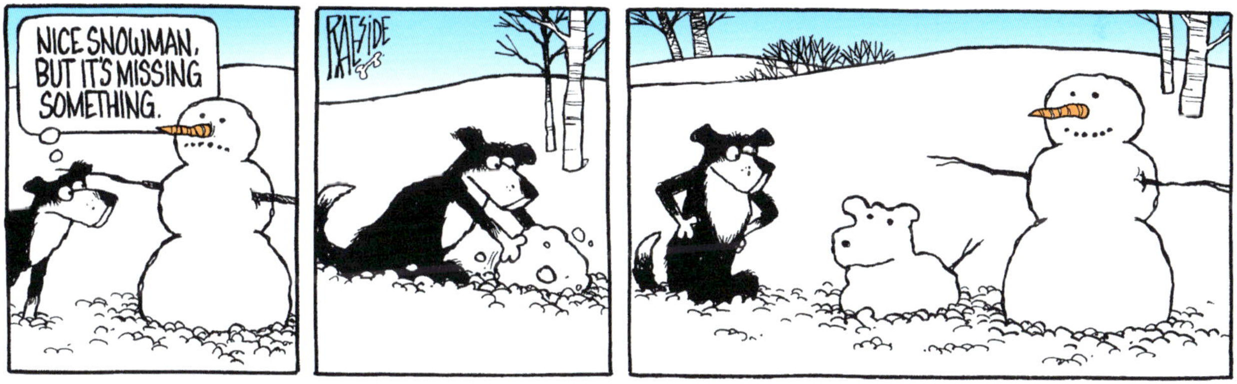
NICE SNOWMAN, BUT IT'S MISSING SOMETHING.

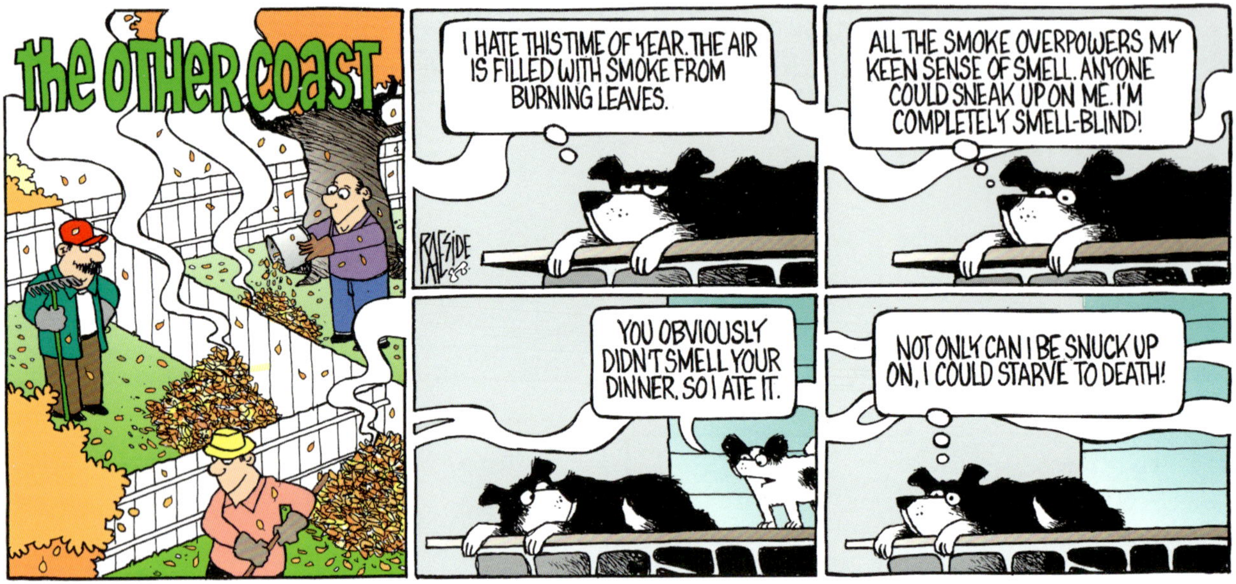
the OTHER COAST
RAESIDE
I HATE THIS TIME OF YEAR. THE AIR IS FILLED WITH SMOKE FROM BURNING LEAVES.
ALL THE SMOKE OVERPOWERS MY KEEN SENSE OF SMELL. ANYONE COULD SNEAK UP ON ME. I'M COMPLETELY SMELL-BLIND!
YOU OBVIOUSLY DIDN'T SMELL YOUR DINNER, SO I ATE IT.
NOT ONLY CAN I BE SNUCK UP ON, I COULD STARVE TO DEATH!

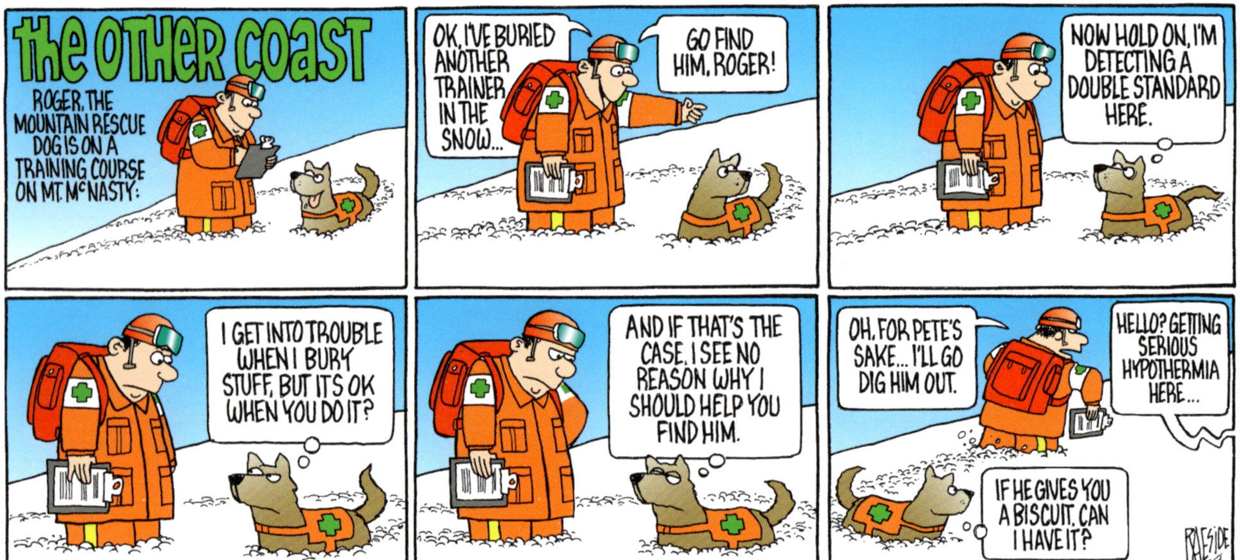
the OTHER COAST
ROGER, THE MOUNTAIN RESCUE DOG IS ON A TRAINING COURSE ON MT. McNASTY:
OK, I'VE BURIED ANOTHER TRAINER IN THE SNOW...
GO FIND HIM, ROGER!
NOW HOLD ON, I'M DETECTING A DOUBLE STANDARD HERE.
I GET INTO TROUBLE WHEN I BURY STUFF, BUT ITS OK WHEN YOU DO IT?
AND IF THAT'S THE CASE, I SEE NO REASON WHY I SHOULD HELP YOU FIND HIM.
OH, FOR PETE'S SAKE... I'LL GO DIG HIM OUT.
HELLO? GETTING SERIOUS HYPOTHERMIA HERE...
IF HE GIVES YOU A BISCUIT, CAN I HAVE IT?
RAESIDE

113

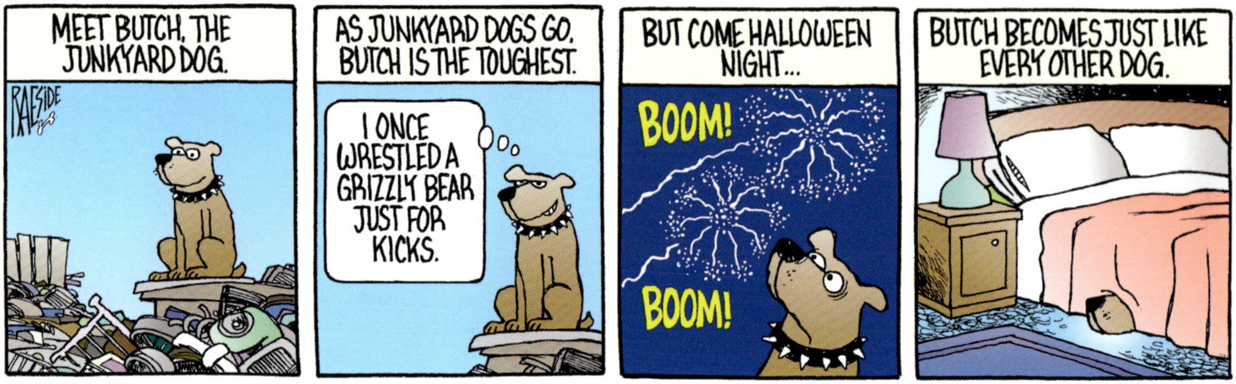
MEET BUTCH, THE JUNKYARD DOG.
AS JUNKYARD DOGS GO, BUTCH IS THE TOUGHEST.
I ONCE WRESTLED A GRIZZLY BEAR JUST FOR KICKS.
BUT COME HALLOWEEN NIGHT...
BOOM!
BOOM!
BUTCH BECOMES JUST LIKE EVERY OTHER DOG.

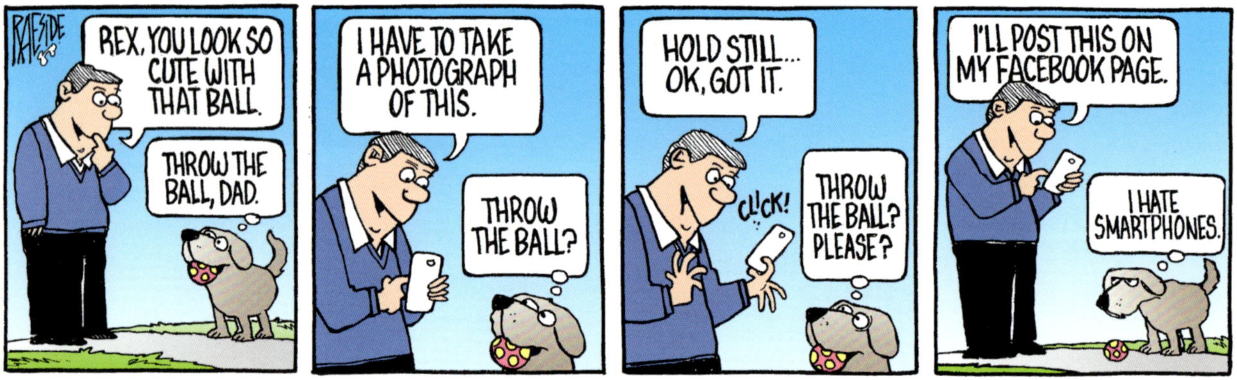
REX, YOU LOOK SO CUTE WITH THAT BALL.
THROW THE BALL, DAD.
I HAVE TO TAKE A PHOTOGRAPH OF THIS.
THROW THE BALL?
HOLD STILL... OK, GOT IT.
CLICK!
THROW THE BALL? PLEASE?
I'LL POST THIS ON MY FACEBOOK PAGE.
I HATE SMARTPHONES.

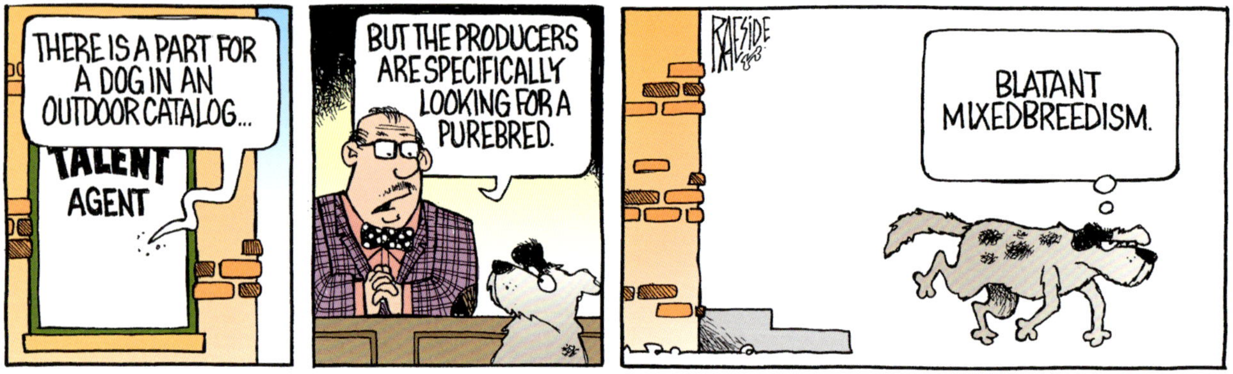
THERE IS A PART FOR A DOG IN AN OUTDOOR CATALOG...
TALENT AGENT
BUT THE PRODUCERS ARE SPECIFICALLY LOOKING FOR A PUREBRED.
BLATANT MIXEDBREEDISM.

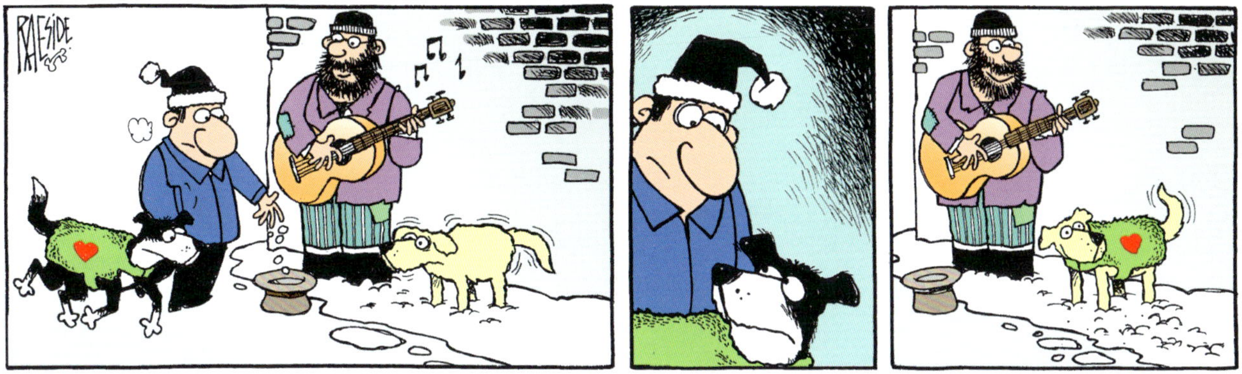

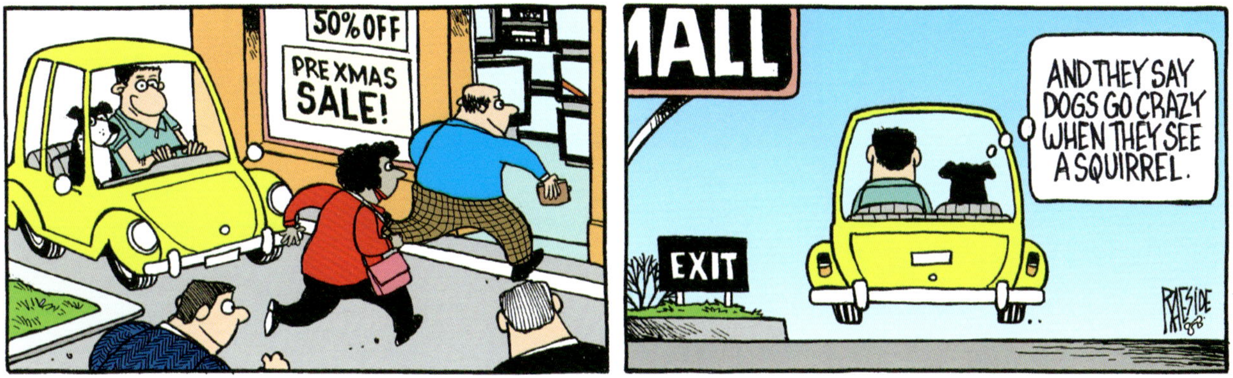

50% OFF
PRE XMAS SALE!
MALL
EXIT
AND THEY SAY DOGS GO CRAZY WHEN THEY SEE A SQUIRREL.

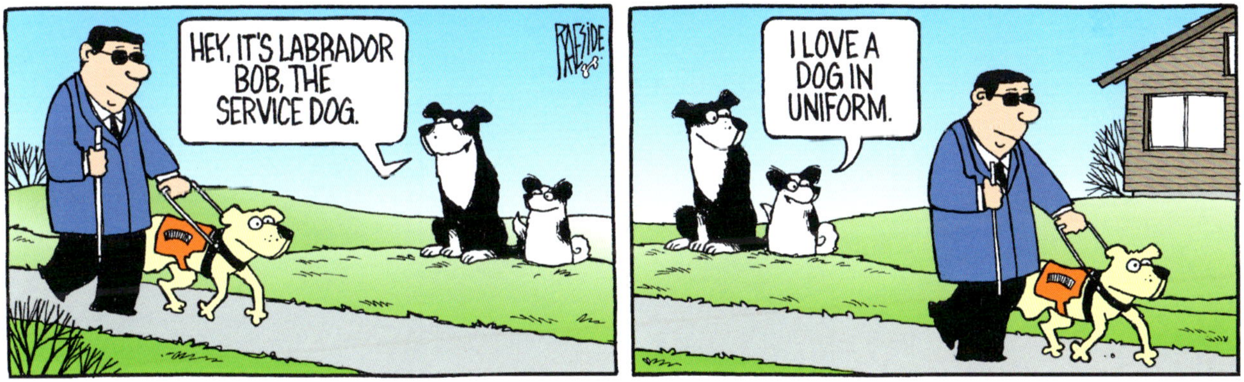

HEY, IT'S LABRADOR BOB, THE SERVICE DOG.
I LOVE A DOG IN UNIFORM.

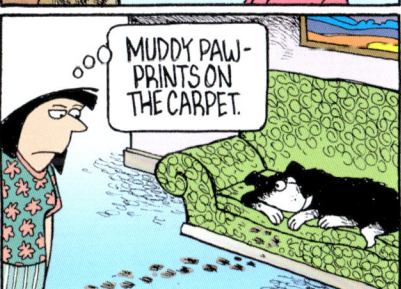

124

ALSO BY ADRIAN RAESIDE...

THE RAINBOW BRIDGE: A Visit to Pet Paradise is a magical tale of adventure and a valuable fable for anyone who cherishes the companionship of a family pet.

Seven-year-old Rick and his beloved dog Koko are inseparable. They cavort in the swimming hole, chase each other through the fields, play fetch and wrestle. But their relationship changes as Koko grows old and his health declines.

With Koko's passing, Rick is devastated. But on Christmas Eve he is woken by Buster, a flatulent but well-intentioned messenger dog, who suddenly appears at the boy's bedside. Buster ferries Rick to a magical paradise for pets where Rick is reunited with Koko; it fills Rick's heart with joy. It's a place where cats burrow through fields of catnip, no couch is off-limits to dogs and Frisbees are flung endlessly. This mysterious adventure is truly a holiday miracle!

Adrian Raeside captures the special bond between humans and their pets, and with marvellous illustrations, brings a gentle humour to a story that will resonate with children and pet lovers of all ages.

ISBN 978-1-55017-584-4
paperback / colour illustrations
8" x 8" / 32 pages

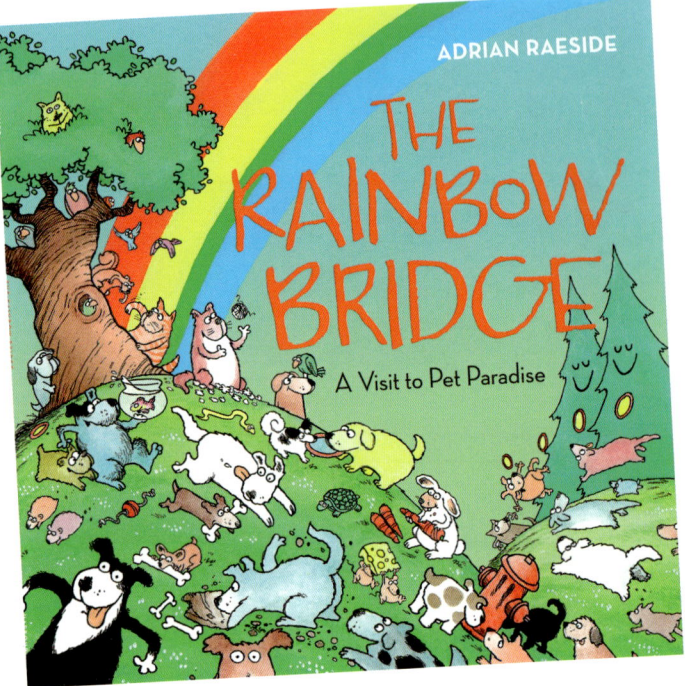

Available at your local bookstore or from

Harbour Publishing
P.O. Box 219
Madeira Park, BC, V0N 2H0
Toll-free order line: 1-800-667-2988

Visit our website for more information on all our titles and authors:

www.harbourpublishing.com

For more laughs visit Adrian Raeside's website:

www.raesidecartoon.com